# Open Minds
# to
# Equality

**Nancy Schniedewind**
State University of New York—New Paltz
**Ellen Davidson**
Phoenix School—Cambridge, Massachusetts

# Open Minds
# to
# Equality

A sourcebook of learning activities to promote
race, sex, class, and age equity

**ALLYN and BACON**
BOSTON  LONDON  TORONTO  SYDNEY  TOKYO  SINGAPORE

*Library of Congress Cataloging in Publication Data*

SCHNIEDEWIND, NANCY, [date]
    Open minds to equality.

    Bibliography: p.
    1. Equality—Study and teaching.  2. Cooperativeness—
Study and teaching.  I. Davidson, Ellen.  II. Title.
HM146.S26  1983        305        82-16610
ISBN 0-13-637264-3

Copyright © 1983 by Allyn and Bacon
A Division of Simon & Schuster, Inc.
160 Gould Street
Needham Heights, Massachusetts 02194

Printed in the United States of America

10  9  8              95  94  93

This book is dedicated to

*Grace Douglass Schniedewind*
and *William Schniedewind*

*Adelaide Heyman Davidson,*
*Henry Alexander Davidson*
and *Ella Yohalem Heyman*

whose nurturance, courage, values,
and love inspired the vision in this book.

*The Authors*

Nancy Schniedewind is Associate Professor of Educational Studies at the State University College, New Paltz, New York. There she coordinates both a Masters Program in Humanistic Education and the Women's Studies Program. She works with teachers and school districts to promote equity in education.

Ellen Davidson is a teacher at the Phoenix School, Cambridge Massachusetts. She is active with community, prison, and camp groups in building cooperation, communication, and conflict-resolution skills.

# CONTENTS

# 2 BUILDING TRUST AND COMMUNICATION 21

# 3 DEVELOPING SKILLS FOR CREATIVE COOPERATION 43

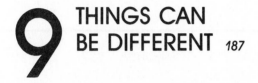

# 9 THINGS CAN BE DIFFERENT *187*

# 10 WE CAN MAKE CHANGES *219*

# ACKNOWLEDGMENTS

*Open Minds to Equality* is truly a cooperative endeavor. The energy and hard work of many people are reflected in its pages.

The creative and zestful artists are Noelle Porter and Laurie Prendergast, and the cartoonist whose work appears most frequently, Bulbul. Thirteen-year-old Noelle Porter has drawn the more youthful pictures in *Open Minds to Equality*. We hope her work captures the spirit and energy of your students. Laurie Prendergast, a Hampshire College student, has drawn the wonderfully detailed characters that reflect the vast diversity of persons whose lives *Open Minds to Equality* addresses. Cinda Raley collaborated with the authors on Chapter One. Her stylistic editing added immeasurably to that chapter. Three Poughkeepsie, New York Public School teachers, Donna Ewing, Kathy Hare, and Joyce Townsend, spent many hours with us sharing feedback and ideas based on their own teaching expertise. Their suggestions were both creative and thoughtful. Gloria Joseph and Eric Perlberg provided valuable comments on the manuscript as a whole. Janet Freeburn and Denise Swiat offered helpful feedback on several chapters.

The outstanding and patient typists were Linda DuBois, Ed Seliger, Pat Clarke, Marni Panuska, and Sadie Caram. People who assisted in a variety of ways were, Dave Porter Jr., Bob Moore, Judy Harkavy, Adam Schartoff, Bridget Fahrland, Janice Giambatista, Geneva Garner, Gregory Finger, and DeCourcy Squire. The title comes from an idea suggested by Lizzie Scott and her family.

Nancy owes special thanks to people and groups whose ideas and energy inspired her work in this book—the students and faculty of the West Philadelphia Community Free School; the staff of The Philadelphia Affective Education Project; friends at St. Mary's State College; colleagues at the University Massachusetts School of Education; and the faculty and students in the Women's Studies Program and Graduate Program in Humanistic Education at State University College, New Paltz. Her very special thanks go to David Porter for sharing his keen intellect and unfailing social vision, and for his ongoing support.

Ellen owes special thanks to many people at Camp Thoreau—campers, teens, and staff—for inspiration, ideas, questions, practice and encouragement. Her thanks go also to the facilitators and participants in the Alternatives to Violence Program for the opportunity to share activities and to learn many new ones, and to her family for frequent and varied help.

We would like to thank the following for permission to include materials: Addison Wesley Publishing Company for use of quotation from *On What is Learned in School* by Philip Dreeben; Asian American Bilingual Center for use of account of Renee Ramos; Women's Re-Entry Project of the Association of American Colleges for use of child care statistics; Women's Studies Program of the Berkeley Unified School District for a modification of Susan Groves and Clementine Duran's *Chicanos Strike at Farah*; Bülbül for use of many cartoons; Council on Interracial Books for Children for use of many quotations and statistics; The Dial Press for use of a quotation from *The Great Brain Does it Again* by John Figzgerald; *The Detroit News* for use of a quotation; Education Research Associates for adaptation of Values Auction idea; *Family Circle* for use of quotation from an article; Gray Panther Network, 3635 Chestnut St. Philadelphia, Pennsylvania for use of materials from its journal; Grove Press for use of a quotation from *White Is* by Preston Wilcox; *The Guardian* for use of an excerpt of an article; Harcourt, Brace, Jovanovich for use of a quotation from *Small Futures* by Richard deLone; The Continuum Publishing Company for use of excerpts from *The Night is Dark and I Am Far From Home* by Jonathan Kozol; Houston Chronicle for use of a quotation; National Commission on Working Women for use of a chart from "An Overview of Women in the Work Force"; Pantheon Books for use of quotations from *Blaming the Victim* by William Ryan; Project on Equal Educational Rights for use of a quotation by Holly Knox; Sidney Simon for adaptation of "I Am Lovable and Capable"—for information on Values Realization workshops and materials contact him at Old Mountain Road, Hadley, MA, 01035; Project Move at SUNY College of Technology for use of a cartoon; Johnny Hart and Field Enterprises Incorporated for use of a cartoon; Thomas Y. Crowell Publishers for use of an excerpt from *Charles Drew* by Roland Bertol; Random House Inc. for use of an excerpt from *The Phantom Tollbooth* by Norton Juster; Universal Press Syndicate and Gary Trudeau for use of two Doonesbury cartoons; A & W Publishers for use of a quotation from *Developing Effective Classroom Groups: A Practical Guide for Teachers* by Gene Stanford, © 1977, Hart Publishing Company, Inc.; Knox Berger Associates for permission to quote from *Sojourner Truth*; McGraw Hill for quotations from "Human Characteristics and School Learning" by Benjamin Bloom; Harper and Row for an excerpt from *Stress Without Distress* by Hans Selye; Resource Center on Sex Roles in Education to quote from "A Student Guide to Title IX"; *Vocations for Social Change* for a quotation from "Work Liberation"; Win Magazine to reprint statistics; *The Washington Post* for an excerpt from "Afro-Alternative to Christmas"; *Heresies* for an adaptation of "Rocking the Docks" by Constance Pohl; Arlene Eisen for a quote from *Women of Vietnam*; Johnson Publishing Company for a quote from L. Bennett, "The White Problem in America"; Noe Valley Ministry for a quote from *Institutional Racism: A Primer* by Carl Smith.

Nancy Schniedewind
Ellen Davidson

# INTRODUCTION

"It's not fair!" How many times have you heard a student in your class say that? This sourcebook of classroom learning activities taps students' fundamental demands for equality. The activities will help them expand their understanding of what is and isn't fair in our society and develop productive strategies for change. We hope that by the end of the year your students will follow "It's not fair!" with "So let's do something about it!"

This volume, geared for elementary and middle school teachers and students, is a sourcebook for learning equality. This phrase has two meanings. First, it is a resource book with many activities for teaching students *about* equality. Students will learn what equality is, how discrimination perpetuates inequality, and what strategies for change can bring about greater justice for all. Specifically, activities examine the ways that racism, sexism, class bias, ageism, and competitive individualism in school and society reinforce inequality. Other lessons present alternatives for change.

Second, it is a book that will generate more equality among students in your classroom, both academically and interpersonally. Unintentional discriminatory practices in classrooms and schools often hinder student learning. When you and students work together to remove these barriers, students will feel more positively about their competencies and self-worth. *All* students will be more motivated and able to achieve academically. Furthermore, by developing greater respect for each other and themselves and by learning to work cooperatively, students will interact more democratically. Your classroom can become a learning laboratory of equality.

*Open Minds to Equality* is for all of us. There are positive benefits for majority, as well as minority, group members in promoting equality. For example, while minority people are more negatively affected by racism, white persons as well lose out on important human experiences and values. Women are more oppressed by sexist institutions, but men also pay a high price. Is it only the losers who benefit from changing competitive values? No, winners do too! We all have something to gain by confronting inequality!

Teachers sometimes devalue their powers as educators. "Well, it really doesn't matter what I do in my classroom anyway, it's parents, the society. . . ." Despite the increasingly frustrating pressures on educators today, teachers *do* have the potential to provide an empowering, democratic learning opportunity for students. Students can experience an egalitarian classroom where, for example, they feel respected whatever their class background; develop empathy for older Americans; understand their skin privilege, if white, or develop racial pride, if they are members of a minority group; feel free to express a range of emotions whether female or male; and work cooperatively toward common goals that benefit all. Students will know that equality is possible because they've experienced it. Such knowledge lasts a lifetime. *You* can catalyze such learning!

**TEACHER LEARNING**   We expect that you too will learn as you use this book. We've worked hard to intersperse intriguing "boxes" of relevant information and challenging ideas. We hope that the full Bibliography will spur you on to further readings.

In the process of using *Open Minds to Equality*, you may come to realize that, unintentionally, you've been reinforcing inequality in your teaching or life. Take heart! It is only when a problem is visible that it can be rectified. Only when you learn that many American Indians today resent the name Indian (because it was given to them by a white explorer who thought he had found India) and prefer to be called Native Americans, do you have a choice to change your vocabulary. Only when you become aware that to talk about issues of race as "a black problem" is to avoid personal responsibility for white racism, can you gain a new perspective to confront racism in your school and community.

It is this kind of growth that we hope you'll look forward to in this book. Such learning is not always easy, but it is challenging and hopeful. Implicitly or explicitly, we have been taught stereotypes and have been socialized not to examine and challenge institutional practices that support inequality. This is not our fault. Once aware of them, however, it becomes our responsibility to change those behaviors and practices.

Change, not guilt, is the intent of *Open Minds to Equality*. Guilt is paralyzing. If we wallow in it, we don't do anything to change things. We encourage you to be aware of the messages you give yourself as you read this book. Instead of becoming guilty or defensive, try telling yourself, "I'm glad I'm aware of this; now I can change it!" That's a powerful statement—and a step to becoming an ever more effective teacher.

**APPROACH TO LEARNING**   The activities in this book promote both cognitive and affective learning. Students will gain much new knowledge. They will also explore their feelings and values and come to better understand those of others. Many activities are personal in that they relate to students' experience, school, and community. Learning, we believe, is most meaningful when it affects a person directly. We could have designed activities about inequality "out there." It is much easier to talk about discrimination against women in United States history or to analyze national figures documenting racism in employment, than to look at our own family, school, or self! This latter focus is harder because it means admitting inequality close to home, but it also is more potent, because within our own sphere of influence changes can be made. Many activities in this book enable students to investigate their environment and take action for change.

Although there are key ideas, themes, and information that we expect that all students will learn, students in different schools and communities will have different experiences doing the activities. This, we believe, is as it should be.

Some lessons are based on an inquiry approach to learning. Students confront problems through data-gathering and investigation, draw conclusions or make generalizations, and then take action. This process involves critical thinking and cooperative processes. Activities in Chapters Two and Three will prepare students for such exploration. In addition, many lessons are participatory and experiential. Students work actively together to get information, share ideas, and solve problems.

**FORMAT AND SEQUENCE**   In our teaching and research, we have found that there is a definite process by which people gain greater understanding about personal and institutional inequality. The format of this book follows that process. First and foremost, a supportive, warm environment is needed for students to feel safe enough to examine their attitudes and explore ideas that may challenge preconceived notions. Equally important, they need to learn the skills for working together. These skills must be taught, just as reading or math skills are taught. Chapter Two, "Building Trust and Communication," and Chapter Three, "Developing Skills for Creative Cooperation," contain activities that develop trust, as well as skills in cooperation, decision-making, listening, critical thinking, interviewing and group work. When students feel secure, accepted, and respected by their teacher and peers, they deal most effectively with issues that create dissonance.

Second, students need accurate information if they are to challenge stereotypes about people of other races, sexes, or class backgrounds. Lessons in Chapter Four, "Expanding Our Vistas: Our Lives to Others' Lives," enable children to gain knowledge about people other than themselves. Students get into others' shoes and, at least momentarily, escape from their egocentric perspectives. New words to define, name, and discuss inequality and its consequences are essential to students' growing awareness. In Chapter Five, students define and recognize prejudice, stereotypes, and the "isms." They learn about the effects such inequality has on people's opportunities in life, and are encouraged to reconsider their attitudes in light of this new information. Students explore the effects of discrimination in Chapter Six, "Discrimination: Prices and Choices."

Once students understand these basic concepts they are ready to apply these ideas to their world. Chapters Seven and Eight use the family, school, and community as a laboratory for students to investigate how inequality is institutionalized. They discover ways in which discrimination and the "isms" affect them in their daily living. They develop a critical awareness and are able to perceive institutions close to them from a new perspective.

By now, students have the knowledge and motivation to act for change. Chapter Nine, "Things can Be Different," shows students realistic ways to foster equality. Resources and activities that enable students to act to change unequal situations are contained in the final chapter, "We Can Make Changes!" Students who have identified sexism in their reading books, for example, can write and illustrate alternative stories. Such an activity not only encourages them to act against sexism, but also develops their skills in creative writing and art. So often we hear, "You just can't change things." Through activities that point out what others have done to change things and through their own initiative, students gain self-confidence, personal power, and experience in collective responsibility.

Thus the activities help students progress developmentally and sequentially in their understanding of inequities and in their ability to foster equality. As students or educators we can best work for equity with accurate information, an understanding of how inequality is institutionalized, knowledge of alternatives for action, and the confidence to act.

**USING THE BOOK**     *Open Minds to Equality* is structured so that you can choose learning activities appropriate for your class within the sequential chapters. The activities vary in their subject matter focus. Some reinforce math or language arts skills, while others emphasize the social studies. Your choice of learning activities within chapter sections will depend on which areas you wish to emphasize, on school and community variables, as well as on the degree to which you're intrigued by various lessons. *Open Minds to Equality* is designed, not as an appendage to your regular curriculum, but as a resource that can easily fit into your current teaching plan and priorities.

First read through this Introduction, Chapter I, and the introductions to the other chapters; then skim through the lessons. This will give you a feeling for the progression of ideas and objectives in the book. We especially encourage you to find another teacher or teachers in your school who will use *Open Minds to Equality* with you. You can provide each other with ideas, feedback, and support—especially helpful the first year you use the book.

In order to build proper trust, skills and knowledge among students, teach chapters and chapter sections sequentially. Within chapter sections choose which lesson or lessons you prefer to teach. You should have ample time to do one or two activities from each chapter section each week. If chosen carefully, these reinforce the cognitive skills you are already teaching.

It's important to remember that *Open Minds to Equality* is not merely a series of lessons, but an egalitarian approach to teaching and learning. You can infuse much of what you typically do in the classroom with the spirit of this book. For example, you can give students spelling sentences that include the names and experiences of minority persons. You can make sure that math problems include low-income people. When you line students up, you can have lines based on creative variables, like sock color, rather than sex. Such an ongoing approach in your classroom reflects a personal and professional commitment to equality.

**TO END, AND TO BEGIN**   As teachers advocating personal and social change through education, we distinguish between long- and short-term goals. We share a vision of an egalitarian society where personal and institutional discrimination based on class, age, sex, and race is eliminated, and where persons cooperate toward goals that benefit all. It will only be after many years and many changes that that vision becomes a reality. However, it is very important for us to have that ideal, to know what we are striving toward. Toward that end we formulate short-term goals, those small day-to-day changes that are building-blocks toward that future. *Open Minds to Equality* provides ideas and activities to achieve such short-term goals. The consequences of these efforts contribute to the broader vision of a just and equal society that many of us share. We're encouraged that you're joining us.

# 1 RECOGNIZING ROADBLOCKS TO EQUALITY

## SECTION A · ROADBLOCKS TO EQUAL EDUCATION

Teachers have a unique and exciting job—a job that influences the thoughts, emotions, and lives of developing human beings. Good teachers do more than just teach the curriculum. They help their students feel confident in themselves and provide them with both knowledge and skills for self-determining lives. *Open Minds to Equality* is written for these educators—those who want the most for all their students.

You may be thinking, "This is fine, but *how* do I develop a classroom based on values of equality? And is it even possible to provide an equal educational opportunity for my students?" These are not easy questions to answer, but this book is designed to provide many tools that will help you make your teaching a catalyst for change. The lessons and resources here should enable you to use your energy and skills to bring equal educational opportunities to all your students and increase their awareness of attitudes and institutions that perpetuate injustice.

### THE EGALITARIAN CLASSROOM

What, then, do we mean by "equality"? Equality, as used in this book, applies both to our classrooms and to society. Equality in society means that all people have respect and dignity, meaningful work at a fair wage, health care, decent housing and food, and opportunities for personal development. Currently, because of institutional and cultural discrimination, people have very unequal chances and choices in life. Activities in this book teach students to recognize such inequality in society and to develop alternatives for change.

Equality in the classroom means that all students have a fair chance to learn and develop as persons. This necessitates changing practices or behaviors that discriminate on the basis of sex, class or race, and those which reinforce competitive individualism. For example, if science books have many fewer references to female than to male scientists, the books would be changed or the issue fully discussed with the class. Omission of role-models gives female students a less than equal chance to be successful in science. Instead of celebrating only holidays in commemoration of white men, such as Washington and Lincoln, holidays would be added to honor the important contributions of minority people and women. Omission of such holidays gives minority students and women a less than equal expectation that their culture or sex is important. Such negative expectations impede learning and personal development.

---

We use the terms "minority," "third world," and "people of color" interchangeably throughout the book. ("People of color" is a contemporary term not to be confused with the racist term "colored.") We find none satisfactory, all acceptable, and realize various readers will prefer one term to another.

All terms refer to Afro-Americans, Latinos, (Puerto Ricans, Chicanos, and people from Central and South American or Caribbean countries), Native Americans, and Asian-Americans in the United States.

---

Specifically, equality means providing an educational environment in which all students develop the cognitive and affective knowledge and skills that will enable them to be self-determining persons. They will understand how societal institutions and values allow some Americans to live full lives while denying that opportunity to others. They will have both tools for changing those mechanisms of inequality, and a vision of a fairer future. Educators teaching toward equality operate with a dual consciousness. We provide students with knowledge and skills to function in the world and *at the same time* awareness and tools for changing that world into a more just and humane one.

Most of us judge ourselves, others, and daily events solely from our own experiences. We seldom stop to consider consciously how others experience life and see the world. We take much for granted and tend to forget that our lives are intricately connected to other people's lives. For some people to have access to opportunities may be possible only because others are denied those same advantages. Equality implies expanding our perspectives to see when privilege for some causes inequality for others. We can help our students discover how this happens, why it happens, its consequences, and what they can do to change this pattern.

Although it is a high expectation, greater equality in student learning is not a "pie-in-the-sky" fantasy. An important condition, we suggest, is an egalitarian classroom. Higher academic achievement for all students is a predictable outcome when teaching for equality. It is our belief that classrooms can be places of equity, and that teachers can stimulate full learning, pride, and justice for all students. Obviously, if you've read this far, this is your belief too.

> If you've started reading Chapter I and haven't read the Introduction, Stop! Go back to the overview of *Open Minds to Equality* found in the Introduction.

**RACISM**   Teaching for equality means that we must challenge many forms of bias that are commonplace in schools. They include bias based on race, sex, class or age, and those individualistic and competitive behaviors that deny some students basic human dignity. Because teachers today are most concerned about racism and sexism, we give special attention to these.

What is racism, and how is it different from prejudice? Racism is a belief that human beings have distinctive characteristics and that one race has a right to power over another; it is a policy, system of government, or society based on such beliefs. Racism is to be distinguished from prejudice, which is a negative personal behavior that discriminates against individuals. When power is added to prejudice, it becomes racism. For example, if a white child calls a black child a demeaning name, he exhibits prejudice. When, however, the policies and norms of a school system, school, or teacher sanction (by action or inaction) such name-calling, we have an example of racism.

> The problem of race in America is a white problem and in order to solve the problem we must seek its source not in the Negro but in the white American and in the structure of the white community. . . . The power is the white American's and so is the responsibility.
>
> Lerone Bennett, Jr. in *White Racism*, edited by B. Schwartz and R. Disch.

Take a look at your school. How many administrators and teachers are members of minority groups? Check the bulletin boards. What percentage of minority faces do you see? Do a survey of your texts and supplementary books. What percentage deal with people of color? What roles do they play? Do the pictures show people with white features tinted black or brown? Do the same for media. What holidays does your school celebrate and what cultures do they represent? Do you incorporate the perspective of a third world person into your lesson?

As you can see from these examples, your school doesn't have to be integrated to be accountable for racism. In fact, children develop their racial attitudes not from contact with people of other races, but from the *prevailing attitudes* about them. If, in a predominantly white school, minority people and their cultures are omitted from reading materials and discussions, and aren't seen on bulletin boards, it isn't hard for students to conclude that minorities are not very important. In fact, if you teach in a predominantly white school, you might ask, "Why is it so white?"

In a racially mixed school you might ask additional questions. If there is busing in your district, who gets bused and who gets to stay in the neighborhood school? Is there a relationship between suspension and race? Is there a double standard in the treatment of minority and white students? Are minority parents and community members encouraged to participate in educational decision-making—for example, evaluation of books for racial bias? Are the cultural values of minority children integral to school norms? Have teachers sought out new knowledge about the cultures of people of color in order to better understand their students' lives? Do some teachers become more concerned if a white child falls behind than if an Afro-American child does?

Racism in schools and society affects both minority and majority students. You have probably seen its effects. Racism causes some minority children to have low self-concepts and consequently, to set low educational goals for themselves. Some minority children act out in aggressive ways or withdraw and give up.

Because of discrimination in standardized testing, tracking, and institutional norms, the learning potential of many minority children is substantially thwarted. A double standard on the part of the school system or the teacher has a powerful effect on a minority student. An overly harsh, punitive standard creates fear and anger. One that is more lenient—sometimes the result of a teacher's fear of confronting minority children in an honest, firm, and supportive way—is equally harmful. Students are cheated of the expectation of meeting the same academic and behavioral standards as others. The message they receive is either that teachers really don't care about them, or that, since they're not expected to achieve, they're probably not capable of it. Positive self-concepts and learning potential diminish.

It is important to acknowledge that, because of previous inequality in education and life-opportunities, minority students often enter a class underprepared. More teacher time and special learning opportunities are required to upgrade knowledge and skills in such cases. Such programming is essential and in no way reflects a double standard. It is the teacher's and the school's expectation, subtly communicated to the student, that minority students *can* achieve and *are expected* to achieve, that is essential for avoiding the negative effects of a double standard.

Majority children, too, are affected by racism. These children can develop a distorted view of themselves, others, and society. Their world is a white enclave that reinforces stereotypes of minority persons, and denies them knowledge of the rich experience of people of other races. Their chances for open communication in the future are diminished. Text books, films, and the examples given in class reiterate the message evident in the broader culture—that white is normal, and therefore "right." They may develop a sense of superiority, and sometimes resort to name-calling and racial pejoratives. The unconscious assumption that what is white is normal can affect their perceptions, values, and interactions with others throughout life. Further, if these children perceive a double standard in teacher behavior, favoring whites, their sense of superiority is reinforced. And if a teacher or school system is lenient towards minorities, white students can harbor resentments and anger that permanently affect their perceptions and actions.

Thus, for everyone, racism takes its toll. *All* children, white and minority, lose an opportunity to work together cooperatively and learn from the richness of others' experiences, world views, and lives. They lose out on valuable friendships and what could be a much fuller education.

> Cultural racism as expressed in educational materials limits the development of white children. . . . It provides them with a false sense of their own self-esteem. Their self-esteem is not based on real things but on the alleged inferiority of someone else. And it frequently gives them a sense that they are owed something because they are white.
>
> Dr. Alvin Poussaint, Harvard Medical School, in *Bulletin, Council on Interracial Books for Children,* Volume 7, Number 1, 1976.

**SEXISM**

Sexism exists when one sex, intentionally or unintentionally, refuses to share power or distribute resources equitably with another. Sexism, again, is different from prejudice in that it is enforced by power. When young boys refuse to play softball with girls because they are "spastic" or "no good," they exhibit prejudice. However, when a school system develops policies to avoid Title IX compliance or when a teacher actively fails to encourage and support girls' participation in all sports, we find sexism. School systems and teachers have the power to enforce and legitimize prejudice based on sex.

Because of recent national efforts to promote sex equality in education, many of you are conscious of sexism in the schools. Despite public attention, however, our schools are still a long way from being anti-sexist. Think about the most recent class or school play. How were women portrayed? If people from another culture were to view that play only, how would they describe the female sex in our culture? What do teachers do when boys make fun of girls in stereotypical ways? To do or say nothing is to sanction their behavior and words. Do teachers allow boys to call other boys "sissies" or "faggots"? To do so reinforces both the aggressive sex-socialization of males in our culture and prejudice about homosexuals. Have teachers actively encouraged fathers to help with class projects? Although more mothers than fathers may be free during the day, there are many things—gathering supplies, making equipment, cooking—that parents who work days can do.

Do teachers assign chores according to traditional sex roles—do girls dust and boys move furniture? Have you noticed that boys seldom choose to read library books about women or girls? Are they encouraged to do so? Are girls' papers expected to be neater than boys'? Check the career education books in your school. Are girls encouraged to aspire to all occupations, including traditionally male occupations like doctor or scientist; are boys encouraged into alternative roles like nurse, dietician, or secretary? At recess when captains choose teams, who gets chosen first? Do teachers use alternative ways for dividing into teams?

> WOMEN IN SPORTS IN CHILDREN'S BOOKS: WEALTHY, WHITE, WINNING.
>
> In many of the books examined in this study:
>
> Minority women were underrepresented.
> Reassurances were given that even though these women were athletes, they were still *real* women.
> The highest praise was to say that the woman played her sport like a man.
> The focus was on winning, not enjoyment of the sport.
>
> Patricia Campbell, in *Bulletin,* C.I.B.C. Volume 10, Number 4, 1979.

You can readily see some of the effects of sexism on the behaviors of both boys and girls. Girls tend to be less sure of themselves than boys in athletics and activities that call for assertive behavior. They often use traditionally "feminine" behavior because of the positive attention they get from peers. For example, if a girl is a captain of a team, she'll often pick boys first because, in the words of a fifth-grade girl, "Then they'll like you better." Girls may choose to wear clothes or shoes that are bad for their physical development and posture, or that prohibit active body movement, because "that's the style" and they want to be "popular" or "feminine."

You can also observe boys feeling the pressures to meet the image of the strong, tough male and giving up a willingness to show their emotions, be supportive of others, and be tender or thoughtful to their friends. When boys call each other "sissies" they not only hurt others, but inhibit gentle parts of themselves. Many boys feel inhibited to play with dolls or stuffed animals when they're young. Do you see boys making pretty things in art, or is a robot or rocket a more familiar image? Do your textbooks show men only in adventurous roles or as athletes, limiting the role-models depicted for boys? While it's okay for girls to dance together at dances, boys wouldn't dare. Sexism inhibits the development of caring, supportive, and warm feeling behaviors in males.

---

**BOYS CAN BENEFIT FROM TITLE IX TOO**

Since physical education classes have begun to be integrated in some schools emphasis is shifting to life-time sports—tennis, swimming, track. Now a majority of children—boys and girls—who are not "superjocks" are learning to make physical activity a regular part of their lives. Title IX can be credited for much change in attitude.

Holly Knox, Director, Project on Equal Educational Rights.

---

The results of the attitudes and behaviors that sexism produces in children take heavy long-range tolls on both sexes. By about the fourth grade, relationships between boys and girls become antagonistic or of the boyfriend-girlfriend type. The potentials for experiencing the fullness of equal friendships with young people of the opposite sex—building-blocks for healthy adult relationships—are often relinquished. Girls often develop the low self-concepts and dependency traits which are disadvantages in personal, and later career, development. The early pressure for boys to compete, to be rational, and to achieve at all costs produce behavior patterns that lead to stress-related diseases in adult men and premature death.

LOOK CINDERELLA...MAYBE YOU SHOULD SKIP THE BALL,
AND JOIN A CONSCIOUSNESS RAISING GROUP INSTEAD.

After twelve years of grade school and four years of college, it's natural that our methods mimic those of our teachers. As a result, some of these methods may inadvertently be racist or sexist.

If you'd like to find out if they are, go through an average day in your classroom and ask yourself these questions. Do you unconsciously segregate the students by race or sex at any time of the day? Do you have them line up by sex? Is the roll called separately by sex? Glance around the room. Have you seated minority students together? Are they seated primarily toward the back of the room? Are you avoiding this issue by letting them sit where they want? When you try to seat them in a more heterogeneous way, is your seating arrangement student-centered so they may communicate with each other, or teacher-centered so they can stare at your desk? (Of course, if members of your class have healthy communication and respect for one another, segregated seating arrangements, if voluntary, may do no harm.)

Be sure to examine the language you use in your classroom. Do you call any of your students "sweetheart" or "dear" or "honey"? Do you use demeaning terms for inappropriate age groups? "Boys and girls" or "children" may be resented by older elementary students; you might want to substitute "students." What terms do you use to refer to minority students? The word "boy," however innocently intended, has negative connotations for older black male students. Do you refer to "their" attitudes and feelings (blacks', womens', Chicanos', and so on) as a group rather than as individuals? This can be a subtle form of discrimination. Have you adopted non-sexist vocabulary? Do you say "fireman" or "firefighter"?

Do you talk more with one group during discussions or let one race or sex take over? It happens time after time in the best of classrooms. Yet how surprised a teacher is when a student says, "We [minorities, females] never get a chance to be heard!" Do you allow for the fact that societal conditioning may have "done the job" on such students before they got to your classroom?

What you say—or do not say—is crucial. Asking the male members of your class to build you something in shop or to pass out books is as sexist as having the girls bring in baked goods for parties and write on the board. The messages: carpentry is a boy's domain; cooking is a girl's job; girls aren't strong enough to carry or pass out books; boys don't have nice enough handwriting to write on the board. If you have chores, are you giving everyone a chance to do them? "Volunteers" all too often end up as "favorites" in the eyes of the students and again subtle messages are sent out, depending on the sex and race of those in the limelight. Punishments must be consistent, and fair. Is it fair to yell at Marie for speaking in what, for her, is a "normal" tone and never to reprimand Tom for using the same tone?

What you don't say can be especially powerful. Not using a student's name, or constantly using it in a harsh or sarcastic way, is a quick way to destroy a student's self-image. If another student or teacher is demeaning a student and you don't say something, you might as well be doing it yourself. Ignoring such statements as "Women can't be doctors," "Blacks live in ghettos," and words like "chick" and "nigger," is very destructive. Not saying anything means you don't care.

Other aspects of your classroom environment are also important. Remember that how you group students can have a racist or sexist implication. Sometimes this is out of your hands; when it is your responsibility, be careful. If you group your students for reading, for example, and your "low ability" group is all boys or all of one race, the message is clear—that group is "stupid." Likewise, if your "advanced" group is predominantly one sex or race, a message is transmitted. Be conscious of, and try to change, sexist and racist outcomes of the grouping process.

Other methods you use, such as citing examples of a skill you have taught, can be examined. Be sure the people you mention in the examples positively represent the diversity of the students in your class. If you use a name that corresponds to a student's name, make sure the statement is positive. For example, suppose you're using the spelling word "commotion" in sentences to illustrate its meaning. Sentences like "Mary sat quietly sewing in her room ignoring the commotion," and

"Jamil and LaMar caused quite a commotion when they fought in class," have sexist and racist messages in them though none may be intended. It is just as easy to think of an apt example which carries a positive message. Perhaps you feel this is making a mountain out of a molehill. Remember, however, that a series of negative images is just like a series of molehills; pile them on top of each other and they become a mountain that can crush a student's self-concept and propagate racist and sexist attitudes in the other students as well.

Images are important and that's why it is vital to examine the images of women, blacks, and other minorities that are projected in the materials you use. Even if you teach art, physical education, or music, you need to examine these materials. The examples, cartoons, and pictures may convey a message that is harmful to the students.

All of this focuses on the sensitivity of the teacher to the student's feeling of self-worth. Creating a classroom atmosphere that promotes personal growth, self-worth, concern for others, and equal education is a heavy responsibility for a teacher. It means constant evaluation and re-evaluation of everything that goes on in the classroom—right down to the minute examples in the textbooks.

---

TARZAN LIVES: A STUDY OF NEW CHILDREN'S BOOKS ABOUT AFRICA

Major findings of this study were:

Only eighteen children's books about Africa were published by major publishing houses in 1977.
Only two of the eighteen were free of factual errors, patronizing vocabulary, or blatant ethnocentrism and racism.

Susan Hall, in *Bulletin*, C.I.B.C.,
Volume 9, Number 1, 1978.

---

**Types of Racism and Sexism**

Most educators are fair, humane people who care about the welfare of their students. Most of us are not intentionally racist or sexist. Often, however, the institutional practices of our schools or classrooms are racist and sexist, and we unwittingly reinforce them.

*Individual* racism and sexism are to be distinguished from their *institutional* forms. Individual racism and sexism are those racist or sexist beliefs that are expressed in individual acts. An example already cited, is that of a teacher calling a black male student "boy" despite knowledge of the history of that term and its racist implications. Another example is that of the media specialist who teaches only boys to run the audio-visual equipment. Most of us try to avoid such acts.

More difficult to avoid, because more difficult to see, are *institutional* racism and sexism—racist and sexist behaviors that stem from social, economic, and political institutions. Some of the policies and practices of our schools fit into this category. For example, most busing programs in this country bus minority children into white schools rather than the other way about. Such a policy not only assumes that white schools are better, and that minority students can benefit by contact with white students, but puts the burden of being bused on the minority students. Only if that burden were shared by minority and white students could we rectify the racist nature of this policy. For another example, look at the percentage of women in the top administrative posts in your school district. If that percentage is tiny, as it is in most districts, you can readily see institutional sexism close to home. In fact, only one percent of current school superintendents are women.

EXAMPLES OF INSTITUTIONAL RACISM AND SEXISM

1. School District of New York

| | Percent White | Percent Black | Percent Hispanic | Percent Asian-American | Percent Native-American |
|---|---|---|---|---|---|
| Students | 29.6 | 38.1 | 39.4 | 5.8 | 2.9 |
| Teachers | 83.0 | 11.4 | 4.9 | less than 1 | less than 1 |

U.S. Commission on Civil Rights, 1979

2. Percentages of Teachers Nationally by Race

white:      89 percent
Hispanic:   1 percent
black:      10 percent
The minority population in the U.S.: 18.9 percent.

1979 E.E.O.C.

3. Women in Public Education

83 percent of all elementary teachers (but 13 percent of elementary principals)
46 percent of all secondary teachers (but 3 percent of secondary principals)
15 to 20 percent of all policy-making administrators
12 percent of chief state school officers (7)
1 percent of school superintendents (182)

American Association of School Administrators, 1981

---

Schools are not the only institutions that reinforce inequality. Institutional discrimination in housing, jobs, and health care affect the lives of your students and their families, especially if these are minority, low-income, or single-parent. Learn more about the powerful effects of discrimination in these institutions and work in collaboration with others for change.

---

A further important distinction focuses on intentionality. *Conscious racism and sexism* are acts which stem from thought-out racist or sexist attitudes. For example, a teacher continues to use a textbook that distorts the images and omits the contributions of black people after that educator has been made aware of the biases. To use the book while training children to see and change the bias is educational; to use it without comment is an example of conscious racism. When a teacher articulates a double standard for the behavior of boys and girls—"boys will be boys"—we find conscious sexism. Such a teacher allows boys to be independent and assertive while reprimanding girls for similar behavior.

While most of us avoid such behavior, many of us unwittingly practice *unconscious* racism and sexism. These are acts which give advantages to whites or males over minorities or females *regardless of conscious motivation*. We may act with the best intentions, but if the *results* give unfair advantages, our actions are racist or sexist. For example, a vital criterion for advancement to administrative and supervisory positions is years of service. The *intent* of this criterion is to get people with the most experience into those jobs. However, in a school district that began hiring Puerto Rican teachers only ten years ago, the *result* of that criterion is to give advantages to whites who have not been previously discriminated against in hiring.

Many schools are now changing from sex-segregated to integrated physical education programs. In a mixed sixth-grade basketball class the girls usually don't do as well as the boys, not because of a lack of innate ability, but because they have had less experience. If the boys make fun of the girls and the physical education teacher continues to teach without comment, we find unconscious sexism. While her intentions in mixing girls and boys are admirable, the *result* is sexist. Instead, she must explain that girls have had less practice in basketball than boys, make ridicule unacceptable, and structure the class in such a way as to allow skilled students to help the less-skilled ones in constructive, cooperative ways. Then her non-sexist intentions will begin to produce non-sexist results. This is the humanistic educator's goal—making sure the methods and materials used in the classrooms promote equal opportunity and fairness. It is a challenging task.

**CLASSISM**     Although *Open Minds to Equality* focuses heavily on racism and sexism, there are other ways in which we can unintentionally distinguish among and discriminate against students.

Classism systematically assumes and enforces the legitimacy, power, and values of a particular group of people—in our society the middle and upper classes. We don't talk much in the United States about class differences because of the prevailing ideology of upward mobility. This claims that if you work hard you can make it; if you don't work hard and succeed, you *deserve* a lower-class position. However, institutional practices and cultural values in American society actively maintain a class structure. Many poor and working-class people are locked into their position, not by a lack of motivation, inventiveness, or hard work, but by policies of institutions that are beyond their control. Let's examine how class barriers to equality may be manifested in our schools.

Do teachers in your school have different academic expectations of children, based on their class background? Do they assume that some will eventually go to college and others won't? Such expectations are often subtly communicated to students and affect their own expectations. Do teachers ask students to talk about vacations and trips, assuming that all children have these experiences? Do they use examples of major consumer products in their lessons, reinforcing the idea that "normal" people have the money and desire to buy them? Look at your texts and reading books. What class of people are portrayed? Look at the messages in the stories in your books. If people work hard, do they always succeed? What message does this give to a child whose parents are struggling very hard and not making it? Are parents expected to provide extra money for additional things? Do students have to pay for books or gym equipment? If students are tracked into reading groups, which social class do students in the low reading class come from? If there are special programs for the gifted, which social class do these students come from? Are there certain lower-class families in your school who are labeled, stereotyped, and made into outcasts?

---

**EXPECTATIONS MATTER**

Teachers were told that their class was tested and found to be "late bloomers" and would be expected to achieve exceptionally well that year. Indeed they did! However the "late-bloomers" were in fact a random sample of students with no special characteristics. Teachers' expectations affected their teaching and student learning.

Imagine what happens to the learning of poor or lower-class students if teachers expect that they won't achieve!

See *Pygmalion in the Classroom,*
by R. Rosenthal and L. Jacobsen.

---

You can probably recognize the effects of classism on lower-class students in your school. Because poor or working-class children don't always have the symbols of status that are "in" among students—a ten-speed bike, x-brand blue jeans—they may be joked about, put down, or ignored by middle-class students. In many schools students give teachers presents at Christmas and Chanukah. You may know of instances where lower-class students have resorted to stealing in order to be "just like everybody else." Lower-class students are often too embarrassed to invite students who are wealthier to their homes or apartments. Some lower-class students don't get academic help at home; they come to school with fewer skills and less self-confidence than their middle-class counterparts—an unequal start to academic equality. Finally, the prevailing mythology of the assurance of upward mobility through hard work prevalent in most texts, media, and children's books can lower self-expectations, self-confidence, and motivation.

The effects of classism are evident in the behavior and attitudes of middle- or upper-class children as well. Students with greater privileges may develop a conscious or unconscious sense of superiority by name-calling or merely through mental comparison. Perhaps you've seen students make fun of children from those lower-class families that, generation after generation, have been marked for ridicule. Privileged children may develop either a lack of empathy for others or an equally destructive feeling of pity that motivates paternalistic behavior. They feel comfortable in school and other institutions which they believe exist to help and support them, and from which they expect returns. They learn to take much for granted.

The effects of the attitudes and behaviors that classism fosters can be life-long. Children of all classes develop stereotypes of each other and a lack of respect, caring, and communication. Although most do not *consciously* think about class, many develop a feeling that "this is my place in life." Lower-class children are reinforced in their sense of inferiority or self-hate. They may feel hostile toward more privileged people or may emulate them while degrading themselves. Some come to accept their position and rationalize that they "deserve" this because they're "no good." Such beliefs lower their academic expectations and impede learning.

The effect on majority children is equally strong. They become accustomed to putting others down, either outwardly or inwardly, to boost their egos. They come to assume that they are "normal" Americans, and that others are different or inferior. Many assume that, because they have enough money, they are somehow better than others. They take for granted the choices they have in school and life and assume that others have comparable choices. Many fail to see how their having privileges is integrally connected to others' lack of them.

Our job is twofold. It is to foster in students greater awareness of the attitudes, policies and practices that reinforce class stratification and help them see alternatives to this form of inequality. It is also to encourage mutual understanding for students of all classes and to help them see their common interests and ways of collaborative action that can foster change.

**AGEISM**   Age is another criterion used to categorize people. Older people are often described as incompetent, listless, and helpless on the occasions that they are present at all in curricula, books, and educational programs. In school, attitudes about both old age and youth are shaped and reinforced. To the extent that old age is denigrated, youth is often praised. This can reinforce a type of superiority similar to that based on race, sex, or class. We can insure that children develop realistic, positive attitudes toward older people. Further, we can help them understand that it is societal neglect of the needs of older people through inadequate health care, jobs, recreational opportunities, and housing that plays a major part in fostering the powerlessness of many older Americans.

Are students given opportunities to develop positive attitudes toward older people? Are older persons sought out to be aides in your school? Many welcome involvement with children, and the children get more adult attention. Check your readers and texts. How are older people characterized? Are they stereotyped or omitted? What do these books imply as the source of older people's powerlessness—themselves or society? Have older people who are involved in active groups like the Gray Panthers been invited to your school to talk about projects to help eliminate discrimination toward elderly persons? Has the awareness of students been raised, for example, by writing an essay on the important part some older person has played in their lives? A bulletin board showing pictures of a significant person—a famous person, friend, relative, or teacher—in various life-stages up to old age can make a vital point.

---

HOW OLDER PEOPLE ARE STEREOTYPED

A comprehensive study of the treatment of older people in children's books found that:

Of 656 books examined, only 16.5 percent contained any older character at all. Three quarters of older characters had no real function or position in the stories. Three words, "old," "little," and "ancient," comprise almost five sixths of all physical descriptions applied to older characters.

The author concludes: "Ageism pervades children's first literature. When older characters are always portrayed as sweet, little or slow and are seldom depicted as capable of self-care or as active or productive, then we must acknowledge that children's literature with it's present focus is a disservice to society."

Dr. Edward Ansello, in *Bulletin*, C.I.B.C., Volume 7, Number 6, 1976.

---

## COMPETITIVE INDIVIDUALISM

A final, but powerful, reinforcer of inequality is the emphasis in schools and society on competitive individualism—the notion that an individual's success or failure in life depends *solely* on his or her efforts and merits, and that each person has an equal chance to compete and succeed. This contrasts with the growing awareness among Americans that one's race, sex, class, or age is often a determining factor in one's chances for success. Individualism places the blame for failure on people rather than on social institutions. Its message is clear—both winners and losers deserve what they get. (Individualism is very different from individuality, which is the growth of each person's unique and full characteristics. Individualism, in fact, hinders the growth of individuality in many people.)

Cooperation, on the other hand, demonstrates that it is through interdependence that people can most effectively learn and develop their competencies while supporting the similar growth of others. Further, by working cooperatively people can change those conditions that bolster inequality. Since most teachers' goals are to have *all* students learn let's take a closer look at your school to explore the effects of competitive individualism.

Do students in your school bicker with each other, name-call, and put each other down? Often the need to put others down comes from a desire to boost one's own ego at someone else's expense. Do students cheat? Cheating arises in a competitive setting where students fear losing and being labeled a failure. Next, take a look at text books, curricula, and library books. Do they reinforce individualism by assuming that if you work hard you're bound to get ahead? Do they subtly blame people for their poverty, ignorance, or lack of success?

*COACH, THE TEAM WOULD LIKE TO RAP WITH YOU ON THE DESTRUCTIVENESS OF COMPETITION.*

Look also for opportunities for cooperation. Have teachers in your school considered structuring learning cooperatively? Do students work in groups toward a common goal—taking responsibility for each other's learning? Have you tried grouping students cooperatively to help each other work on behavior problems?

How does competitive individualism affect students? Young people often develop antagonistic feelings toward each other when competing for grades, teacher attention, or peer approval. Mistrust is inevitable, and the possibility of friendships with all students discouraged.

---

**A good answer may not be good enough. It has to be better than someone else's.**

Philip Dreeben in
*On What Is Learned in School.*

---

Competition reinforces the negative self-expectations of students who don't usually win. Failure isn't fun, and if it happens too often students tend to give up and drop out, cheat, or act aggressively and defensively toward school. If the culture, the texts, and the teachers tell students that they can make it if they try, they blame themselves for failure. Students who tend to succeed also pay a price. To further bolster their self-image, they verbally or mentally make negative judgments about others. They can be unwilling to share, because the fear of others achieving as well as they do threatens the basis of their positive self-image. They tend to disregard the needs of others and to look out primarily for themselves.

The long-term effects of competitive individualism face us daily. Drug-abuse, vandalism and lack of positive motivation and commitment are evident among young people. As one young woman remarked, "If no one cares about me, why should I care about them?" Winners easily justify their success with a rationale of individualism and feel no responsibility toward—or connection with—the situation of others. Another effect is the lack of experience and skills to look at a problem and work cooperatively toward creative, effective solutions that benefit all people. We miss out on the power of synergy—the coming together of unique persons to create a whole greater than the sum of the individual parts.

A restructuring of some of our classroom activities can help to reverse this trend and create a more humanistic atmosphere in our schools. With effort, this atmosphere can foster attitudes and behaviors that are more people-centered than me-centered. *Open Minds to Equality* contains lessons that are structured cooperatively, providing an alternative to competitive individualism.

> Competitiveness and individualism are tied in with the racial question. If one is very competitive and needs to feel superior, one is more open to prejudice and scape-goatism. If there were less competitiveness and individualism in our society, there would be less need for scape-goating and for feeling threatened by other people's achievement.
>
> Dr. Alvin Pouissant, in *Bulletin*, C.I.B.C.,
> Volume 6, Number 1, 1975.

## TEACHERS AND STUDENTS: THE POWER TO CHANGE

You, as a concerned educator, need to make a commitment to be sure the methods and materials used in your classroom foster equality—that they are not racist, sexist, or classist. The course of study is the ultimate tool; the resources included in this book will help you build the curriculum you desire. Some of these lessons you will be able to use successfully in their entirety with no revisions; some you may want to revise to fit your particular student population or teaching style. Still others you will try and the results will leave you unsatisfied. Don't cast these aside; they may work another time with a different group of students.

Center whatever you do on the students, because their feelings, experiences, and evaluations are crucial. Let these activities and resources be your building-blocks as you help your students understand and deal with issues of equity. Although the materials deal with various age groups and subject areas, read all of them. They are all exciting, and you will find valuable ideas in every one.

It is our hope that you too will learn about inequality as you use these lessons with your students. We expect that you will become more conscious of examples of racism, sexism, classism, ageism and individualism in your own school. With this awareness, you can take action that will improve not only interaction but also learning, for the more students feel worthy and understood, the better they learn. In sum, we hope you will become a role-model for your students.

---

### MEETING RESISTANCE

It is our experience that activities in *Open Minds to Equality* can be taught in most school districts. That is not to say that you shouldn't be prepared for resistance. Some teachers, administrators, and parents, either out of ignorance, closed value systems, or political viewpoints, are not committed to teaching toward equality. Your commitment to give all students a meaningful education and help to recognize and change bias and discrimination will be important in meeting this resistance. No doubt other educators and parents share your aims—enlist their support! After all, education in a democracy should mean teaching toward equality.

---

As you try these activities, set clear goals for yourself and your students. Expect that students will learn more. When *all* students feel respected, a basic precondition for learning is met. Aim to see that minority children, girls and lower-class students no longer internalize the inferiority that schools and society attempt to instill in them. Expect that majority children, males and middle-class students will understand causes of inequality and make changes.

While your focus of energy and time is in the classroom, the integral relationship of school to society necessitates action in the broader community. Seek consistency between your goals and actions in the classroom and in society. To introduce anti-racist materials into the classroom while violating anti-discrimination laws in renting an apartment, for example, betrays inconsistency. A teacher offering meaningful options to students strives to support those local and national struggles that aim to create a society that will provide *all* people with significant alternatives.

We encourage you to make changes. In both personal and social spheres, people are often afraid to take risks, imagining catastrophic results. We have more

"And now friends, how to make this happen.... !"

power and flexibility than we think—especially when working together. The challenge is to begin where we are and do what we can.

In this book, we aren't providing a "bag of tricks" for promoting equality. We *do* offer activities and ideas toward that end. Your honesty, critical thinking, commitment, and action are what ultimately will assure not only a democratic classroom, but an egalitarian society as well.

## SECTION B  INTEGRATING *OPEN MINDS TO EQUALITY* INTO YOUR CURRICULUM

*Open Minds to Equality* is written to fit easily into your standard curriculum. Provided here are both general suggestions to help you look at your curriculum with a more egalitarian perspective, and ideas for use of the specific types of lessons.

At the beginning of each lesson plan you will see one or more of the following abbreviations: M–mathematics; LA–language arts; R–reading; C–communication; SS–social studies; S–science; A–art; PE–physical education. By using these you can glance through each chapter to find lessons in appropriate curriculum areas. If you are looking for lessons in a specific subject, use the "Activity Chart" at the back of the book. All lessons are charted for their content areas, skill areas, and grade levels.

**READING**

*Open Mind to Equality* is useful for reading lessons, especially those involving comprehension and vocabulary skills. Several lessons are also relevant when you teach the use of an index and table of contents, and dictionary work.

In many lesson plans, students must understand the difference between connotations and denotations. You can use the activities in this book when first introducing these terms, or for reinforcement. Many lessons encourage students to look at familiar words in new ways. They learn to examine words for "loaded" meanings, to understand how language influences thinking, and to use new non-sexist vocabulary. The new words introduced in this book can be taught as sight words. They appear frequently, allowing opportunities for mastery. By teaching the roots of the words, students gain greater understanding of their meaning, as well as remember better. This can be a follow-up lesson anytime your reading series teaches root words.

Many lesson plans help students to empathize with others, an important inferential reading skill. As students learn to empathize through the activities in *Open Minds to Equality*, they can do so similarly with their reading book stories. The frequent critical reading and the comparison of different perspectives on the same situation teach point of view.

Students will read fiction, biographies and historical nonfiction as part of these lessons. Assign whatever standard book reports or research papers you regularly do. If you assign historical fiction, you might ask that students choose a book with a central female character, or one portraying the life of a working-class family. You might, while studying biographies, have students choose those of people of color. They can compare sex roles in a modern novel with one of twenty or thirty years ago.

There are lessons in *Open Minds to Equality* which promote awareness of detail. Use these when preparing questions which stress literal comprehension. Students will see good reasons for reading carefully when they are discovering important information about their own lives or the lives of people who are becoming "real" to them.

**LANGUAGE ARTS**

Language arts curricula teach children skills in communicating—in speaking, listening, writing, and spelling. The lessons in this book can be adapted to fit your standard language arts goals for the year.

For example, if you teach handwriting, you may have students copy from the board. Why not have their copying include paragraphs about famous Americans who were people of color, or who were women? Or give them passages which present people in nonstereotypical roles. They will get the handwriting practice, as well as exposure to egalitarian values. Students are more inclined to write neatly if someone in the world outside of school is to read their writing. *Open Minds to Equality* provides many opportunities for this. Students can be encouraged to do careful copies because they want to make their points, they want their letters read and respected, and they want responses.

Mechanics can be stressed through the use of lessons in this book. In addition to letter-writing, where proper mechanics is in order, you may give your pupils paragraphs to correct. Why not use a paragraph which will support equality and will stretch their view of the world!

Often you create sample sentences to teach a specific language arts skill, such as the use of commas in sequence. Here is a perfect opportunity to present your pupils with people of both sexes, of many races and classes, in divergent roles. Carry this over into your spelling sentences. If you prefer a traditional spelling series, you can still create your own sentences for tests. Use students' names in sentences where they can see themselves in various roles. If you give students additional words, teach them non-sexist words to replace ones they have previously learned.

In both spelling and vocabulary-building, encourage appreciation of other cultures. Look at words in our language which come from Native American words, or words which were originally Spanish. Students can learn to spell these words and to use them correctly, as well as to realize how much we learn from other cultures.

Note-taking may be part of your language arts program, especially in middle school. Many of the activities in *Open Minds to Equality* provide opportunities for practice. Students interview people in their school, community, and homes. This teaches specific skills in interviewing as well as note-taking from oral sources.

Gathering information provides ample opportunity to learn to classify and categorize. Many activities promote skills in observing. Students increase their awareness of the world through looking at bulletin boards, television advertisements, packaging of goods at stores, and magazines. They learn to listen more carefully for racism, sexism, ageism, and classism in what people say. This careful listening leads to more critical thinking. Students are encouraged to analyze what they hear and to understand the reasons for different viewpoints.

Creative and expository writing are the basis for many of the activities in this book. They are also, assuredly, a major part of your language arts curriculum. Why not choose topics from this book, thus giving your students practice in expressing themselves in writing and, at the same time, a chance to gain a more egalitarian look at the world?

**MATH** This book contains many activities which teach and reinforce mathematics skills, from the elementary level through middle school. As you use this book, you will begin to use more topics concerning equality when developing your own word problems, charting tasks, and work with ratio and percentage.

Many of the lessons involve graphing. For some students, this may mean picture graphs with appropriate keys. For those who can go beyond picture graphs, use bar graphs. For greater diversity, go on to circle graphs.

For middle school students, there are lessons with ratio and proportion. These are usually follow-ups from the graphing lessons, and present students with another way of looking at information. Students will develop math skills in setting up and reading ratio and proportion and will, at the same time, be reinforcing the information. For students at this level, there are lessons on percentages and on working with fractions and decimals. In some activities they read statistics, which they will learn to understand in both mathematical and humanistic terms. Thus students use numbers in a way which is both personally helpful in gaining mathematics skills and meaningful in the information it teaches.

For younger children there are calendar lessons, an integral part of most beginning mathematics curricula. Have children calculate the number of days or weeks between holidays, the greater number of holidays in some months than others, the number of years ago certain events happened, and so forth. Give practice in the basic processes of addition and subtraction. Middle school students can do more sophisticated work with fractions, ratios, and percentages with these calendar lessons.

*Open Minds to Equality* may help you look at your word problems with stereotyping in mind. Word problems provide an excellent opportunity to develop small situations which present children with a variety of sex and age roles, and with open race and class values. Show children various types of life-styles, work, and income-levels without judgments. Similarly, create problems in beginning algebra for middle school students.

**SOCIAL STUDIES**

*Open Minds to Equality* ties in particularly well in the area of social studies. Elementary school social studies curricula often teach about family living, communities, and different cultures. Since American history appears as the major focus in at least one year of upper elementary and middle school social studies, all the lessons which examine our country are relevant there. For middle school students, the emphasis on local history and historical perspective ties into *Open Minds to Equality*. If you choose several lessons a week from this book, a majority will fit well into your social studies curricula.

For younger students to comprehend the world around them, they must understand their own immediate world. Included here are lessons on students' closest environments—their home and school. When you study families, children can do the lessons which allow them to look more clearly at some of their family patterns. As they compare these to other families', they will find both commonalities and differences and learn about alternative family structures.

Chapters Four and Five are concerned primarily with our lives and those of others. No matter what your social studies topics for the year, these can easily be incorporated. You can help students to look at their life-experience as one of many, with some advantages and some disadvantages. They can see how their life-situation was determined, in part by choices they and their families made, in part by how society sets up expectations and possibilities for them. They can look at others' lives in the same way.

A broader grasp of economics is encouraged in the book. Students look critically at television programming and advertising and compare the life-experiences there to actual ones. Examining stores, food products, and toys, students develop a greater insight into the effects of our economic system.

Critical reading is encouraged throughout *Open Minds to Equality*. As students read texts and books, they learn to recognize prejudice and stereotyping. They thus develop an important critical skill to understand how textbooks influence their view of the world. When they do social studies reports from reference or library books, they will read more critically and write from a more objective perspective. For middle school students, research from several sources for a single report supports skills emphasized at that level.

**ART**

In *Open Minds to Equality*, frequent opportunities are presented to create displays. There are also chances to develop new game box covers, posters, advertisements, packaging for canned goods and other products, and so on. The students will thus get practice in lettering, design, and displaying in nonsexist and nonracist ways.

Many lessons involve drawing. Some lessons involve cooperatively creating murals or posters; others stress such technical skills as planning and measuring. Students illustrate stories in some lessons and in others draw pictures to analyze and change stereotypes. Use art in lessons as you assess its suitability in addition to or in place of writing tasks.

These ideas will help you integrate activities from *Open Minds to Equality* into the curriculum. You can simultaneously fulfill the academic goals you have for your students and teach toward equality.

# 2 BUILDING TRUST AND COMMUNICATION

Trust and communication

Egalitarian classrooms don't emerge overnight! They're the result of a great deal of hard work on the part of teachers and students. Just as a gardener prepares the soil for seeds and potential growth, so an educator must prepare students for working democratically. This chapter provides activities that teach basic skills which we feel are vital to a supportive classroom environment where students feel free to question, let down their defenses, and learn.

Explain to your students why these interactive skills are important. We often say something like this to students or people with whom we work: "We're in this class together this year to learn many things. You'll improve your reading and math, and learn lots of new information in social studies and science. . . . We're also here to learn about ourselves and each other. Everyone in this class is as valuable and special as anyone else and we'll be working together as a group in cooperative ways. *How* we do things is as important as *what* we do. Therefore we'll be taking time to practice listening to each other, working in groups, and using cooperative skills." Explain that these skills are applicable to many life-situations and once students learn them they will be able to use them at home in groups, and in future work.

These activities are sequential. Students initially learn simple skills and move on to more complex ones. They begin with lessons with a low level of risk and progress to more challenging activities. First, it's important that students get acquainted with each other and learn about their peers' lives and interests. This is a basis for trust and further communication.

Activities that teach students to listen to each other are followed by those that enable them to understand and improve their group process skills. These activities let students step back from the group, think about how well the group is working together, and pinpoint areas for change. Essential to successful group work is teaching students to identify and share feelings and to give each other feedback. With these skills, students can communicate honestly and change disfunctional individual or group behavior.

The value of the activities in this chapter is brought out in the discussion. *Processing questions* are those questions you ask after an activity is over. These enable students to look back on the activity and draw learnings from it. Some questions refer to the task—*what* students did; others refer to the process—*how* students worked together. As a rule of thumb, ask questions about the task first, then go on to questions about the process. Be sure to ask both types, and to allow plenty of time for them at the end of an activity. They are an extremely important tool to improve student learning, communication, and cooperation.

Don't be discouraged if activities don't go perfectly at first. As you well know, it takes time and practice to develop new skills. Keep on teaching activities, processing them thoroughly, and reinforcing the skills in all aspects of your classroom procedures. Your efforts will be worth it, for not only will students have skills they can use throughout life, but you will have laid the groundwork for trust and communication for this school year and subsequent ones as well.

The content of Chapters 2 and 3 does not always address itself to issues of equality. It is often difficult for students to concentrate on new process skills and on challenging content at the same time. Therefore we have chosen some non-threatening topics for the activities that teach listening, group process and feedback skills. Once your students have practiced these skills, you can use them again and again with lessons throughout the book.

"I believe . . . "

---

**PLAN AHEAD!**

To complete later lessons in *Open Minds to Equality* you'll need the following books. Why not ask your school librarian to order them now? They're all excellent and will be a valuable asset to your school library or curriculum center. (See Bibliography for addresses and publication information.)

*Unlearning "Indian" Stereotypes.* Council on Interracial Books for Children.
*Guidelines for Selecting Bias-Free Textbooks and Storybooks.* Council on Interracial Books for Children.
*Rosa Parks*, by Eloise Greenfield.
*New Life: New Room*, by June Jordan.

## SECTION A GETTING ACQUAINTED

## Name Game _____ C

**OBJECTIVES**  To have students learn the names of the other children in the class at the beginning of the school year.
To validate those things that children do well.

**IMPLEMENTATION**  Gather children in a circle. Ask children to think of something they like to do or are good at. Give some examples—"I'm good at singing," "I'm good at making friends," "I like to read."

Ask children to turn what they're good at or like to do into an "ing" word and to preface their name with that word—for example, singing Bob, making-friends Daryl, reading Jennifer.

One child introduces himself by saying, "My name is _____ and I like to/am good at _____." The student on his left introduces herself and then repeats the name and gives "ing" word of the person before her—for example, dancing Mel. This process continues, as each person introduces himself and then repeats the names and "ing" words of all the students before him.

Urge the children to concentrate hard. Also remind them it's not a memory test, and if they forget that's perfectly okay. To make this activity easier and more fun, you might have students briefly act out their "ing" word—or give creative clues—if someone is stuck. In this way the responsibility is on the group for every-one's success.

**DISCUSSION**  1. What did you learn about someone you didn't know before?
2. How hard or easy was it for you to think of something you're good at?
3. What would happen and how would we feel if more of us told each other the things we think they're good at?
4. How did members of the group help each other remember names and "ing" words?

---

**COOPERATIVE PEOPLE MACHINES**

Divide students into groups of six to ten. Tell each group to think of a machine, which they will act out, without words, using all their members as parts. Allow about ten minutes for planning and rehearsal time in groups. Gather together as a class. Each group in turn acts out its machine and other class members guess what it is.

---

## Concentric Circles _____ C

**OBJECTIVES**  To have students get to know each other at the beginning of the school year.
To encourage students to share information about themselves with others, that can foster communication.
To begin to think about experiences in which inequality or discrimination has af-fected them.

**IMPLEMENTATION**  Divide the class into two groups. Have one half of the class move their chairs into a central area and form a circle facing out. Or have children sit on the floor in that same formation. Ask the other half of the class to form an outer circle, facing in. In this way each person has a partner.

Tell the students that you will give them a question to talk about with their partners. (See examples at the end of this lesson.) Each person has about a minute to respond. Give a signal at the minute mark so the other child gets enough time. Then say, "Children on the outside circle, please each move one chair to your right." The inner circle stays stationary. Now each person has a new partner. Give them a new question to which they can respond.

Continue having students in the outer circle rotate to new partners as many times as seems appropriate or until they have come back to their original positions.

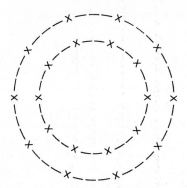

**DISCUSSION**
1. How did you like talking with your classmates?
2. Think of a person you talked with who you felt was really listening to you. Without naming that person, share some things that person did to make you feel listened to.
3. What's some new or surprising information that you learned about someone in your class?
4. Some of the experiences you talked about were about being treated unfairly or unequally. How does that feel? What can we do to change those situations?

**Sample Questions**  Note that there are two types of questions—those that are relatively unthreatening, and those that focus on feelings or experiences of inequality.

1. Tell your partner what you like to do in your spare time.
2. If you could have one wish granted, what would it be?
3. Describe an experience where you didn't get to do something you wanted to do because of your age.
4. Describe something you did recently to help another person.
5. Tell your partner about a time where you were treated unfairly by someone else.
6. How are you like and unlike your father or mother?
7. Describe a time you couldn't get to do something because you were a girl/boy.
8. If you could pass a law to make the world a better place to live in, what law would you pass?
9. Describe an experience you were part of or know about where someone was discriminated against because that person was a member of a minority group— black, Puerto Rican, Chicano.
10. Describe something that someone did with or for you recently that made you feel good.

---

SUPERB MATERIALS!

For some of the best materials on communication skills written for teachers by teachers, write to the Philadelphia Affective Education Program. Their *Together Book* is packed full of excellent activities that help students learn group process skills.

# People Scavenger Hunt C, M, A

**OBJECTIVES**   To have students find out more about each other.
To encourage students to interact with a wide variety of their classmates.
To find feelings we share in common with others.

**MATERIALS**   Copies of "Worksheet: People Scavenger Hunt" p. 35; paper and pencils.

**IMPLEMENTATION**   Ask students if they've ever been on a scavenger hunt. Tell them that on this scavenger hunt instead of finding things they will find their classmates!

Pass out worksheets. (If you prefer to make up your own, be sure that there are items relevant to all groups of students in your class.) Tell students they are to move around the room and try to find a person for each item and write that person's name in the blank next to the item. They may use each classmate only once.

Tell children that some of the items are feelings. For those items they should tell what situations caused them to have those feelings. Explain that many times we think we're the only people to have the kind of feelings we do, but usually we're not.

After ten minutes, or when students seem to have finished, have them gather in a circle. Start down the list and ask them, "Who in our class plays a musical instrument?" Call on students to tell who they found. Continue until all items on the scavenger hunt have been discussed.

**DISCUSSION**   1.   With whom did you find you had something in common? What was that "something in common"?
2.   What did you learn that you didn't know before about someone in your class?
3.   Was it hard or easy to talk about feelings? In what ways?
4.   Which feelings did you find others felt too? Were the situations that caused those feelings similar?
5.   What can we do to create more positive feelings and reduce the number of negative feelings?

**GOING FURTHER**   1.   Make a chart of class commonalities either with names and items or by having children draw themselves.
2.   Make a bar graph with number of children as one axis and categories as the other.

---

COOPERATIVE ENERGIZER: CREATE A PLACE

The whole class can participate in this cooperative energizer, which can be done either outside or inside. If you do it in the room, you will need to push desks and chairs back to create a large central space.

Ask a student to think of a place in which a number of people might be doing different things. An example is a grocery store. The person who thinks of the place does not tell anyone else. He moves into the central space and marks off the boundaries of that place by pacing them out. Then he begins taking the role of someone in that place. All is done *without talking.*

In the grocery store example, he might walk through the doors, get a cart, and start walking down aisles, getting products off shelves. Once someone else thinks she knows where the place is, she enters and begins doing something else appropriate to the place. For example, she might be the shopper's child who keeps nagging the father (non-verbally of course) to buy things. This can continue until all children who wish to participate have come into the place. If others don't want to, that is fine. Only at the end does everyone say where they think the place is.

## SECTION B  DEVELOPING LISTENING SKILLS

### I Feel Good About Myself _____ C

**OBJECTIVES**    To have students identify and share positive points about their own personalities and skills and learn about those of classmates.
To give students the opportunity to hear about their own good traits from two other people.
To create a supportive classroom feeling.

**IMPLEMENTATION**    Explain to students that this is an "affirmation" activity, one which helps them feel good about themselves. They will have the opportunity to share their positive feelings about themselves and then listen to these said back. Divide students into pairs. Try to pair those who do *not* know each other well. Give students in the class one minute to think of ways they like themselves and of skills they have. You can give a range of examples such as: things you're good at, like bike-riding, cooking, carpentry; things you do well as a person, such as helping your friends when they're in trouble, doing chores for neighbors, not criticizing people; and personality traits, such as being fair, cooperative, understanding of others' feelings, not being mean to people. Have younger children make a list so they can remember.

   When you tell them to begin, one person in each pair spends three minutes or less telling her partner these positives. The listeners may not talk except to give the speakers one-word reminders not to put themselves down in any way or qualify what they say! For example, it is okay to say, "I am a good guitar teacher because I was just recently a student myself and can remember how hard it is to begin." It is *not* okay to say, "I am a good guitar teacher but only for very beginning kids because I'm not really a very advanced player." If the second part of that second sentence is true simply leave it out. In the activity students only look at what they do well and how they help others. If the speaker runs out of things to say, both sit quietly until the time is up. At the end of the time, switch roles.

   Each pair now gets together with another pair. Then each person in the group of four introduces her partner to the other two people. She tells the other two as many good things about her partner as she can remember. All four get a turn to do this.

**DISCUSSION**    1.    How did it feel to talk about yourself?
2.    Did you have trouble thinking of enough to say?
3.    Did you feel you were bragging? Did you feel bad about doing that?
4.    When you were listening, was it hard not to interrupt?
5.    How did it feel to listen to your partner tell the other two about you? Was it easier or harder than the original talking?
6.    How hard was it to remember what your partner had said about himself?
7.    What did you learn about yourself in this activity? about your partner?
8.    What is one thing you can do in the next few days with what you learned?

**GOING FURTHER**    Sometimes a re-do of this activity, with different partners, is helpful later in the year if class feelings are less supportive than you wish. Sometimes even a reluctant or hostile group can do this well and come out with significantly changed feelings.

---

**A SUMMER CAMP ANECDOTE FROM ELLEN**

We tried this activity one day in a van with eight boys between seven and nine years old. They were tired and had been fighting constantly the whole ride back from a county fair. Almost immediately they understood the directions and were delighted with the opportunity to be encouraged to talk about themselves and to get to say so much that was good. They became absorbed in the process and we had the treat both of a peaceful ride and of hearing them in such a supportive, positive mood.
   This works equally well with much larger groups of young people.

**OBJECTIVES**     To learn a communication skill, "listening-checking," that will improve group discussion and empathizing skills.

To encourage students to hear what others are saying, rather than spend all their energies formulating their next contributions to a discussion.

To help students realize that often we don't express ourselves clearly and others misinterpret, or that we may be expressing ourselves well but others may be mishearing.

**IMPLEMENTATION**     This is an excellent way to build class discussion skills. It works best with a controversial topic where students are giving opinions and supporting those with facts.

Use a topic where interpretation and understanding of what others are saying is necessary. Here are a few suggestions. What, if anything, should the school do to include retarded children in regular programs? If you were making an advice booklet for parents what would you put in it? What are some effective ways you have handled put-downs from other kids? What are some of the things you would like about being another race, another sex? What should parents or teachers do when you hit another kid (or swear at another kid)? What are some of the ways to better get to know people different from yourself—different race, neighborhood, age, other sex?

Explain that after the first person speaks, the next person is to re-phrase what the first speaker said. This must be done in the second speaker's own words, but accurately enough so that the first speaker is satisfied that she was understood. If the second person cannot do that, then the first should re-say what she said until the second can re-phrase it correctly. The third speaker must re-phrase that before giving his contribution. Discussion proceeds in this manner. Before any student can join in the discussion, she must re-phrase the previous speaker's contribution.

This is awkward and time-consuming. However, it helps students concentrate on other people and greatly reduces people's tendencies to think through what they want to say while others are talking.

You certainly wouldn't want to do this every time you have a discussion. You might want to do it near the beginning of the year, when working on these methods, and then again later if poor listening is a problem.

**GOING FURTHER**     This is an activity that you could suggest families try at home. After one of the authors did it with a Girl Scout troop, several girls, on their own initiative, tried it with their families. The author got some very positive feedback from parents.

---

"Listening-Checking" is a skill. It can be used throughout the year, as needed.

---

### COOPERATIVE ENERGIZER: GROUP JUGGLE

*Needed:* Three balls of different sizes.

Gather students into a circle. Ask if anyone knows how to juggle. If so, have that student give an example. Tell students that they will learn to juggle as a group.

Begin by tossing one ball to a student. Tell the students they must remember two things—who they received the ball from and who they threw the ball to—because they will continue to receive balls from that person and throw balls to that same person. The student who has the ball throws it to another student, and so on.

For the first round, and the first round alone, have students raise their hands once they have thrown the ball. Others must throw to a person whose hand isn't up. In this way, all students become part of the pattern.

Once one ball has reached everyone in the group, the group's basic pattern has been established. Practice until students know it well. Now, start the first ball again, in the same sequence, but add a second ball, and then a third, so all three balls are being thrown in the group's pattern at the same time.

Slowly increase the speed of the juggle. Sometimes the group gets very proficient and sometimes all goes haywire—either is fine if you're playing for fun. If you are trying to develop psychomotor skills and cooperation, strive for group success.

# Adjective Attributes

**OBJECTIVES**
To learn a process for checking and improving listening skills that can be used throughout the year.
To build positive self-concept.
To learn new vocabulary and practice creative writing.

**MATERIALS**
Copies of Worksheet: Listening, p. 36; 3x5 index cards; magic markers.

**IMPLEMENTATION**
Tell the class they should try to listen better to each other in this activity. Go over the "Listening Worksheet" with them. Tell them they will fill it out at the end of the lesson. Tell students they will work together in groups to select positive adjectives that describe each other. They will help each other learn new words, have a chance to talk about positive qualities they see in each other, and practice careful listening.

On the board, make a list of adjectives that *positively* describe others. Here are suggestions: friendly, helpful, competent, athletic, tolerant, hard-working, kind, honest, strong. Add others relevant to your grade level. Define them together.

Divide students into heterogeneous groups of three or four. Students write down the adjectives and definitions of difficult words. They check others' work to make sure each student has correct words and definitions.

Then students choose an adjective that describes each member of their group. They do this by focusing on one group member at a time. He must sit quietly while the others agree on an adjective and the reason for their choice. Continue for all students. Remind students that all discussion regarding people must be positive. Monitor groups to catch any put-downs.

Next, each group has fifteen minutes to write a very short story in which each person in the group shows the quality described by the positive adjective the group picked for him. Groups read the stories to each other. Other groups try to guess the adjective the group chose for each person.

Have the students write their adjectives on a 3x5 card with a magic marker. They tape the card to their desks or chairs as a reminder of the positive quality their peers see in them.

The final, and very important, step in this activity is to have each student fill out the Worksheet.

**DISCUSSION**
Task (The content of the activity).

1. How did you feel about the adjective your group chose for you? Would you have chosen that one or another adjective for yourself?

2. How hard or easy was it to decide on an adjective for another person? Why?

Process (How people work together—in this case, listen).

3. Discuss all four questions on the Worksheet in some depth.

Keep the emphasis positive by focusing on what they learned about listening and how they can improve. Tell students they'll be using the Worksheet throughout the year as a way to check their improvement in listening. Return their Worksheet to them after you check them. Next time they do a group activity have them look at their answer to number 4 and work hard at that goal.

---

Use the "Listening Worksheet" throughout the year with any academic lesson that involves listening. Watch student improvement!

---

# SECTION C   BUILDING GROUP PROCESS SKILLS

## The Equal School _____ C, A

**OBJECTIVES**  To have students heighten their awareness of group process by use of a group process observation form.
To have students think about what makes schools just and equal.

**MATERIALS**  Copies of "Worksheet: Our Group," p. 37, one per student; copies of "Worksheet: Our Group Tally," p. 38, one per group; paper and pencils.

**IMPLEMENTATION**  Divide students into heterogeneous groups of four. Make sure students of different sexes and races are mixed within the groups, where possible.

Explain to students that there are two important areas to be noticing about working in a group—the task and the process.

TASK—*What* the group is trying to accomplish or complete, (for example, make a social studies map, draw a mural).
PROCESS—*How* the group is working together, (for example, how well students are helping each other, the amount of listening).

Reiterate to students that the task—the goals they are working toward—and the process—their group interaction—are equally important. Tell them they will have an opportunity to practice doing a task and to evaluate their group behavior.

Tell students that they are to work together to think about what would be a very fair and equal school. These things would not matter: race, sex, handicap, how much money their family has, or how much help their families can give them at home. Groups are to write down what students and teachers would do and say in such a school. They can also write down special rules, equipment or programs such a school might have. There is one paper per group. Give them about twenty minutes.

After completing the task, and before discussion, ask each student to check questions 1 through 4 on the Worksheet. Collect their Worksheets and make a quick composite tally for each group on the Tally sheet. Put a hypothetical group tally on the board and ask students what they could learn about that group from the tally.

---

**EXAMPLE:**

1. How much did I contribute to the group?    1 ✓    2 ✓    3 ✓✓
2. How well did I listen to the ideas of others?    1 __    2 ✓✓    3 ✓
3. How much did I ask other people for their ideas?    1 ✓✓    2 ✓✓    3 __
4. How well did our group work together?    1 ✓    2 ✓    3 ✓✓

---

In this example, one person felt left out and students didn't ask each other for their ideas too often.

Now distribute the Tally sheets to each group. Ask students to study their tally and see what they can learn about their group. Finally return individual Worksheets and have each student answer the last question.

**DISCUSSION**  "First, let's talk about the *task* of your group."

1. What are some student behaviors you'd see in a fair school? teacher behaviors?
2. Did any groups have rules that would be important to encourage equality?
3. What disagreements did you have in developing your school?
4. How can we apply what we've learned to our own school?

"Now let's talk about the *process*."

1. What did your group learn from the Tally sheet?
2. How can you tell if group members are listening to each other?
3. How can you improve your group behavior next time you work in a group?

**GOING FURTHER**   Use the Worksheet again, on academic as well as other tasks, until students become familiar with looking at the process of groups.

*Good Team Work*

---

GROUP LEADERSHIP SKILLS

Do *you* feel confident about structuring effective groups? If you'd like a refresher see:

*Developing Effective Classroom Groups*, by Gene Stanford
*The Together Book*, Philadelphia Affective Education Project

---

## Gum Drop Inventions ———————————————— C

**OBJECTIVES**   To become aware of the roles students can play in groups.
To recognize the role a student usually plays in a group, and to try out an alternative to that role.
To give students the opportunity to work collectively.
To challenge students to think of a priority in our nation's problems.

**MATERIALS**   Several boxes of toothpicks; about 150 small gumdrops; copies of "Worksheet: Roles People Play in Groups," p. 41.

**IMPLEMENTATION**   Pass out the Worksheet and discuss it with the class. Have students give examples of times they have played one of the roles mentioned. Ask them to think about what role they typically play, and what role they want to play today, then fill in the worksheet. Share a few responses.

Divide students into heterogeneous groups of five. Give each group 20 to 40 toothpicks and about 30 gumdrops. Tell them that they have five minutes to discuss, within groups, an invention which would help make our country a better place to live in. During the five minutes they should decide on the type of invention, how it works, and how they can build a model of it with toothpicks and gumdrops. They may look at the materials during this time but not touch them. Explain that once they start building they may not talk at all, so they should reach whatever decisions they can before they begin.

After five minutes, announce that there is now no talking and groups may begin building. While the groups are working, circulate around the room. When all the groups are finished, talk together, but keep groups near their own projects.

Going to the first group, ask others to guess what the invention is and how it works. If no one guesses, the group which created it can give hints. Finally, the group describes its invention in detail. Continue around the room for all the inventions. Then go on to the group discussion, which follows the pattern of beginning with questions about the task and continuing with questions about the process.

**DISCUSSION**
1. What are some new things you learned about other people?
2. Think of a word that you feel describes your invention.
3. What roles did you play in the group?
4. What did you do so other people could recognize that role?
5. What role did others think you were playing? What did you do to give them that idea?
6. How did you feel playing the role you did?

7.  Did you learn anything new doing this activity? If so, what?
8.  How will you use what you learned in other groups this week?

**GOING FURTHER**   Assign students roles to play in other group activities to give them an experience of an alternative. They can learn that they're not "stuck" in roles they typically take on.

## Who's Doing The Talking? _____ C

**OBJECTIVES**   To make students more conscious of the role they play in group discussions and to encourage them to make more critical decisions about that.

**MATERIALS**   Ball of yarn; two bags of dry beans or peas.

**IMPLEMENTATION**   Explain to students that often when we get very involved in a discussion we lose our awareness of how much we are contributing, or not contributing. Often some people do almost all the talking while others are silent or nearly silent. Sometimes a dialogue will take place between two people while other group members are excluded. The following activities help focus awareness on these issues. (They are probably *not* ones that you will want to use regularly, but only when the need arises.) For some discussion topics, see "No Interrupting," p. 45.

METHOD ONE.    Students sit in a circle. The first speaker starts with a ball of yarn, tying the end loosely around her wrist. When she is done talking, she gently throws the ball of yarn to the next speaker. After that person is finished, he winds it once loosely arond his wrist and throws it onward. In this way students can keep track of the pattern of a discussion. After the discussion, and before rewinding the yarn, discuss the questions listed below.

METHOD TWO.    Students sit in a fairly tight circle. Give each student ten, or more dried beans or peas. Place a large container, such as a garbage can, in the center of the circle. Each time someone talks he must throw one of his beans into the container. When a student uses up all his beans he may not participate any more in that discussion. Again be sure to process this at the end when some students still have left-over beans.

**DISCUSSION**   1.  What did you discover about your group participation? What could you have predicted?
2.  Do you think you behaved any differently in these activities than you would otherwise in a group discussion? Why or why not? Are those differences ones which please you?
3.  Were some people not participating in the discussion? Think of reasons which have to do with their choices and the choices of other class members. How is this helpful? harmful?
4.  Were some people participating a great deal? What causes this to happen? How is this helpful? harmful?
5.  Look at the yarn. Are there some people who always responded to the same people? Are there some people who got responses from a variety of people? Think back on these people and what they said and try to come up with reasons.
6.  Did having to give up beans make you more cautious about what you said, more reluctant to speak? As the discussion came to a close, how did you feel if you had many beans left?
7.  What could you do differently the next time you have a class discussion because of what you learned today?

**FOLLOW-UP**   "Fantasy Problem-Solving," p. 54.

LOVE AND FRIENDSHIP FOR THOSE OF
US WHO CANNOT HEAR...

## SECTION D  SHARING FEELINGS AND GIVING FEEDBACK

### Color Me Lovable and Capable _____ C

**OBJECTIVES**  To increase and share positive feelings about self.
To become more sensitive to one's own feelings and those of others.

**MATERIALS**  Paper and crayons.

**IMPLEMENTATION**  Tell children that we can help ourselves like ourselves, and help others like themselves, by what we say and do. Tell them the phrase IALAC stands for "I Am Lovable and Capable."

STEP ONE.   If you have access to Sidney Simon's *I Am Lovable and Capable*, read that to the class. See pp. 39–40 for our short adaptation of the story.

Before telling the story to your students write IALAC in very big letters on a piece of paper. Hold this up in front of you as you tell the story. At each point where Josh's IALAC is chipped away (marked * in our adaptation) rip a piece of the IALAC sign. By the end of the story there should be nothing left.

In discussing the story with your students the following questions can be starters: How would you feel if you were Joshua? What do people do to you that tears away at your IALAC? What has someone done to you to increase your IALAC? Only discuss briefly, as the rest of this activity allows students to go into more detail.

STEP TWO.   Divide students into heterogeneous groups of about three or four and distribute materials. Have each student make wide letters spelling IALAC on their papers. Their letters should be open, so that they can color them in.

# IALAC

Tell students there are three ways we can increase IALAC. They are through the things we say and do to others; the things others say and do to us; and the things we do or say to ourselves.

Students tell each other how their IALAC—their feeling of being lovable and capable—was boosted recently, in any of the three ways. One student starts and they proceed around the circle, telling of an experience and coloring in a letter. Continue around the circle five times until all students have told of five experiences and colored their IALAC signs. Hang these around the room or on their chairs or desks.

**DISCUSSiON**
1. What did you learn about yourself?
2. What did you learn about someone else?
3. How can you build up a friend's IALAC?
4. How can someone increase your IALAC?

**GOING FURTHER**   Remind students about their IALAC as you proceed through the year. Return to this activity periodically to build up positive individual and group feeling.

---

COOPERATIVE JOURNALS

Students can build trust, communication, and writing skills with cooperative journals. Students write an entry to a partner, who answers in writing, and then is responded to, and so on. As the year progresses, issues about equality and inequality can become the topics for the journals.

From Kathy Hare, Morse School,
Poughkeepsie, N.Y.

---

## Feeling Messages _____ C

**OBJECTIVES**   To practice sharing feelings.
To practice giving feedback in the form of "feeling messages."

**MATERIALS**   Oak tag; marker.

**IMPLEMENTATION**   Introduce "feeling messages" to the class: "When people work in groups, it helps to let others know how they are feeling about what's happening. This is true when things go well and when they go badly. One way to give feedback is through 'feeling messages' or 'I-messages'."

Write the format for a feeling message on oaktag.

"When you _____, I feel _____, because _____.
      [behavior]       [feeling]       [explanation]

Examples: "When you helped me understand the math problem, I felt thankful, because I had been very confused." "When you pushed ahead of me in line, I felt angry because I had been waiting patiently." "When you asked me to play soccer, I felt accepted because sometimes no one asks me to play."

Explain to students that by using feeling messages we can tell other people how particular behaviors of theirs make us feel. The feelings can be positive or negative. Feeling messages don't label the whole person as bad or good, they only point to specific behavior. Only if a person knows how he affects you, does he know either to continue or change his behavior. (See Thomas Gordon's *Parent Effectiveness Training* for a full discussion of "I-messages.")

Brainstorm a list of feeling words. Put them on oaktag and post in the class. Have students write down two or three feeling messages for the teacher or other students in the class. Ask a few students to share theirs with the class in order to reinforce the correct format.

Ask students to each pick one feeling message they would like to share with the person they wrote it for. Tell them to go to that person and give him the message. Sit down as a class and talk about how they felt giving and receiving feeling messages.

1. How did you feel giving your feeling message?
2. How did it feel to get a message, if you did?
3. Why is it sometimes hard to give feeling messages?
4. How could giving and receiving feeling messages help us get along better in our class? At home? On the playground?
5. Think of one more feeling message you would like to give today. Find a good time to do it and tomorrow we'll talk about how it went.

**GOING FURTHER** Leave the oaktag with the list of feelings, feeling message format, and examples up in the classroom. Remind students to use feeling messages often. Model them yourself. Periodically give the class time to write these messages to each other as a way to reinforce good feelings or helpful behavior, or as a way of working through tense or highly charged situations.

Create a mail box in your classroom for "Feeling Messages." Have a stack of blank forms (see p. 42) next to it. Allow students to fill in slips when they wish and have these delivered at the end of the day. Be sure they know they can send messages to you too. Allow time for discussion after students give and receive messages.

---

AFFECTIVE LEARNING

Need resources for sharpening *your* ability to deal with affective classroom learning? Read *Human Teaching for Human Learning*, by George Brown; or *Toward a Humanistic Education* by Gerald Weinstein and Mario Fantini; or *Reaching Out: Interpersonal Effectiveness and Self-Actualization* by David Johnson.

---

FINDING COMMONALITIES

It's easier to be with people and work with them when you feel you have something in common. This is a good quick activity for anytime, but especially helpful if your class is going through a tense period or a time when there are cliques working against each other. Have students take a piece of paper and list their classmates' names down the left hand edge. Then have each student go up to another student. They must find something that the two of them have in common—an interest, a skill, a like or dislike, etc. As soon as they establish that, they write the commonality by the other peron's name on their sheets. They should each then immediately move on to a new person and find a new commonality. Do this at several intervals until everyone has gotten to everyone else in the class.

Worksheet:  PEOPLE SCAVENGER HUNT

Find someone who:

1. Plays a musical instrument_____

2. Felt proud recently (share what
   happened)                      _____

3. Had a scary dream recently_____

4. Has recently read a book
   about people of a different race_____

5. Was born in another state     _____

6. Cooked a meal for his/her
   family recently               _____

7. Can whistle                   _____

8. Felt left out recently
   (share what happened)         _____

9. Helped someone out recently_____

10. Spends time with an older
    person--like a grandparent_____

11. Is good at something that
    isn't typical of his/her sex_____

12. Knows a game from another country_____

13. Felt angry lately (share
    what happened)               _____

14. Laces his/her shoes in an
    odd pattern                  _____

15. Repaired something that was broken_____

16. Has a regular job in his/her family_____

17. Can say a sentence in a language
    that is not English          _____

18. Felt happy recently (share
    what happened)               _____

19. Stuck up for a person being "put down"_____

20. Has learned a new skill in the last month_____

Worksheet:   LISTENING

1.  Who listened to you?


    What makes you think so?


2.  How well did you listen to other people?


    How would they know that?


3.  Was anyone easy to listen to?


    What makes them easy to listen to?


4.  One way I will improve my listening next time I work in
    a group will be to:

Worksheet:  OUR GROUP

Let's see how well your group worked together!   Answer each
question by putting a circle around a number.

|  |  | none,<br>not well | some-<br>what | a lot,<br>very well |
|---|---|---|---|---|
| Example: | How well do I play<br>kickball? | 1 | 2 | 3 |

Try these:

|  |  |  |  |  |
|---|---|---|---|---|
| 1. | How much did I contribute<br>to the group? | 1 | 2 | 3 |
| 2. | How well did I listen to<br>the ideas of other people? | 1 | 2 | 3 |
| 3. | How much did I ask other<br>people for their ideas? | 1 | 2 | 3 |
| 4. | How well did our group<br>work together? | 1 | 2 | 3 |

Look at your answers.


Write down one thing you'll try to do better when you work in a
group next time.

Worksheet:  OUR GROUP TALLY

Your teacher has put a check next to the number that each person in your group circled for each question.

1.  How much did I contribute              1___   2___   3___
    to the group?

2.  How well did I listen to               1___   2___   3___
    the ideas of other people?

3.  How much did I ask other               1___   2___   3___
    people for their ideas?

4.  How well did the group                 1___   2___   3___
    work together?

As a group, study this tally sheet.  What can you learn about your group process?

THE IALAC STORY

All people are born with a big IALAC--a feeling that "I Am Lovable and Capable." Sadly, as we grow up other people and events in life chip away at our IALAC. I'll tell you about a day in the life of Joshua, so you'll see how this happens. He is a ten-year-old boy, who's perhaps very much like you.

On this particular day, Joshua was awakened by his father who was yelling, "Joshua, you overslept again. What's the matter with you? Hurry or you'll be late for school."[*] Nevertheless, Joshua said to himself, "I'll hurry and will be ready on time."

Joshua got dressed and tried to get in the bathroom. His older brother had the door locked and wouldn't let him in. "You can wait your turn, squirt, I was here first."[*] Josh waited, and waited, and waited. . . .

Joshua had been looking forward to his yummy, crispy, crackling cereal. As he entered the kitchen his mother remarked, "My, Josh, you certainly are the poke of our family."[*] He hung his head, sat down, and there was a bowl of mushy, soggy cereal.[*]

Not to be discouraged, Joshua gathered his homework and started walking quickly toward his bus stop. He was very proud of his science homework. It had taken a lot of time and research. He was eager to show it to Ms. Vega, his teacher. As Joshua was heading toward the bus stop, a huge gust of wind blew up behind him and his science papers flew into the air and landed in a puddle!  He tried to gather his wet papers, but they were completely soaked.*

Josh was so discouraged!  He'd just have to explain things to Ms. Vega.  He started quickly toward the bus stop.  With only two blocks left to walk, he looked up and saw the bus pulling slowly away.*

Josh decided to walk the rest of the way to school.  As he walked in the door of the school, the principal, Ms. Johnson, stopped him.  "Joshua, you should be ashamed of yourself--twenty minutes late.  I want you in my office during recess."*

By this time Josh was feeling so low!  He got to his class-room and began doing his work.  Then Ms. Vega said, "And now students, please take out your science homework."  Joshua slowly raised his hand and said, "Ms. Vega, I know you might not believe this, but as I was walking to school a huge gust of wind. . . ."

Ms. Vega straightened up and said in a loud, stern voice, "Students, if you don't do your homework please do not make up ridiculous stories and excuses.  I want people to tell the truth in class."  She gave Joshua a very serious look.*

Joshua had very little IALAC left.  As he walked to lunch he said to himself, "Well at least a good lunch will make me feel better."  As he carried his tray across the lunchroom, someone tripped him.  Crash, down everything fell.  All the kids laughed at him.*

Adapted from "I Am Lovable and Capable" by Sidney Simon.

Worksheet: ROLES PEOPLE PLAY IN GROUPS

HELPFUL

1.  <u>idea-giver</u>

    gives helpful ideas to the group   I'VE GOT AN IDEA!

2.  <u>idea-seeker</u>

    asks other people for their ideas HEY JILL, WHAT'S YOUR IDEA?

3.  <u>friendly helper</u>

    is friendly to people and thinks
    of other people's feelings  TYRONE, WE MISSED YOU IN THE GROUP LAST WEEK!

4.  <u>peace-keeper</u>

    tries to help people who disagree or
    fight to understand each other  WHY ARE YOU TWO ARGUING?

5.  <u>organizer</u>

    encourages people to get the job done  WE'D BETTER GET BUSY IF WE'RE GOING TO FINISH!

6.  <u>supporter</u>

    tells people things he likes about them  I LIKE YOUR PLAN, LATISHA!

<u>NOT HELPFUL</u>

1.  <u>boss</u>

    acts like a "know-it-all" DO WHAT I SAY!

2.  <u>do-nothing</u>

    sits to the side and doesn't help  I'M NOT GOING TO DO THAT!

3.  <u>talker</u>

    talks and talks and talks and talks  YAP YAP YAP YAP

4.  <u>dart-thrower</u>

    makes fun of other people and their ideas  OH THAT'S A STUPID IDEA!

<u>Questions</u>:

1.  Which do you usually play in a group?_____

2.  Which role will you try to play today?_____

Worksheet:  FEELING MESSAGE FORM


_____, when you _____,
          (name)                        (behavior)

I feel _____,
                (feeling)

because _____.
                (explanation)

------------------------------------------------------------


_____, when you _____,
          (name)                        (behavior)

I feel _____,
                (feeling)

because _____.
                (explanation)

------------------------------------------------------------


_____, when you _____,
          (name)                        (behavior)

I feel _____,
                (feeling)

because _____.
                (explanation)

------------------------------------------------------------


_____, when you _____,
          (name)                        (behavior)

I feel _____,
                (feeling)

because _____.
                (explanation)

# 3 DEVELOPING SKILLS FOR CREATIVE COOPERATION

We have the potential to learn more from others, and with others, than we can on our own. Sometimes we expect students to have the tools for productive collaboration at their fingertips. This, however, isn't usually the case. Explicitly and implicitly our culture teaches competitive values and skills, and much less often cooperative ones. This chapter provides lessons which give students important tools for interdependent learning.

The first lessons provide opportunities for students to see that several heads are usually better than one, and that each group member has positive contributions to make. Skills in not interrupting, helping, and coming to consensus are introduced. Interviewing skills, needed in many data-gathering activities throughout the year, are taught.

It's when people work cooperatively that the most creative problem-solving and divergent thinking result. The final lessons in the chapter give students experience with brainstorming, creative controversy, and role-play.

A number of lessons in *Open Minds to Equality* use cooperative goal-structuring. When learning is structured in such a manner, students work together in a group on a common task and are accountable to the group. Each person succeeds if, and only if, the group succeeds. Cooperative goal-structuring enhances not only students' responsibility for themselves, but for their peers. David and Roger Johnson's book, *Learning Together and Alone: Cooperation, Competition and Individualization* is an excellent resource describing the rationale and methodology of this approach.

As you go through the chapter, continue to remind students that they can learn as much, or more, by working together as by working alone, and that they can learn as much from other people as from books. Help them understand that learning is a many-faceted experience.

In this chapter, as in Chapter 2, the content does not always directly focus on issues of equality. Students are still learning process skills with some nonthreatening topics, so they will have had practice with those skills when they study discrimination. But if students are learning those skills, your classroom process will already be reflecting more equality!

## SECTION A  LEARNING COOPERATIVE SKILLS

# Brainstorming _____ LA, C

**OBJECTIVES**   To teach students a skill in drawing information out of themselves and sharing it with others.
To encourage more creative thinking and generation of ideas.
To show students how others' ideas can help them come up with more ideas of their own—and how a combination of ideas from many people can often be more exciting than any single one.

**MATERIALS**   Chart paper; magic markers.

**IMPLEMENTATION**   Explain to the students that brainstorming is a method which is helpful in getting people to think creatively and in getting many solutions to a problem. Often hearing others' ideas helps get one thinking better. Discuss the rules of brainstorming, below, then post in front of the room. Remind students to follow them during the lessons.

1.   All ideas are accepted—everything gets written down.
2.   No one comments (positively or negatively) on anyone else's ideas.
3.   Say anything that comes to mind, even if it seems silly.
4.   Think about what others have suggested and use those ideas to get your brain moving along new lines.

   Divide into heterogeneous groups of four to six students. Each group needs several pieces of chart paper and a recorder. If ideas come too fast for one person to write, have two recorders. Printing should be big enough so everyone can read it while brainstorming is going on.

BRAINSTORMING TASK ONE.   Each small group must come to agreement on a name for this product: sneakers which have striped fluorescent uppers, waffle bottoms, Wilma Rudolph's signature, double holes up each side for fancy lacing, and autograph space around the edges. After ten minutes call "time" and have each group share the title it created.

BRAINSTORMING TASK TWO.   Students come up with composite solutions for how to do a task. Tell each group that often the process for picking teams in gym class or on the playgound isn't helpful because some people are always picked first and others last. Come up with new ways of picking teams that would be fun and make everyone feel good! After five minutes have groups share their ideas.

BRAINSTORMING TASK THREE.   Students come up with a problem-solution of a more subjective nature. Tell them: "You told your best friend that you think your parents are getting a divorce. You explained clearly that this was confidential and not to be told to anyone. A few days later you discover that your friend has told everyone. What are you going to say to your friend? What are you going to do?" After ten minutes have all groups share their ideas.

1. Was it difficult not to compliment or criticize other ideas? Why do you think this is a rule of brainstorming?
2. In what ways was each of the three tasks easy or hard?
3. Which task did you find easiest? hardest? Why?
4. In what ways did brainstorming as a group help you come up with a solution that you wouldn't have thought of on your own?
5. How could brainstorming be used in some of our regular classes? Think of something we did in any subject last week that might have been helped by using brainstorming. Explain how.
6. Are there any other rules we should set up as a class when we use brainstorming in the future?

**GOING FURTHER** Many other lessons in this book use brainstorming. If your students need further practice in this technique, before you use it as a crucial part of the content of other lessons, try some additional topics.

---

COOPERATION FOR SURVIVAL

Microbiologists agree that the extraordinarily rapid development of penicillin was possible only because groups of scientists in many countries were impelled to rise above all questions of national pride or personal scientific credit and pool their efforts to make this efficient antibiotic available for wounded soldiers in field.

From *Stress Without Distress,*
by Hans Selye.

---

# The Bean Jar                                                                           C, M

**OBJECTIVE** To examine how the involvement of different numbers of people in decision-making affects accuracy.

**MATERIALS** A jar filled with beans. You must know the number of beans in the jar.

**IMPLEMENTATION** Set the jar of beans in a place where all children can see it. Have each student estimate the number of beans in the jar. Record the estimates.

Have children form partners and repeat the process. Record the estimates. Do the same for groups of four. Encourage children to discuss their reasoning with their group members as they make their group estimates. Have the quartets pick another foursome and record estimates.

Tell the children the number of beans in the jar and have them compare it with their various estimates.

**DISCUSSION** 1. How did you feel during each decision-making process—alone, with partners, with groups?
2. How did sharing ideas with others and cooperating in a group affect how close you came to guessing the right number?
3. Why did the number of members in the group affect your accuracy?

---

# No Interrupting                                                                            C

**OBJECTIVES** To give students a method to eliminate interrupting each other when having a group discussion.
To eliminate hand-raising while others are talking.

**MATERIALS**  A rolled up clean sock.

**IMPLEMENTATION**  Tell students they will learn a method to promote better group discussion techniques. List some problems in group discussions on the board. For example, "No one really listens to anyone else," or, "People always cut each other off." Then list reasons for these. Students may realize that often people don't mean to be rude, but interrupt because they want to be sure to get a turn. Understanding that, and knowing that methods can be developed to cope with it is helpful in instituting a new approach.

Explain the following method. In the group discussion, the first person to speak will be handed a rolled up sock. While he is speaking he holds the sock in his hand on his lap. During that time none of the other students may say anything or raise their hands. When the speaker is finished, he holds up the sock in front of him. This is the signal for other people to raise their hands if they wish to speak. The speaker then throws the sock to someone with a raised hand. If that person is going to speak directly on the topic, she does so; everyone else must put hands down until she holds up the sock as the signal that she is done speaking. If, however, she is going to go off on any kind of tangent from what the previous speaker said, she must say so and give anyone who wants to speak more directly to the original point a chance to go first. In that case, when that person is done, the sock comes back to her before going onward. No one may say anything when not holding the sock except for the facilitator who may make "points of order," such as reminding people not to interrupt or not to repeat what has already been said. No one may raise a hand except when the sock is being held up.

Here are some suggestions for topics:

1.  A classroom project, such as a luncheon for the parents and children, that the whole class could work on cooperatively.
2.  A local issue that involves race, sex, or age discrimination—such as unequal funding for girls' athletics or funding for public health nurses for homebound older persons.
3.  A problem relevant to your students and their age group, such as teasing and put-downs.

**GOING FURTHER**  You can use this as a model whenever you do a whole-class discussion. Once students master the technique it is automatic, not distracting, and an excellent way to encourage more considerate group practice. Often it is helpful even when working in small groups, especially with a high-energy topic.

> Once we discovered this technique for our bunk at camp it completely changed our way of working as a group. It took us a few meetings to perfect it. The first few times people still raised their hands too soon, before the speaker had raised the sock. After that they relaxed and realized that they really would get called on. As soon as we all began to appreciate not being interrupted, and not seeing hands flying in our faces as we talked, we became committed to this method and worked with it easily. Later we found it equally effective with bunks of 8 and 9 year olds as with our bunk of 15 and 16 year olds. It was also a wonderful help with a mixed age group. I found this equally effective in a highschool computer center with a group of students I'd only known for a day. They now use it regularly at their meetings.
>
> Ellen Davidson

## Helpful Hints for Helping _____ C

**OBJECTIVE**  To practice some "do's and don'ts" of helping other students in a cooperative group.

**MATERIALS** Large poster board or piece of newsprint for chart; copies of "Worksheet: Do's and Don'ts of Helping," p. 60, two per student.

**IMPLEMENTATION** To simplify this activity it is broken down into three days. Schedule it in any way that works best for you.

**Day One** A) MAKING THE CHART, "DO'S AND DON'TS OF HELPING." With the whole class together, students think of a time that someone was teaching them on a one-to-one basis or in a small group setting. They close their eyes and picture that experience as clearly as possible in their minds. Allow a minute or two. Ask them to think of the ways that that person's interaction with them helped or hindered their learning the new skill or information.

They open their eyes and list these helpful and unhelpful behaviors on the board in two categories: "Do" and "Don't." Add items yourself.

When the list is complete, select the most important items from each category and put them on a large poster. It probably will be a variation of the following, depending on your grade level.

| DO | DON'T |
|---|---|
| 1. *Give Praise.* ("Great, I think you're catching on!") | 1. *Tell the answers.* ("Listen, here's the answer.") |
| 2. *Have the learner explain the information to you.* ("I think you've got it! Now teach it back to me.") | 2. *Give put-downs or embarrass the learner.* ("Do you mean you don't understand how to do this?") |
| 3. *Try varied ways of going over the same skill.* ("Fine, you know this multiplication table. Now I'll give you problems with multiplication in them.") | 3. *Pressure.* ("Hurry up! What's taking you so long?") |
| 4. *Find relevant examples.* ("Write a sentence using these vocabulary words to describe a person you know.") | 4. *Ignore a person who doesn't understand something.* ("Jim doesn't get this. We've got to hurry and finish the project, though.") |
| 5. *Quit while you're ahead.* ("You've got it! Now let's continue solving the group task.") | 5. *Pile on too much information.* ("You learned it, but there's a lot more you're behind on. Now listen to this. . . .") |
| 6. *Find the person's learning style and use it.* ("You learn your spelling best when you write the letters in the air.") | |

B) LEARNING STYLE. Explain that different people learn in different ways. Give some examples. Sue, a fourth-grader, learns spelling best by writing the letters in the air. John likes to spell his vocabulary words out loud in order to reinforce them. Ask students to name some of the strategies they have used to help themselves learn. Discuss them together. Each person completes these statements: "I learn best when. . . ." "I learn best by. . . ." Remind the students that when they are helping each other, they are to use the learning style that works best for the person with whom they are working.

**Day Two** A) PRACTICING HELPING SKILLS. Students work in trios to practice the "Do's and Don'ts of Helping." They number off. During the first stage of the activity #1 helps

#2, and #3 observes. Person #2 receives five "hard-but-intriguing" vocabulary words that she helps person #1 to learn. (A list of possible words is below.) Remind helpers to try to use the "Do's" of helping and to avoid the "Don'ts." The observer receives a dittoed copy of the "Do's and Don'ts" in the form of a checklist. (Use Worksheet, p. 60 if applicable, or make up your own based on the list your class generated.) Each time the helper manifests one of the behaviors, the observer makes a mark on the checklist. When person #2 has mastered the words, rotate so that #2 teaches #3 and #1 observes. Lastly, #3 teaches #1 and #2 observes. Each new process-observer gets a new checklist.

B) PROCESSING.   When finished, process the activity. Remind students that this was a practice session and the use of the checklist was to help them see the strengths and weaknesses of their helping skills, not to judge anyone. Also point out that since process-observing is a new skill for students, it wasn't expected that the checklist would be 100 percent accurate. This activity was to give practice to observers too! Don't worry about omissions or errors.

One at a time, students share information from the checklist with others in their group. The observer makes comments about what the helper did particularly well and in what area improvement is needed.

Come together as a class and discuss students' experiences in doing and processing this activity.

**Day Three**   STORY.   Students return to their original groups of three and use the new words to write a story together. Allow thirty minutes. Come back together and read the stories to the class.

**GOING FURTHER**   During future cooperative academic activities in which some members have higher skill levels than others, assign a process-observer to use the checklist for helping.

Set as one of the main criteria upon which the activity will be evaluated students' scores for helping. In this way the use of helping skills and the accomplishment of the task are equally important to group success.

## HARD-BUT-INTRIGUING VOCABULARY

| | |
|---|---|
| kudos | faux pas |
| en loco parentis | mukluks |
| pompous | titinnabulation |
| euphemism | empathic |
| epidermis | vivacious |
| pagination | acrophobia |
| prima donna | |

*HAVE YOU GOT A GAME THAT DEVELOPS SHARING AND COOPERATION ?*

## Zebulon's Fall _____ S, R

**OBJECTIVES**
To encourage the use of consensus.
To help children realize that pooling their information can often help them make more accurate decisions than if each child works independently.

**MATERIALS**
Copies of "Worksheet: Zebulon's Fall," p. 61, 25 percent more copies than there are students in the class; paper and pencils; library books on first aid.

**IMPLEMENTATION**
Go over the Consensus Guidelines listed below and posted in your classroom.

Distribute copies of the Worksheet. Students work individually to fill out Worksheets. Collect those.

Divide students into heterogeneous groups of four students. *Note:* in this case "heterogeneous" means mixed in terms of their knowledge about first aid—reading and writing levels are irrelevant. In fact, this is a good chance for some of your students with good health-care information and poor academic skills to be leaders and extra-helpful group members.

Give each group a clean Worksheet. Each group must reach consensus on the items. When they're done, collect the sheets.

Score the individually-done Worksheets and the group Worksheets. (The correct answers are given on p. 50.) Usually the group ones will be better than any individual one since students have combined their knowledge. Hand back both group and individual sheets. Discuss the content and then the process.

---

**CONSENSUS GUIDELINES**

Consensus is a way of working together as a group to reach a decision with which everyone is comfortable. It is informal discussion involving talking things through, understanding what other people are saying and feeling, and trying to work out decisions which are acceptable to everyone. Everyone must be part of the decision and satisfied with it. When a decision is reached the group shapes it and puts it into words which everyone understands.

Here are some helpful attitudes in consensus:

*Unity*—trying to come up with things the whole group can go along with.
*Cooperation*—understanding that the needs, feelings, and ideas of everyone are important.
*Openness*—keeping checking our own beliefs and changing them if new ideas make us feel differently.
*Diversity*—bringing out disagreements and seeing value and truth in what everyone says.
*Creativity*—coming up with new ideas.
*Patience*—working until we find something acceptable to everyone.
*Respect*—recognizing that everyone has rights, whether they agree with us or not.

---

**DISCUSSION**
1. How did you feel doing the Worksheet by yourself?
2. How much did you think you knew?
3. How did you feel when working with the group?

4. Did you think your group was getting better answers than you did individually? Than any of you did individually?
5. How was your group process? Did some people talk too much? Too little? Did everyone listen?
6. Looking at the class as a whole, how well did people do individually compared to the group scores? Why do you think that's the case?

**GOING FURTHER**     Students interested in content may want to look up more information.

Students may want to make up their own quiz sheets for their classmates to do individually and then in small groups. Many social studies and science content topics lend themselves to this.

---

Here is a fine exercise to convince students that more heads are better than one! Show a film or read a story which has a complicated multi-step ending. Don't read or show the ending. Have students first predict it on their own. Then have them work in small groups to do so. Then read or show the actual ending and compare individual with small-group predictions.

---

ANSWER SHEET FOR ZEBULON'S FALL

1. No. Poking in the wound might cause more injury. The wound will be cleaned with antibiotics in the hospital.
2. No. If nothing else is done until help arrives, serious bleeding could lead to shock, coma, and perhaps even death. Proper first aid treatment will also lessen pain.
3. Yes, do this second. Direct pressure over the wound site is the best method for stopping bleeding.
4. Yes, do this fourth. Using traction to hold the leg steady while straightening it lessens pain, reduces the chance of making the injury worse and allows splinting.
5. No. Unnecessary motion by Zeb will make the injury worse.
6. No. Zeb will have to have surgery. Fluid in the stomach may be vomited and go into the lungs when Zeb is placed under general anesthesia.
7. Yes, do this first. One person should go to call for help, and then wait until it arrives to lead the rescuers to the victim.
8. Yes, do this fifth. Splinting a broken bone stops motion so the injury won't get worse; it also reduces pain.
9. Yes, do this sixth. Preserving body heat is one way of preventing shock.
10. No. Zeb would be unable to stand because of his injury, and would most likely fall again, causing further injuries. His confidence can be restored after his fracture has completely healed.
11. No. It is better to let trained personnel move the victim; they will most likely have special equipment to permit them to do so without hurting Zeb more.
12. Yes, do this third. Comforting Zeb, letting him know that help is on the way, and finding out what are his injuries, all help to calm him (which reduces shock). Also Zeb might have other injuries which are not as obvious but which may be serious.
13. No. Tourniquets are used ONLY after all other methods of controlling bleeding (direct pressure, elevation) have failed.

---

# SECTION B   PRACTICING INTERVIEWING

## Intriguing Interviews ——————————————— LA, C

**OBJECTIVES**     To practice interviewing skills.
To learn more about people in the class.

**MATERIALS**  Paper and pencils.

**IMPLEMENTATION**  Have students write down three questions they would like to ask another person in order to get to know him better. Encourage students to ask unusual questions. Rather than, "Where do you live?" ask questions like, "If you could be granted one wish, what would it be?"; "What's one thing you've done that you're proud of?"; "Where in the world would you most like to visit?"

Students mill around the room. Each finds another student to speak with, and asks one question. The other person asks one in return. Students write down the name of the person interviewed and a summary of how that person answered the question. When finished with one person, they move on to another, with another question.

Remind students to ask their questions clearly and write enough of a summary to be able to remember their interviewee's answer.

When students have had an opportunity to interview three or four people, come back into the large group and sit in a circle. Begin with one student. Call out her name. Ask everyone who interviewed her to share the question they asked and what they learned about her. Go on to the next student and continue until everyone has had a chance to be highlighted.

**DISCUSSION**
1. What new and intriguing things did you learn about your classmates?
2. How hard or easy was it to interview your classmates?
3. What did you learn about doing a good interview? What could you do in the future to improve your interviewing skills?
4. How did you like being interviewed? What could the interviewer have said or done to make you feel more comfortable or talk more?

---

COOPERATIVE ENERGIZER: ATTRIBUTE-LINKING

In this fast, lively energizer, students move around the room quickly from one group to another.

You will call out an attribute and students must quickly move around the room to find all other children with the same attribute. For example, if you call "birthday month," students call out their birthday month and move around to form a group with all others with the same month. When students are finally in their groups ask each group to say its month, one at a time. Then name a new attribute and have students form new groups.

Other possible attributes include place of birth, color of socks, favorite season, favorite subject in school, hobby or pastime, birth order in their family.

This is a fun and fast way to enable students to find out what they have in common with each other.

Compliments of The Philadelphia
Affective Education Project.

---

## "Hello, I'd Like To Know . . ." _____ C, LA

**OBJECTIVES**  To help students learn to interview peers and adults in a way which is interesting and comfortable for all participating.
To help students become skillful enough in interviewing so that it is a useful means of gathering information.

**MATERIALS**  Paper and pencils; a resource person for one session; copies of "Worksheet: Guidelines for a Successful Interview," p. 62.

**IMPLEMENTATION**  Explain to students that interviews are ways of getting information and learning about other people. Sometimes they are done alone, sometimes as part of other research. Background research is often needed for a successful interview.

**Day One**    Post a large copy of the Worksheet. You can simplify it for younger grades. Go over it in class. Students brainstorm topic areas appropriate for interviewing the teacher. Encourage questions around issues of equality and inequality—for example, how being female or male, white or black affected your childhood. Then they divide into groups of four or five. Each group picks a topic and brainstorms a list of relevant questions. The group then decides on four or five questions and puts them in a sensible order. One group then begins to ask questions while the other students observe and fill in the Worksheet. After members of the first group have asked their questions, they evaluate themselves. Other students help them with their evaluations. Continue until each group has had a turn. During these interviews the teacher should be a cooperative interviewee.

**Day Two**    Brainstorm more topic areas. Next, tell students that not all interviewees are relaxed and cooperative. The class then brainstorms a list of the various kinds of personality styles an interviewee might have—hostile, verbose, friendly, confused, and so on. Write each personality style on a slip of paper.

Students then divide into heterogeneous groups of four or five; each group picks a topic area and brainstorms questions within that area. When they are ready, the teacher draws a slip of paper and uses that personality style as the first group asks questions. Evaluate before going on. Draw another slip for the second interview and proceed until all groups have had their turns. Discuss what they learned. Pinpoint strategies for working with difficult interviewees.

**Day Three**    Quickly review what has been learned about interviewing. Add to the Guidelines, if desired. Students divide into pairs. Each person interviews his partner for ten minutes on any topics he chooses. You can suggest topics relating to equality and inequality. Then they switch roles for another ten minutes. Following that, in pairs, students give feedback to each other on how they felt.

Pairs now combine with other pairs to make groups of four or six. The groups list what they learned about interviewing. For example, "I learned to ask simple questions before asking anything hard," or, "I learned not to tell my interviewee that I thought something he said was bad." As a whole class, discuss what has been learned and techniques for improvement.

---

TOPICS RELATING TO EQUALITY

1. What are the problems/good things about being male/female?
2. What are the advantages/disadvantages of being minority/white?
3. What are the positive and negative aspects of being young?
4. What are times in your life you've been taken advantage of? What are times you've stood up for other people who were being taken advantage of?

---

**Day Three**    HOMEWORK.    As a class, decide on the type of person to be interviewed—for example, previous teachers, parents, children over five and under ten. Agree on an interview topic. In pairs, students make out a list of initial questions. The interviews are done after school. One student asks the questions of the interviewee while the other takes notes. Then they find a second interviewee and switch roles. Evaluate the next day.

**Day Four**    Students are now ready to interview an outside expert. This should be a person who can speak about issues relating to equality—for example, someone doing a job which is not sex-role typical; someone who has recently been discriminated against because of age; someone who has just contributed in some way which is pro-equality. Use the format from Day One for students to brainstorm topics, then specific questions, then the order of questions. As a class, agree how the interview will be conducted. Will everyone get a turn? Will you set up an order beforehand? Are people allowed to use questions as they think of them or only the set ones? Conduct the interview, in the ways that you have decided. If possible, evaluate afterwards with the guest speaker; if not, evaluate on your own as a class.

**DISCUSSION**

1. How hard was it to think of topics? Was this harder with your teacher? Your student partner? Your homework interviewee? The expert resource person?
2. How did your actual interview questions compare to your projected ones? In what ways was it helpful to have a list ahead of time? Is there a way you could make that kind of list even more helpful?
3. How comfortable was the interviewee? If comfortable, what did you do to help create that? If not comfortable, what could you do differently another time?
4. What did you learn in content? Are there ways you could learn more content?
5. What did you learn about interviewing style? What advice can you now give yourself for future interviewing?

**GOING FURTHER**

Interviewing is used in many lessons in *Open Minds to Equality*. It can also be an excellent part of your curriculum for all other subject areas.

**FOLLOW-UP**

". . . And How Do They Feel About That" (p. 151); "Please Buy Me One," p. 167; "On the Horns of a Dilemma," p. 171; "Stop, Don't Take It for Granted," p. 189; "The Children's Place," p. 196; "Removing Those Hurdles," p. 240.

---

EVERYBODY GETS A TURN

A strategy to:

Develop equal participation in group discussion.
Encourage students to observe and change the pattern of participation.
Improve listening skills.

During a discussion, explain that no one may speak a second time until each member of the group has spoken once. *Variation:* Students may speak a second time if it is to encourage another student to participate. For example, "Juanita, what do you think about this?"

We suggest you use this activity with care because sometimes it puts too much pressure on some quiet students. One safe way to try it is in smaller groups, that tend to be less threatening to reserved students.

Also, pick a topic about which everyone *does* have something to contribute—for example, where we should go for a class trip, a suggestion for change in classroom procedure, and so on.

# SECTION C   ENCOURAGING CREATIVE
# THINKING AND PROBLEM-SOLVING

## Fantasy Problem-Solving ⎯⎯⎯⎯⎯⎯⎯⎯⎯⎯⎯⎯⎯⎯⎯⎯  C, LA, S

**OBJECTIVES**    To free students' thinking.
To help them evolve more creative, divergent solutions to problems.

**MATERIALS**    Chart paper; markers; clock with a second-hand, or a timer.

---

AN EXAMPLE OF FANTASY PROBLEM-SOLVING

*1—Brainstorm on Problem Ideas*

Sometimes some boys make fun of girls who aren't good at kickball.
There's a boy in our class who's two years older than the rest of us who gets teased
    a lot.
A few of the same kids keep failing all the spelling tests.
Many girls don't want to let the boys play jump rope with them.
When we go on class trips some kids have lots of spending money and some have
    none.
Two kids in the class speak only Spanish and no one else tries to talk with them or
    play with them.
The librarian keeps giving us "girl" books for girls and "boy" books for boys.

*2—Pick one problem and brainstorm fantasy solutions for it*

Problem:   When we go on class trips some kids have lots of spending money and
    some have none.
Go outside and pick money off of trees.
Ask the principal for money for the kids who don't have it.
Do trips where there is no way to spend any money.
Plant money seeds in our window boxes.
Sell stuff for money.
Put all the money kids bring in a bag and split it equally.
Go to the teachers' room and beg for money.

*3—Develop one fantasy idea*
Idea Chosen:   Sell stuff for money.
Sell our younger brothers and sisters.
Make mashed potato and bean-sprout sandwiches and sell them at lunch time.
Sell wishes.
Auction the teachers off to the kids.
Sell tickets to adults to ride on the school buses on weekends.
Get car lot to donate new cars to us; sell those.

*4—Pick one idea (or a combination of ideas) and brainstorm practical steps for
    carrying it out*
Idea:   Sell wishes and split the money earned equally.
Create a wishing well out of a carton; all paint it.
Make a sign for different kinds of wishes and the prices we'll charge.
Make a magician costume.
Put wishing-well in hallway for teachers and students to use at recess.
Sometimes on weekends put wishing-well outside for parents and other people to
    use.
Take turns being in magician costume in well.
Have people throw in money with a written-down wish. Magician jumps out and
    catches wish and money.
Get together as a class and decide how to carry out each wish and which kids in
    class will do what parts.
Carry out wishes.
Split all money made among whole class for next class trip.

---

**IMPLEMENTATION**  Explain to students that they will learn a problem-solving technique where they get to use their imaginations, starting out with seemingly "silly" solutions to problems and making those practical.

Make a copy on chart paper of the Sample Fantasy Problem-Solving, p. 54. Discuss with the class. Then have class brainstorm for several minutes on either classroom problems, community problems, or personal ones. After you have a list of eight to twelve items, stop. Then have the class as a whole pick one of those problems to discuss. Write the chosen problem on the top of another sheet of chart paper.

Now brainstorm, again as a whole class, on fantasy solutions for this problem. The single requirement is that the students may give only ideas which they think are impossible to implement. These include science fiction solutions or those which necessitate wishing on stars. This approach is partly to loosen thinking and partly because often a fantasy solution can become a real one. Go on until you have ten or fifteen ideas.

Take a clean sheet of chart paper and have students pick one of the fantasy solutions. Either the class can pick one in a consensus manner, or the student who originally suggested the problem can pick one he particularly likes.

Next, brainstorm on practical ways to develop this fantasy solution. As you start those, some of the "practical" ways may also be fanciful, but usually some realistic possibilities will emerge. Be careful to allow yourself and your students to see as "realistic" some ideas that you might reject initially.

Then, on a final sheet of chart paper, pick one of these ideas and develop very specific practical steps for how to carry it out. Finally, try the idea.

**DISCUSSION**  1.  How did you feel giving fantasy solutions? Did you see any point in it? Was it fun?
2.  Can you see the practical value in these? What happens when we only let ourselves see sensible solutions? What is to be gained from fantasy ones?
3.  Think of a problem other than the one used. Can you, on your own, think of both practical and fantasy solutions? Can you combine those into something that might work? What is the advantage of doing this as a group? on your own?

**GOING FURTHER**  Use this technique when you have a real problem in the classroom which needs solving.

## We All Own the Problem _____ C

**OBJECTIVES**  To help students realize that they can generate constructive ideas for the solution of both their own problems and those of their peers.
To help students learn that group problem-solving is often more effective than isolated independent problem-solving.
To give students practice in "walking in another person's shoes."

**MATERIALS**  Scrap paper; pencils; clock with a second-hand or a timer.

**IMPLEMENTATION**  Instruct each student to write on scrap paper a brief answer to the following question: "What is a way that you are or might be treated unfairly in school by your peers?" (Students should not write their names on the paper.) Then have them fold the paper in quarters.

Divide students into groups of six. Students within a group put their slips of paper in a container and mix them up. Students draw a slip. If anyone gets her own, they all go back in and get reshuffled.

When all students have a slip, they read these silently and spend a minute thinking about the problem and possible solutions. Each group chooses a first speaker. That person reads aloud, to others within the small group, the problem on her sheet. She must *own* the problem, reading it as though it is her own. Then she spends a minute talking about how she is going to deal with the problem, again in the first person. After a minute call "Time." The group has two minutes to discuss the problem and give other ideas, before moving on to the person sitting on the original speaker's right. Continue in this manner until all problems have been discussed. Be careful to call "Time" promptly, and to see that groups move on.

**DISCUSSION**

1. What was it like to hear your problem read by someone else as though it were that person's problem?
2. What was it like to have to talk about a problem as if it were your own, when it wasn't?
3. Did your group members have similar problems?
4. Did you get any good ideas on your own problem? on others'?
5. What ideas that the speaker didn't think of came up during the two minutes of group discussion on a problem? Why do you think some new ideas came up in that way?
6. What are some advantages of this technique? of having your problem be anonymous? What are some disadvantages?
7. How could we use this method at other times in our classroom?

**GOING FURTHER**

This activity can be used during the year when there is a particular issue involving the class, or in connection with problems of racism, sexism or class bias. Anonymity allows for more openness than your students may have when having to "own" their own problems.

In using this approach with your students in connection with specific topics you might want to try: "What is one way racism (sexism, class bias) has affected you personally and how did you handle it?" "What is a worry you have about being an adult female (male)?" "What is a concern you have about an elderly person in your family or neighborhood?"

---

CLASS ACHIEVEMENT GOAL

Set a class achievement goal in an academic area to encourage students to work together as a group.

For example, set the goal that the class will get 95 percent of the words on the weekly spelling test correct. At the beginning of the week set up small peer-tutoring groups in which students help each other learn the words. They study at home and later in the week the groups meet to test and further help each other. The small group is working to see that *everybody* can spell all the words!

Have students decide on a special kind of pictorial chart on which they can record their weekly progress as a class. Ellen's class used a rocket ship. A flower with petals that gets fully or partially filled in is another of many possibilities. Have a group of students make the pictorial chart.

At the end of the week, students take a quiz, and after correcting papers, record their class score on the chart. They work in subsequent weeks to improve it. Students are achieving *as a class!*

---

# Role-Play Guidelines and Techniques

C, LA,

**OBJECTIVE**

To help students learn skills for good role-playing.

**MATERIALS**

Clock with a second hand, or a timer.

**IMPLEMENTATION**

Role-plays are designed to help students see the choices they have in situations and to show them that they do not have to continue in past patterns. They encourage creative problem-solving and enable students to experiment with solutions. Take notes during role-plays. Write down any crucial moments, body-language, strategies used, quotations, changes in tone of voice. Caution the rest of the class not to laugh, cheer, boo or clap during a role-play, since these behaviors are distracting.

Role-playing can be threatening to many students. Others will participate eagerly but sometimes not thoughtfully. "Facing Lines" and "Group Decisions" are preliminary activities for role-playing. You will stand a better chance of having more participation and better involvement, if you use these, or other warm-ups, first.

**"Facing Lines"** This involves only brief action and creates less self-consciousness than role-playing because no one is watching. The activity encourages a variety of solutions to the same problem and forces people to think and act quickly. Students can observe their own and others' body-language.

Ask for two rows of partners facing each other. Use the whole length of your room. Designate one line "X" and the other "Y." Read the scenario to the students. Then allow thirty seconds for all students to stand quietly and think about their roles and get in character. When you say "Begin," students start talking with their partners. They may physically act out the scene as long as they stay more or less in the long line. They continue until you say "Time," which should be about two minutes later. They must then freeze in place.

SCENE ONE.    Line X is Robin. Line Y is Leslie. Leslie asks to use an old school paper of Robin's as Leslie's own work. Although Leslie is a good friend of Robin's, Robin is generally against cheating.

SCENE TWO.    Line X is Tracy. Line Y is Toby. Tracy has just teased Toby because Toby speaks English with a heavy Chinese accent.

SCENE THREE.    Line X is Lee. Line Y is Terry. Lee tells Terry that Lee doesn't want to spend the weekend at Terry's house because Terry lives alone with Terry's eighty-five-year-old grandfather.

**DISCUSSION**
1.   How did it feel when you were in each role? Which made you most comfortable? most uncomfortable? Why? In which scene were you playing a part with which you could identify?
2.   What happened in each scene? Share your solutions to the problems. As a class compare solutions. Were there many different ones?
3.   In what ways were the solutions you tried successful? unsuccessful?
4.   What kinds of behavior in your partner were helpful in coming to solutions? What kinds of behavior turned you off? Why? What suggestions do you have for yourself of what you might have done differently in each, or some of, the scenes? How about for your partner?

**"Group Decisions"** This requires people to think quickly in stressful situations and with a time-pressure. As a small group they must reach agreement. Conflicts often necessitate such quick thinking. Several possible solutions usually come up in different groups; thus, divergent problem-solving is encouraged. Because acting per se is not involved, students who are uncomfortable "on stage" often participate more.

Divide students into groups of three or, if necessary, four. Read the first situation to the class. Then allow thirty seconds of quiet thinking time. Then each group has one or two minutes to talk together and reach a decision of what it will do. Students are playing themselves—they are to decide what they would do if the three of them were actually in the situation. After you call "Time," have each group share its decision with the class.

SITUATION ONE.    You* are on a school trip. You get separated from the group and cannot find them. You see a truant officer questioning another group of kids—a group that looks suspicious. He'll be over to your group in one minute.

SITUATION TWO.    You are in the classroom at recess. The principal comes in with a

---

*In all cases, "you" means the three students.

new girl for your class. Serena uses crutches and has metal braces on both legs. Instead of her right arm and hand, she has a plastic arm with a metal hook at the end.

SITUATION THREE.    Your class has been planning a trip to a local fair. All of you would be able to bring a few dollars each. It is the day before the fair and you realize that several kids in your class won't have any money to bring along.

**DISCUSSION**
1. How did you feel in each situation? Which were easy? Which were hard?
2. In which decisions could your group reach consensus? In which could they not? Why? In what sorts of real-life situations do you have to reach decisions quickly? In what kinds can you wait?
3. What types of group behavior were helpful? harmful? What suggestions can you give yourself for functioning in a group which must decide something quickly?
4. What are some values which are important in making the decisions in these situations?

**Traditional Role-Play**

"I believe..."

This activity is a more standard role-play. When using role-play, give the characters names not belonging to anyone in your class. After the role-play ends, have participating students stay where they are in the scene. Using character names, ask each in turn how she is feeling. As each person answers she then returns to a regular class seat. Then ask the students, now back to their real names, how they feel as themselves. When discussing the role-play, it is important to direct questions in either character names or real names—depending on what you are asking. Ask the students who participated if the problem was resolved. If they reached a resolution did the characters feel satisfied?

ROLE-PLAY ONE.    Pat, twelve years old, and Devin, seven years old, are in the grocery store. Devin is staring at a black man ahead of them on line.
    Do this a second time, but this time have Devin staring at a woman in a wheelchair.

ROLE-PLAY TWO.    Eduardo has been at his friend Mark's house. Mark's father gets home from marketing and finds Eduardo and Mark playing. Mark's father calls Mark aside and says he doesn't want Eduardo at their house because Eduardo is Puerto Rican.

ROLE-PLAY THREE.    Tillie finds spelling difficult. Everytime she writes a story she asks her classmates for help with many words. Today she is just asking, "How do you spell 'please'?" Jayral and Gilbert begin, as is typical for them, to tease her. Nereida is a quiet student who is often teased herself. In this case, however, she feels it is necessary to come to Tillie's defense.
    Do this role-play a second time leaving Tillie, Jayral, and Gilbert the same. This time, though, Nereida is a popular, outgoing student who never gets teased.

ROLE-PLAY FOUR.    The setting is a baseball field and Carlene, who almost always strikes out, steps up to the plate. Immediately the in-field, consisting of Anselmo, Josh, and Airin, begin heckling Carlene with, "Hey, no batter, no batter," and, "Easy out, easy out," and, "Carlene can't hit nothin' but air."
    In the second role-play the in-field is heckling a batter, but this time it is Maura who is known all over school as one of the very best batters.

**DISCUSSION**
1. In what ways did the actors make choices which resolved the problems?
2. What choices did they make which made problems greater?
3. Give some specific examples of what people said or did that was helpful, that you might want to try in similar circumstances.
4. What other ideas can you think of that might work well? In what ways is it sometimes easier to think of more ideas when you are not directly in a situation? Thinking about that, how can role-plays help you to learn new behaviors for your own life?

5. How could we use role-plays to help us solve some of our own classroom problems? How could we use them to learn about other people and their problems?
6. Are there any new guidelines we have to establish to make role-plays work better in this class?

**GOING FURTHER**    If you decide to use role-plays as a way of understanding classroom conflict, there are some suggestions which can help. Try to isolate the conflict, understand its basis, and then create a role-play which speaks to the same issue but is different enough so that students don't say, "Oh, this one is about Samantha. . . ." Try to put students in a variety of roles.

**FOLLOW-UP**    "If Only We Had More Money," p. 70; "Seeing Eyes Glasses," p. 72; "M. and S. Auto Repair," p. 90; "Health or Home," p. 97; "Assignment Research Paper," p. 132; "What If It Hurts," p. 174; "Say It So They'll Hear It," p. 219; "Relearning About Native Americans," p. 226.

GUIDELINES FOR ROLE-PLAY

1. Set the scene for both the actors and the audience, to make sure everyone knows what is going on.
2. Make sure the actors know their roles very clearly (conducting an interview of the actors is a good way to do this and help them get into their roles).
3. Give the audience something(s) to look for as they watch the role-play.
4. If side coaching is necessary, break in and do it obviously, so everyone knows what is going on.
5. If the scene is not coming to its own resolution, make it do so. Say something like, "Take two minutes now for a resolution."
6. After role-play is finished, ask a sharp, focusing question to get discussion going and students focusing on the significance of what they saw.

From the Philadelphia Affective
Education Project.

Worksheet: DO'S AND DON'TS OF HELPING

Make a check each time the person you are observing shows one of the behaviors below.

| DO'S | | DON'TS | |
|------|---|--------|---|
| 1. Gives praise. | _____ | 1. Tells the answer. | _____ |
| 2. Has the learner explain the information back to the helper. | _____ | 2. Gives put-downs or embarrasses the learner. | _____ |
| 3. Tries a variety of ways for going over the same skill. | _____ | 3. Pressures the learner. | _____ |
| 4. Finds relevant examples. | _____ | 4. Ignores the person being helped if she doesn't understand. | _____ |
| 5. Quits while ahead. | _____ | 5. Piles on too much information. | _____ |
| 6. Uses helpee's learning style. | _____ | 6. | _____ _____ |
| 7. | _____ _____ | 7. | _____ _____ |
| 8. | _____ _____ | 8. | _____ _____ |

Worksheet:  ZEBULON'S FALL

It is a late fall afternoon.  On their way home from school, a group of six seventh-graders stop to play ball in an area several minutes walk from the street.  After a while, Zebulon climbs up to the top of an old wall.  He shows his friends how he can hop along the wall on one leg.  Suddenly he falls to the ground.  His friends see Zebulon lying on his back with his left leg tucked under his right one.  The bone on his left shin is sticking out through the skin.  The wound is bleeding.  Zebulon is screaming and complaining about the pain.

Which of the following should the friends do?

1. ____ Poke in the wound to get the dirt out.

2. ____ Send one friend for help while the other four comfort Zeb;  do nothing else.

3. ____ Wrap a T-shirt or jacket tightly around the wound to stop the bleeding.

4. ____ Have one friend lift Zeb's right leg, while another puts her hands on Zeb's ankle and pulls gently to straighten out the left leg.

5. ____ Help Zeb to his feet and support him while he hops to the street.

6. ____ Give Zeb a soda to drink since he complains he's thirsty.

7. ____ Send one friend for help.

8. ____ Take two strong sticks and use belts to tie sticks onto Zeb's left leg so it won't move.

9. ____ Put friends' jackets on Zeb to keep him warm.

10. ____ Cooperatively lift Zeb back up to the top of the wall so he won't develop a fear of heights.

11. ____ Carry Zeb out to the streets so that his injured leg does not move.

12. ____ Have one friend ask Zeb, "What hurts?" and talk quietly to comfort him.

13. ____ Tie a belt tightly around the top of Zeb's left thigh to stop bleeding.

Now number your "Yes" choices in the order you think they should be done.

Worksheet:   GUIDELINES FOR A SUCCESSFUL INTERVIEW

1.   Create a safe atmosphere.                                    _____

2.   Begin with some door-opener, "at ease" type of
     questions.                                                   _____

3.   Go from general questions to specific ones.                 _____

4.   Mix intellectual with emotional questions.  (Don't
     start the emotional ones until at least half-way
     into the interview.)                                         _____

5.   Make eye-contact with the respondent.                       _____

6.   Give the respondent the right to refuse to answer
     questions without having to explain why.                    _____

7.   Don't fire questions too fast.                              _____

8.   Keep questions short and simple.                           _____

9.   Ask open-ended questions, not loaded "trap door"
     ones.                                                        _____

10.  Don't debate questions with the respondent.  (You're
     there to listen, not give your opinions.)                   _____

11.  Write down key words to help remember what the
     respondent said.                                            _____

12.  At the end, ask the respondent if there is anything
     else to be added.                                           _____

13.  Thank the respondent.                                       _____

14.  Write up the interview as soon as possible.                _____

# 4 EXPANDING OUR VISTAS: OUR LIVES TO OTHERS' LIVES

The activities in this chapter will help students understand and experience ways in which they are similar to and connected with other people, and ways in which their life-situations and opportunities are different. It is difficult for all of us—adults and children alike—to step outside our own lives and examine our perceptions and behaviors as observers. It's also hard to get inside others' shoes to understand how others view the world and experience reality. That's why your thoughtfulness, sensitivity, and willingness to risk stepping outside your own experience will be so important for student learning in this chapter, and in *Open Minds to Equality* as a whole.

The first section of this chapter is entitled, "New Perspectives to See the World." Many of us grow up with a very ethnocentric world view, assuming that our life-experiences are "typical," when this is often far from true. Activities in this chapter will enable students to see how their perceptions of reality shape their ideas, values, and behaviors. Further, it will expand their vistas and help them understand that when they see only part of a picture, their perceptions may be inaccurate.

An apt metaphor to explain this is to say that all of us grow up with a pair of blinders on our eyes. Our particular life-experiences, values, and opportunities are those blinders. The purpose of Section A is to help students see that they might be wearing blinders. The goal of the chapter as a whole is to help students take those blinders off so they can see a bigger picture and legitimate the many points of view and life-experiences that are not their own. Often it's when we take off our blinders that we can most creatively solve problems and work in cooperation with diverse groups of people.

Section B, "Others' Shoes: Others' Views" is comprised of activities that will increase students' abilities to get into other peoples' shoes and empathize with their feelings and life-situations. They will see those things they have in common with people different from themselves and better understand and appreciate the very real differences.

Particular emphasis is placed on helping students examine how differences of race, sex, class are used to hurt people, and to think about the ways they as individuals might inadvertently be contributing to that process. Other lessons help students feel the effects of competitive individualism, as compared to cooperation.

The lessons in this section aim to help children *feel* the feelings of those hurt by differences and inequality. Upcoming chapters of this book will help them move a step further and *name* and *analyze* the processes at work.

## SECTION A   NEW PERSPECTIVES
## TO SEE THE WORLD

### It's All in How You Look at Things _____ R, LA, A

**OBJECTIVES**

To have students realize that their own perspective is not necessarily the only way to see the world.
To help them realize that there may be advantages in various viewpoints.

**MATERIALS**

Copies of "Worksheet: Phantom Tollbooth," p. 75; paper and pencils.

**IMPLEMENTATION**

Distribute copies of the Worksheet to all students. Have them meet in pairs, being sure that one student in each pair is capable of reading the Worksheet. Students can take turns reading aloud to each other.

When they have read the Worksheet, each pair takes a piece of paper and divides it vertically in half. At the top of one half they write, "Advantages of growing upward" and at the top of the other side, "Advantages of growing downward." Then using the ideas from the Worksheet, plus their own, they list as much as they can in each column.

Pairs get together with one or two other pairs to form groups. Each group picks, or is assigned, one or more of the following tasks:

1. Draw a picture of a specific scene from your point of view. Then draw it from the point of view of someone your age in the land where people grow downward.
2. Act out a scene taking place in the land where people grow downward. Show some of the problems they might have and also some of the advantages. Act out the same scene from our point of view.
3. Hold a debate or discussion between Milo and the boy in the story. In addition to what the story says, be sure to point out any other advantages you can see—from both points of view.
4. Suppose we could choose and sometimes be in the land we're in, and sometimes be in one where we start with our heads at the top. When would you choose each? Write some journal entries for a week in your life, each time saying whether you were in our land or in the land in the story. Tell about what you are doing and why you made the choices you made.

The following day in class you can stretch students' perspectives further by having them open themselves up to other differences which might exist in a fantasy world. Students get into new heterogeneous groups of three to five. Each group comes up with a different fantasy world—a world where everyone looked identical, for example, or one where people grew younger instead of older, or one where there was no such thing as money. Then the group does one of the above four tasks, using our world as one alternative and their new world as the other. When completed, share with the whole class.

**DISCUSSION**

1. What did you think when you first read the passage from *The Phantom Tollbooth*? Explain.
2. Do you think that kind of world could really exist? Why or why not?
3. Would you ever *really* want to live in a world like that? Explain.
4. What was it like to design another type of world? Did you have trouble thinking of ideas? making a group decision?
5. In what ways can looking at the world from such very different points of view make it easier for you to understand other people better and learn about equality?
6. In what ways are you "locked into" your point of view, such that you sometimes are not as open as you might be to someone else's way of seeing the world? Give one example of when that was harmful and explain something you could do about it.

**GOING FURTHER**    Students may want to finish *The Phantom Tollbooth*. They could design their own lessons on point of view using another chapter in the book, since there are many suitable ones.

---

STOP!

Are you remembering to have students process their group work? If not, look back to Chapter 2. Don't forget that the process skills students learned can be used with many activities throughout the year.

---

WINGO WANGO TAG

Pick a heterogeneous group of about one-fifth of your class to work with you secretly. Tell them that they will run around the game area pretending to tag other students. They will make more noise as the game goes on, so that it sounds like more people are doing the tagging. They should be careful *not* to tag anyone.

When you get ready to play, blindfold all children not in the planning group. Sit blindfolded children cross-legged, far enough away from each other so that they cannot touch with outstretched arms. Tell them they may not remove blindfolds, stand up, or speak until they are tagged by having both of their hands held by an "it." Then they get up and become part of the "it" group.

After everyone is seated and blindfolded, your planning group runs around pretending to play, but not actually tagging anyone. After about five minutes, everyone removes blindfolds and remains seated. After they have seen the arrangement, discuss what it felt like not being chosen when they thought other people were being chosen. Discuss how it felt when some people were in on the planning while the others did not know what was going on. Compare to situations in society.

From Lane Arye, counselor, Camp
Thoreau, Thetford Center, Vermont.

---

## What's In The Picture? _____ LA, C

**OBJECTIVES**    To enable students to see how easy it is to make assumptions when only seeing part of the whole.

To help students understand that their perspectives about other people and the world may be only partial pictures, limited by their life-experiences.

To encourage students to look for the "whole picture" when examining issues of equality and inequality.

**MATERIALS**    Copies of pictures 1-A and 1-B, 2-A and 2-B, p. 77, for all students; copies of "Worksheet: What's In the Picture?" p. 78.

**IMPLEMENTATION**    Examine the pictures yourself before you begin the lesson. Pictures 1-A and 2-A each represent the central portion of a larger scene. Picture 1-A portrays a woman pouring from a measuring cup. The larger scene (1-B) shows her as a chemist in a laboratory. Picture 2-A shows a black woman holding back a white girl. Picture 2-B places them at a busy street corner, where the woman is trying to keep the girl from being hit by a car.

Divide students into heterogeneous groups. Be sure they're mixed by race and sex, if possible. Give each student a copy of the Worksheet and pictures 1-A and 2-A. Have students look at picture 1-A and answer the questions on the Worksheet. Repeat for picture 2-A.

Now ask students to discuss their feelings in their groups. Ask them to compare their ideas about what's going on in the two pictures. Have a recorder in each group take notes on the different ideas. Then, without having students move their desks, discuss their feelings and ideas as a whole class.

Now tell students they will work silently again. Give each a picture of 1-B. Have them look at it and answer the questions on the Worksheet under "Follow-up." Repeat for 2-B. Then have them share their feelings in the small group. Finally come together as a whole class for discussion.

**DISCUSSION**

1. What was the difference in your feelings about the pictures when you saw part of the picture compared to the whole picture? Why was this so?
2. What assumptions did you make when you saw part of the picture alone?
3. When in real life have you only seen part of a "picture," or looked at a situation from one point of view, and later changed your mind when you saw the "whole picture"?

Tell students that because we grow up with limited experiences, we often see only "part of the picture." Sometimes we don't even know we're doing this. Explain that learning to see situations from others' points of view helps us perceive larger pictures. End by saying that in exploring issues of equality and inequality this year, this point is very important. For that reason, you will be asking them to remember this exercise as they deal with lessons and ideas about fairness and equality throughout the year.

---

AN IDEA FROM BRIDGET

One day have all the students describe the previous day. Be sure that day was a school day. Ask them how quickly the day went, whether they liked the weather, what the mood was, and so forth. Compare the results. It is likely that they will vary a great deal. Use this to reinforce how different our perceptions are, how different people at different times see the world. We are used to seeing only through our own eyes. The more we can understand that that is only one view, and often not an absolute one, the more we can understand other people.

---

## The Nine Dot Problem _____ LA, M

**OBJECTIVES**

To show students that sometimes they must step outside usual limits in order to solve problems creatively.
To understand that we unconsciously limit our perspectives and alternatives.

**MATERIALS**

Pencils and paper.

**IMPLEMENTATION**

Draw nine dots on the board as indicated below. Have students copy the same configuration onto their papers. Their task is to try to connect all nine dots with four straight lines without taking their pencils off the paper. Give them several minutes to work at it. They might try in pairs. If no one gets it, give clues like, "You might have to go outside the dots."

When a student solves the problem, have her go to the board and connect the dots.

**DISCUSSION**

1. Why is it that most of us didn't think of going outside the boundaries to solve the problem?
2. When in your life have you found new alternatives by looking at a situation from an expanded perspective?

Tell the students that in this unit they will be asked to step outside their own perspectives and look at the lives of others from a new viewpoint. Explain to them that most people grow up thinking that the way they see the world is the way everyone else does, but in fact that's not so. We'll be learning to see the world from many different points of view.

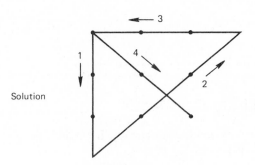

Problem
Shape

Solution

WHAT'S THE REAL STORY?

Get a few students to plan this with you. Stage an occurrence in the middle of class. It should have quick action and several props in it. There should be conversation. After it is over, finish whatever you were doing in class. Then have students each write a description of the occurrence. You'll find that the on-lookers have a range of ideas about what really happened. Often in confusing, fast-moving events we don't all remember or observe accurately.

## SECTION B  OTHERS' SHOES: OTHERS' VIEWS

### If I Were. . . . _____ R, LA ,C

**OBJECTIVES**  To have students appreciate their library book reading as an opportunity to empathize with another person in a life situation different from their own.
To have them see what they have in common with other people as well as positively appreciate differences.

**MATERIALS**  Copies of "Worksheet: If I Were . . . ," p. 76; assorted children's books; paper, pencils, and drawing materials.

**IMPLEMENTATION**  Ask each student to pick any fiction book that she is reading, or has recently finished. Distribute the Worksheets and have each student do one or more of the tasks listed or cut up sections and distribute individual task cards.

This lesson can be done independently or in reading groups. For sharing results, you may want to use a bulletin board or small discussion groups.

**DISCUSSION**  1.  How did these lessons help you look at your book differently?
2.  How did they help you look at the world differently?
3.  What are some advantages in being able to do this?
4.  What positive difference would it make for you and others to see the world through the eyes of people of different cultures, races, and backgrounds?
5.  What difference would it make in the world if we were all better at doing this? Give some examples.

GOING FURTHER    Make these task cards a part of your regular choices for book reports. Create some more of your own, or have students create them, following the same sorts of themes.

FOLLOW-UP    "Here's What Some People Did," p. 187.

> Equality of learning outcomes can be a goal of education rather than equality of opportunity.
>
> From *Human Characteristics and School Learning*, by Benjamin Bloom

## A Girl On Our Team!      LA, R

**OBJECTIVES**
To encourage understanding of what it feels like to be teased and put down because of your sex.
To help students learn to be supportive of equal opportunities and diversity in participation in activities.

**MATERIALS**
Copies of "Worksheet: Rebekah's Journal," pp. 81–82; paper for additional entries; pencils.

**IMPLEMENTATION**
Hand out copies of the Worksheet to all students. Have them staple on additional sheets of the same size to create something like a notebook.

    Students can read the Worksheet to themselves or work in small groups if the reading is hard. Explain any difficult vocabulary to the class. Assign students to write several additional entries. They can write a few at once, or one a day.

    After each student has written several new entries, divide the class into groups of five and share journal entries in the small groups. Gather for discussion. Then, as a class, brainstorm on what you would like to see happen. Agree on one idea. Then assign several more journal entries, the first being a description of what happened, and the other continuing in any way each student desires. (Save these for another lesson on Rebekah on pages 247–48.)

"MAIL-CARRIER"

**DISCUSSION**
1. How did Rebekah feel? Explain why she felt that way.
2. How would you feel if the same thing happened to you?
3. Why did Rebekah keep trying?
4. What would you do? Explain your decision.
5. What different things did the other children on the team do? What do you think of their choices?

## That's What You Brought for Lunch?      LA, A, SS

**OBJECTIVES**
To help students understand what it feels like to be made fun of because of racial or ethnic background.
To help students realize that people from different racial or ethnic backgrounds are people with whom they have many things in common.

**MATERIALS**
Copies of "Worksheet: Consuela's and Marita's Lunch," p. 79, one for each student; copies of "Worksheet: A Time I Felt Different," p. 80, one for each group; paper; pencils; drawing materials.

**IMPLEMENTATION**
Divide students into heterogeneous groups of four or five. Hand out Worksheet: Consuela's and Marita's Lunch to each student and have them either read silently, or

read aloud in small groups. (Be sure someone in each group can read the worksheet comfortably.)

After students have finished reading, ask if there are any questions or difficult vocabulary words. Then direct each group to write a lunchroom dialogue. This can be done in one of two ways, depending on the level of English mechanics of your class. If they can write conversation, in standard form with quotation marks, that is better language arts practice. If they are not yet at that level, they can use drama format, such as,

*Consuela:*

  *Marita:*

  *Heather:*

Each group comes up with a one- or two-page dialogue of how they think the lunchroom conversation might go. Move among groups to assist those having trouble getting started. Then gather as a class and have each group read its dialogue aloud. After each one, or at the end, go through the discussion questions.

Students then get back into their small groups. This time each group writes a dialogue about how they would like to see the conversation go in a way that would make it *supportive*, or even more supportive, *for all the children*. Again, these are read aloud and discussed.

On the following day students work in groups to either illustrate their new conversations, or to copy them over in comic strip format with the dialogue in balloons. Then groups go on to the second Worksheet, "A Time I Felt Different." When these are completed, they are shared with the entire class and discussed.

**DISCUSSION**

1. Why did Consuela and Marita get teased? How do you think they felt?
2. Consuela and Marita are Chicanas—Americans of Mexican descent. In what ways are people of different races or cultures teased because of their ethnic background?
3. What are some reasons that we tease people who are "different?"
4. How do you feel when you are teased?
5. In what ways did your group have the other children react to Consuela and Marita? Do these things happen in your school? In what ways?
6. What new solutions did you make up in the second set of conversations? How can you make those more likely to happen in your school?
7. How can you help yourself not to tease people who do things differently from the way you do?
8. How can you help each other not to do that?

**GOING FURTHER**

If parents of children in your class, or your school, cook food of various ethnic groups (for example, German, Afro-American, Mexican, Jewish) have them come in and do so with you. If not, use cookbooks which teach about food of different cultures. See Bibliography for ideas.

---

**INVOLVE PARENTS**

Are you wondering about parental responses to activities in *Open Minds to Equality*? Why not:

Write a letter to parents describing the expected academic gains, new learning opportunities, and increased self-confidence that will result for all students from these activities.

Invite parents into your class to participate in lessons. Urge them to ask questions. Encourage their involvement.

---

## Falling Behind

**OBJECTIVES**    To understand the feelings of someone who is left out because of competitive individualism.
To help children think through creative solutions to problems of conflicting needs.

**MATERIALS**    Copies of "Worksheet: Norman and Essie," p. 83.

**IMPLEMENTATION**    Tell students you are going to describe a situation that takes place in a class like theirs. They should try to understand the feelings of these two students. They are going to have to make a decision. This is the situation:

> Norman has been out of school sick for a week and he just came back. This is not his first absence this year—he's been sick again and again. Norman is getting behind in his work. He's scared that he might not catch up.

> Norman found out that the class is having a big unit test on multiplying and dividing fractions. He decides he will ask his friend Essie to spend her study period and lunchtime recess reviewing the math with him before the test. His teacher told him she wants him to take the test today. Norman is worried that he won't pass. He hopes Essie will help him.

> Essie has a report due in social studies at 2:30. She has a little more work to do on it. She's trying for an A. Essie works hard and likes to get good grades. The teacher said that for each day the report is late that grade will be lowered a full grade. For example, what would have been an A will be a B.

> Norman asks Essie to help him—just when she is putting the finishing touches on her social studies report. To help Norman might mean she won't get an A. She wants an A very badly.

Divide students into heterogeneous pairs. Give each student a copy of the Worksheet. Each starts out in Norman's shoes and fills in the first part of the worksheet. They trade papers and respond as Essie. Finally each concludes as Norman.

**DISCUSSION**
1. How did you feel as Norman before Essie's decision?
2. How did you feel as Norman after her decision?
3. Was the decision you came up with as Essie based on what was best for you or best for Norman?
4. What were some solutions that met both people's needs?
5. When were some times you have felt left out, when others were thinking only of themselves? Give examples.
6. When were some times you had to decide between helping someone else or helping yourself? Give examples.
7. What are some things we can do to help ourselves be more cooperative—to make choices that involve working with others?

## If Only We Had More Money

**OBJECTIVES**    To help students understand what it feels like to be left out because of class background.
To help students realize how economic differences in families effect social interactions.

**IMPLEMENTATION**    These are role-plays. Be sure you have done some work on role-playing from the lesson on p. 56. Choose one or both situations to role-play.

ROLE-PLAY ONE—OUT FOR A SODA.    There are four students in this role-play: Gwen, Amanda, Ashley, and Lloyd. Ashley comes from a home with very little money. The other three all get allowances of approximately $1 a week, which they are allowed to spend in any way they wish. The scene takes place right outside the building one day after school. Amanda has suggested to the other three that they all go out for a soda to continue working on their group social studies project. Gwen,

Lloyd, and Amanda have been out for sodas together before. This is the first time they have done a school project with Ashley. They enjoy him and want to include him in their activities. All four children normally walk home.

ROLE-PLAY TWO—THE BUDDING ARTIST. Tom, Ramon, Lois, and Gloria are friends. They're very excited about the new after-school program in drama, cooperative games, and art that is about to begin at their school. Gloria is an excellent artist and Ramon and Lois have been trying to convince her all week to sign up for the after-school program. This would help her in her goal of being an artist. Tom knows Gloria can't sign up because she has to go home to baby-sit for her younger brothers and sisters, Gloria has been avoiding the issue by saying, "Oh, I'm not interested in the after-school program." She doesn't admit she has to baby-sit. All four friends are now together. This is the last day to sign up.

**DISCUSSION**
1. How do you think Ashley felt? Explain.
2. Have you ever felt that way? When? What did you do?
3. What did you think of the ways Ashley handled the situation in the role-play? Can you think of anything else he could have done or said?
4. What do you think of what the other children said or did? Are there any other more creative ways they could have handled the situation?

Repeat discussion questions 1 through 4, substituting Gloria for Ashley.

5. Are there other times in your own lives when there have been problems for you or children who come from families with little money? Give examples.
6. How do you feel in these situations, when you don't have enough money to do what others are doing? What would you like others to do or say?

**MORE IS NOT ALWAYS BETTER, ROGER.**

## Seeing-Eye Glasses*                                                    R, C

**OBJECTIVES**   To enable students to understand how a point of view effects how one acts in a situation.

To help students understand the choices people have in life regarding individualism and cooperation.

To help students experience the feelings resulting from individualism or cooperation.

**MATERIALS**   Copies of "Worksheet: Concetta's Choice," p. 84, one per student; pairs of sunglasses and frames of old eye glasses (ask students to bring these from home the day before).

**IMPLEMENTATION**   Tell students that they are going to get to wear some very special glasses—"seeing-eye glasses." Each pair of glasses enables them to see the world in different ways.

PART ONE.   Assign students to heterogeneous groups of three. Explain the following situation to them:

> In Bill's family everyone takes turns cooking dinner. Each person has a night to cook. Tonight is Sam's turn. Sam is Bill's older brother. Sam calls Bill on the phone and says he's working on a play at school and will be late. He asks Bill to cook for him.

Have ready different sets of glasses—angry glasses, empathic glasses, creative glasses, fussy glasses, and so on. Define words and feelings as needed. Use actual sunglasses or old eye glass frames. You should role model the difference in glasses by putting them on and speaking briefly. For practice, have one group come to the front of the room and role-play the situation. One person is Bill, one Sam, and one the observer.

*Adapted from an activity in *Toward a Humanistic Education*, by Mario Fantini and Gerald Weinstein.

Begin the role-play with the phone ringing. Give Bill one of the four pairs of glasses and have him respond to Sam. Correct any misinterpretations. Have them have a dialogue with each other for about thirty seconds. Then give Bill a different set of glasses and have them continue. The observer is instructed to watch for changes. Next have students switch roles and give the new Bill yet another set of glasses. Continue the process until all have played each role and tried on at least a couple of pairs of glasses each.

Now that class members have the idea, let each small group of three do this, or a similar, role-play. Students change roles as above. After they're finished, talk together about the experience.

**DISCUSSION**

1. How did the kind of glasses you wore affect how you saw the situation?
2. How did your perspective change as you changed glasses?
3. When you were the observer, how did you see other people change when they switched glasses? What else did you notice?
4. In which glasses did people think mostly of themselves? In which did they think of others?
5. In real life when we look at a situation only from one point of view, it's like wearing only one pair of glasses. When has this happened recently in your life? Watch for this during the day. Why not try another pair of glasses!

PART TWO.   Have students read the Worksheet, Concetta's Choice. Explain that for this role-play there are two types of seeing-eye glasses—"me first glasses" and "we first glasses." When you wear "me first glasses" you are thinking about only what's best for yourself. When you wear "we first glasses" you are thinking of what's best for *you and other people;* your friend's need or wishes are as important as your own.

Students form pairs. One person is Concetta and the other the observer. Concetta is at home, trying to decide what she's going to say to her boss tomorrow. Concetta puts on the "me first glasses" and begins "thinking aloud." At thirty seconds call "Time" and have Concetta put on the "we first glasses." Again, she thinks aloud. The observer watches for the change in her point of view. Have her switch two more times and then ask students to reverse roles.

Finally, with glasses off, give pairs a minute to come up with their suggestions for a good solution.

**DISCUSSION**

1. How did you feel with the "me first glasses" on? with the "we first" on?
2. When you were the observer, what did you note as the difference in Concetta when she was wearing different glasses?
3. What solution did you come up with regarding Concetta's choice?
4. When in real life have you gotten ahead at the expense of someone else? How do you feel about that?
5. When in real life have you had to choose between what was best for you as an individual and what was best for the entire group? Did you make an individual or cooperative choice?
6. If we want *everybody* in our class to feel happy and successful, which glasses will help make that happen?

**GOING FURTHER**

The "seeing-eye glasses" technique can be used throughout the year in a variety of ways to help students see things from different points of view.

---

**TEACHER ALERT**

**Is it still September or October? If so, stop right here!**
It's important that your students have practiced skills in listening, group work, and sharing feelings before you continue. If you go back to Chapter Two and Chapter Three and reinforce those skills to your students, you'll have more success with the rest of *Open Minds to Equality*.

USE THAT VERITABLE VERSATILITY!

Are some lessons not exactly right for your grade level? Feel free to adapt them. The objectives for the lessons are clear. Why not change vocabulary words or adapt the Worksheet? Choose processing questions that are realistic for your grade level, or reword them.

You can use most lessons—given a dash of your veritable teacher's versatility.

Worksheet:  PHANTOM TOLLBOOTH


     "I said it's all in how you look at things," repeated the
voice.
     Milo turned around and found himself staring at two very
neatly polished brown shoes, for standing directly in front of
him (if you can use the word "standing" for anyone suspended in
mid-air) was another boy just about his age, whose feet were
easily three feet off the ground.
     "How do you manage to stand up there?" asked Milo, for this
was the subject which most interested him.
     "I was about to ask you a similar question," answered the
boy, "for you must be much older than you look to be standing on
the ground."
     "What do you mean?" Milo asked.
     "Well," said the boy, "in my family everyone is born in the
air, with his head at exactly the height it's going to be when
he's an adult, and then we all grow toward the ground.  When
we're fully grown up or, as you can see, grown down, our feet
finally touch.  Of course there are a few of us whose feet never
reach the ground no matter how old we get, but I suppose it's
the same in every family.
     "You certainly must be very old to have reached the ground
already."
     "Oh no," said Milo seriously.  "In my family we all start
on the ground and grow up, and we never know how far until we
actually get there."
     "What a silly system."  The boy laughed.  "Then your head
keeps changing its height and you always see things in a different way?  Why, when you're fifteen things won't look at all the
way they did when you were ten, and at twenty everything will
change again."
     "I suppose so," replied Milo, for he had never really
thought about the matter.
     "We always see things from the same angle," the boy
continued.  "It's much less trouble that way.  Besides, it makes
more sense to grow down and not up.  When you're very young, you
can never hurt yourself falling down if you're in mid-air, and
you certainly can't get into trouble for scuffing up your shoes
or marking the floor if there's nothing to scuff them on and the
floor is three feet away."
     "That's very true," thought Tock, who wondered how the dogs
in the family liked the arrangement.

                              From The Phantom Tollbooth,
                              by Norton Juster, pp. 102-106.

Worksheet:  IF I WERE . . .


Pretend you are a character in the book.  Write about a day in
your life which is not already described in the story.  Give
your thoughts and feelings, not just what you do.

_____

Pretend you are a character in the book.  Write a sequel about
some time in your life taking place after the book ends.  Give
your thoughts and feelings, not just what you do.

_____

Take one scene in the book.  Describe it three times, from
points of view of three different people in the story, explaining how each would see it.  Illustrate those.

_____

Be yourself.  Write a letter to a character in the story.  Then
write a letter from that character back to you.  Write a correspondence back and forth with at least four letters in it.

_____

What do you and one of the characters in the book have in
common?  List five adjectives that describe both of you.  List
five skills you both have.  List two problems you both have.
List three things you would like to do together if that person
visited you.  List five words which you and that character
would both use to describe your families or your schools.

_____

Pick a character in your book.  What are some ways you would
like to be like that person that aren't true for you now?

_____

Picture 1-A

Picture 2-A

Picture 1-B

Picture 2-B

Worksheet:  WHAT'S IN THE PICTURE?

Picture 1-A
How do you feel about this picture?




Describe what you think is happening here.




Picture 2-A
How do you feel about this picture?




Describe what you think is happening here.




Follow-up
Picture 1-B
Have your feelings changed now?  If so, how?  why?




Picture 2-B
Have your feelings changed now?  If so, how?  why?




What have you learned by doing this activity?

Worksheet:  CONSUELA'S AND MARITA'S LUNCH

It was the third week of school.  At lunchtime the children got in their usual two lines.  One line was for children who bought lunch.  The other line was for those who brought lunch from home.  Consuela, a fifth-grader, had her lunch in a bag from home.  She stood at the back of the line so she could leave the line quickly.  She always joined her sister, Marita, when the fourth-graders came in to eat.

Consuela and Marita's family had moved to town in August. Their parents were both working on one of the citrus farms.  The girls felt funny in their new school, which was almost all white.  Most of the other girls wore jeans to school, but they wore cotton dresses.  Their English didn't sound like the other students'.  The worst time of the day was lunch.  Everyone else who brought lunch seemed to have peanut butter and jelly or bologna sandwiches.  The first day Consuela had wanted to sit with the other fifth-graders.  Her parents had told her to try to be friendly.  She had sat down and taken out her tortillas. Right away three of the other kids in her class started laughing.  They laughed and laughed.  Then they started saying that she had a strange lunch and they would never eat anything like that.

That first afternoon Consuela and Marita told their parents about lunch at school.  They didn't want to be teased every day, but they liked tortillas.  They also liked doing something the way they were used to.  It felt safe and reminded them of home.

After that day they sat at a table away from the other students.  That way they could have their tortillas and not be teased.  But they could never quite enjoy it.  They felt ashamed that they had a lunch other kids thought was strange.  They wanted to make new friends and worried about what the other kids thought.

Now it was late September.  This day, right after Consuela and Marita sat down, two of Consuela's classmates, Heather and Deborah, sat down with them.

Now write the conversation that took place among the four girls and anyone else who came over.

Worksheet:   A TIME I FELT DIFFERENT

1.  As a small group, review how Consuela and Marita felt.
    Write down some of those feeling words.

    _____

    _____

    _____

2.  Review what had caused them to feel that way.  Write down
    at least two examples.

    _____

    _____

3.  Now brainstorm some times when each of you has felt
    different and has been teased.  List those examples.

    _____

    _____

    _____

4.  Pick one of those times and work together to write a
    description of what it was like.  If not all of you have
    been in the situation, those who haven't should imagine
    the feelings.

    _____

    _____

    _____

    _____

5.  Now think about what some other kids could have done to
    make you feel better.  Write down some suggestions or
    advice.

    _____

    _____

    _____

September 15

Dear Diary,

I'm so glad I got you for my birthday. The most exciting thing happened today. I got the best birthday present. You're a good present, but I got another one which is maybe a little better. Our town finally realized that they have to let girls on the town soccer teams. Finally I get to play on a real team. What a perfect present for my eleventh birthday.

My father said he would take me down to sign up tomorrow after school. I can't wait.

Oh, I also got a great new long skirt for folk dancing and the best book of mystery stories!!

Love,
Rebekah

---

September 16

Dear Diary,

You're not going to believe this. I sure didn't! My dad and I went to sign up for soccer. Well, this real big man with no smile on his face just stared at me. Finally he said, "You mean her?" Then he looked at my brother, Scott, and said, "Doesn't he want to play? What kind of family you got, Mister?"

Scott just laughed. He can't understand why I want to play on a town team. He likes playing soccer with me in our yard, but he'd much rather be building stuff on his clubhouse up in the woods, than be going to practice all the time.

My dad said he meant me and the man signed me up. But we knew it was just because he had to and that he was going to make it as hard as possible.

Aren't some people mean?

Love,
Rebekah

September 17

Dear Diary,

I can't write too much today since Dad and I are making egg-rolls for dinner and that takes a long time. I had my first soccer practice this afternoon. I'm not one of the best kids on the team, but I'm not one of the worst either. It's a good thing Norbert had practiced with me a lot before he moved away. It's bad enough how much the boys tease me as it is. The coach is just as bad.

They all say, "Why does she got to get to play?" and, "I never would have signed up if I knew I'd be playing with a girl."

I wonder if they'd be nicer to me if I was better than they all are. Maybe they'd be even meaner.

Love,
Rebekah

September 20

Dear Diary,

I'm sorry I haven't written for three days. Life hasn't been much fun. The second day we had soccer practice the boys were just as mean. One of them purposely kicked me at least ten times. The coach asked me if I wouldn't be happier mending uniforms. Mending uniforms, he's got to be kidding!

Then we didn't have practice one day, and would you believe I was actually glad? Well, today's practice wasn't much better. I'm playing okay and I'm getting better at passing. It really helps to be able to play with a whole team. But if no one will include me, what kind of team game is it?

Tonight I'm staying over with Tammy. We're going to try out a new chocolate cake recipe. But what should I do about soccer?

Love,
Rebekah

Worksheet:  NORMAN AND ESSIE

A.  Get into Norman's shoes.


    1.  I feel...




    2.  Essie, what I'd like you to do is...




B.  Trade worksheets with your partner.  Read what Norman says.
    Get into Essie's shoes and decide if you will help Norman.


    1.  I feel...




    2.  What I will do is...




C.  Trade papers once more.  Read what Essie says.  Get into
    Norman's shoes.


    1.  Now I feel...

Worksheet:   CONCETTA'S CHOICE


Concetta is a worker in a fast-food restaurant.  She works with ten other teenagers.  Concetta is earning money to help support her younger brothers and sisters.  She feels good that she can work to help the family out.

Working at the restaurant has been getting worse because the manager has made several new rules lately.  One is that if a worker drops any food she must pay for it herself.  One worker slipped on a wet floor and dropped a huge pile of hamburgers--it cost him $40.

Another new rule is that workers must do the clean up. The manager used to hire another person to do this job.  Many of the workers, however, cannot stay later because they have school the next day.

Concetta and the other workers are very upset about the new rules.  They are all very careful, but once in a while accidents do happen.  The leaky dishwasher--which the manager hasn't had fixed--makes the floors very wet.  One slip can cost them two days' pay.  Many workers can't possibly stay late to clean up, but the manager has said,"Well that's your problem. You <u>must</u> be here or lose your job."

The workers have decided to go to the manager as a group and tell him they'll all quit if he won't sit down with them and find ways to work out these problems.  They feel if they all stick together they can succeed.  After all, he can't run a restaurant without experienced workers!

The day before the meeting, the manager called Concetta into his office.  He said, "Concetta, you're such a good worker, I'd like to make you my assistant.  I'll give you a raise and you won't have to pay for any dropped food.  Also you won't have to stay late.  What do you say?  Of course, if you want the job, you'll have to convince all the other workers to stop all their complaining about the new rules.  Let me know tomorrow."

# 5 NEW WORDS: NEW EYES FOR SEEING

As students have an opportunity to feel what it's like to be hurt by differences and inequality, they will begin to name and recognize ideas and actions that reinforce inequities.

In "Prejudice and Stereotypes," students learn to recognize and examine these two types of attitude and behavior. They will pinpoint experiences in their own lives when prejudice and stereotypes have been involved, and will identify the accompanying feelings. Through the stories and accounts of other people, many of them their own age, they will understand the feelings of people who are stereotyped on the basis of their age, race, class, or sex. They will explore ways in which *all* people are hurt by prejudice and stereotypes, both those on the receiving and those on the giving ends. It is intended that students will develop an awareness that stereotypes are learned and that they therefore can be changed.

Section B, the "Isms," contains lessons that take students a step further in their understanding of inequality—that is, to a knowledge of institutionalized discrimination. The term "ism" is used throughout the book. Sometimes a word with an "ism"—racism or ageism, for example—threatens people. That need not happen if you and your students deal with the words with open minds. All "ism" implies is that a form of inequality is institutionalized. Using an "ism" word is to take institutional norms, practices, and power relationships into account. It is an accurate and inclusive description of inequality. Help your students understand the isms without being scared by them!

Explain to children that prejudice and stereotyping are sometimes practiced by *individuals*. (For example, John calls Tyrone a name that is based on a racial stereotype.) They can also be practiced by *institutions*—the school, family, workplace, government—and it is then that they become "isms." (For example, when such name-calling is a pattern in a school, and when a principal or teacher fails to take action to stop it after student and parent complaints, we have an example of racism.) Thus, an "ism" is a discriminating behavior practiced in a consistent pattern, often through the policies of institutions. A way to help students understand this is to use the equation—"ism = prejudice + power."

The lessons are planned so that students can experience the feelings of people affected by "isms" and understand how their options and opportunities in life are negatively affected. Through your careful use of discussion questions, they can learn to pinpoint the ways in which policies and practices of institutions reinforce such inequality. Explain that the situation described in particular case studies in the lessons are typical for *many* people in the United States today.

As you can tell, your role in this section is especially important! While the lessons will enable students to recognize institutional and cultural discrimination and see its effects, your leadership in the discussion can help students see broader connections to our society. The ways in which the "isms" divide people who otherwise might have common interests, and the ways they serve to maintain the status quo, can be discussed with some students, particularly those in the upper grades. Again, it's important to encourage students to discuss how we *all* lose out by the effects of the "isms."

Finally we encourage *you* to do new reading about institutional discrimination, so that you feel the excitement of new learning along with the students. Some fine books are listed in the box below; there are many more in the bibliography.

---

**USEFUL READING**

Non-fiction

*Institutional Racism in America* by Louis Knowles and Kenneth Prewitt
*Sexism in School and Society* by Myra Sadker and Nancy Frazier
*The Hidden Injuries of Class* by Richard Sennett
*Why Survive? Being Old in America* by Robert Butler

Fiction

*Daughter of the Earth* by Agnes Smedley
*The Bluest Eye* by Toni Morrison

---

Your test scores are excellent but your grovelling and snivelling scores are low.

# SECTION A   PREJUDICE AND STEREOTYPES

## What Are They?—Prejudice
## and Stereotypes _____ LA

**OBJECTIVES**   To define prejudice and stereotypes.
To have students think of times when prejudice and stereotyping affected them and
to identify the feelings involved.

**MATERIALS**   Chart of definitions, (below); paper and pencils.

**IMPLEMENTATION**   Remind students that this year we are working together to try to create a classroom
based on equality. One way to enforce inequality is through prejudice and
stereotypes.

Post the definitions of prejudice and stereotypes on newsprint and, if you wish,
pass them out to students on dittoes. Discuss these definitions with the whole class.
Ask the students to share examples from their lives.

Now ask students to think of one specific time that they were the victim of
prejudice or stereotyping. Have them write a short account of what happened and
what their feelings were during that experience. Then have students find partners
and read their accounts to each other. Ask them to talk particularly about their
feelings. Come together in a large group to share accounts and find commonalities in
emotions.

**DISCUSSION**   1.   What are some feelings you had when you were stereotyped or felt prejudice
directed at you?
2.   Are your feelings similar to those of others in our class? How?
3.   How do you think the person or people who showed prejudice against you felt?
When we stereotype people, how do we feel?
4.   Why do people show prejudice or stereotype others? How can we or they
change?

---

DEFINITIONS

*Prejudice.*   An unfavorable opinion about a person or group of people formed
without knowledge. For example:
Joey says, "I don't like Puerto Ricans!"
Joey has never met a Puerto Rican. He is prejudiced against Puerto Ricans.

*Stereotype.*   A *general* viewpoint about a group of people not based on fact.
For example:

*Stereotype*—Girls are lousy baseball players.
*Fact*—Many girls are excellent baseball players.
*Stereotype*—Older people are sick and helpless.
*Fact*—Many older people are healthy and independent. Others have illnesses
and need support.
*Stereotype*—Native Americans were savage and wild.
*Fact*—Many Native American nations were peace-loving and only fought whites
when their land was being invaded.

## No Grandmothers Wanted ⎯⎯⎯⎯⎯⎯⎯⎯⎯⎯⎯⎯ LA, R

**OBJECTIVES**  To have students recognize a stereotype based on age.

To have students realize how stereotypes of people are harmful to those who have the stereotype, to those who are stereotyped, and to others who are part of the situation.

To encourage an awareness that stereotypes are learned and can be unlearned.

**MATERIALS**  Copies of "Worksheet: No Grandmothers Wanted," p. 106; paper and pencils.

**IMPLEMENTATION**  Divide students into groups of four. Give each student a copy of the Worksheet. If possible, have some students work in the hallway so that groups can rehearse without too much interference. Each group assigns parts for the skit. They read aloud the script as written, write their own endings, and rehearse those.

Come back together. Each group acts out its script. After all the groups are done, discuss the issues. Pick one script, or a combination, to present to another class.

**DISCUSSION**
1. What was Ms. Yung's stereotype about older people?
2. What reasons do you think there might be for Ms. Yung having that stereotype? How do you think we learn stereotypes?
3. Why did Angela suggest her grandmother for the hike? Why didn't Angela have the same stereotype about older people that Ms. Yung had?
4. How do you feel about the different endings to the script you made up? Did the endings correct the stereotype?
5. What can you do when you see someone acting in a certain way because of a stereotype she has?
6. Think back over the last week about some decisions you or someone else made because of some stereotype? Where did you get that stereotype? What can you do to unlearn it?
7. What would the class have lost out on if Ms. Yung's stereotype were enforced?

## Renee Ramos _____ R, LA

**OBJECTIVES**
To have students recognize stereotypes based on race, in this case Asian-American. To have students compare the stereotype to the actual situation of a person, in this case an Asian-American student.

**MATERIALS**
Copies of "Worksheet: Renee Ramos," p. 101, one per student; Group Questions: Renee Ramos, p. 102, one per group.

**IMPLEMENTATION**
This is a cooperative group project. Students work together as a group and hand in one assignment. Divide students into heterogeneous groups of four. Make sure that a strong reader is in each of the groups.

As a group, ask students to brainstorm words that describe Asian-American people. You might ask them to think about what Filipino, Chinese, or Japanese people their age are like. If you have Asian children in your class, ask students not to think of the particular people in the room, but of Asian-Americans in general. After about five minutes have someone from each group read off that group's words or descriptions. Put these on the board.

Now, in small groups, have students read the story of Renee Ramos, a Filipino-American. Assign the slowest reader in each group the paragraphs numbered 4 and the strongest those numbered 3. Students read their paragraphs to themselves first. Tell them to ask for help from others if they don't know the words. Then students read the account aloud.

Together, they decide on the answers to Group Questions: Renee Ramos. They fill out and hand in one Worksheet for the group.

**DISCUSSION**
1. First, discuss responses to the five questions on the Worksheet.
2. What negative stereotypes do some people have of other people of color—blacks, Latinos, Native Americans? How do these stereotypes affect people?
3. How does your understanding of Renee Ramos compare to the words your groups came up with about Asian-Americans? How are they the same? How are they different? Why do you think this is?
4. How much of your description of Asian-Americans was a stereotype? How do we learn stereotypes? What can we do about them?
5. What do we lose out on when we stereotype people?

**GOING FURTHER**
Using ideas from "'Famous' Stereotypes" (p. 88) talk with students about stereotypes of other groups of people. Have them watch for examples in books, advertising, or on TV.

Encourage them to read books that have non-stereotyped portrayals of ethnic minorities. (See bibliography.)

## Lizzie Gets Old Clothes _____ C, LA

**OBJECTIVES**   To have students recognize stereotypes based on class bias.
To understand how someone who is poor feels when faced with class bias.

**MATERIALS**   Copies of "Worksheet: Lizzie Gets Old Clothes," p. 103–5, one set per pair.

**IMPLEMENTATION**   Tell students that they will be working in pairs to read a story aloud to each other. Mix students from different class backgrounds when possible.

Have students work together to fill out one Worksheet. Encourage them to discuss their answers first and try to come to agreement before writing. Tell them to alternate writing down the answers to questions, and have the student not writing check the other's spelling and punctuation.

**DISCUSSION**
1. Begin the discussion by asking students for responses to questions 2 through 4 on their Worksheets.
2. How did you finish the story? Let's hear some examples.
3. When you have been hurt by prejudice or stereotypes, do you sometimes "not show it"? How do you do this? Why do you do this?
4. How did you answer question 5?
5. What can you do in your life when people act in hurtful ways toward others because of prejudices or stereotypes?
6. Sometimes people try to make themselves feel better about themselves by putting other people down because they are different. What are ways to feel good about yourself without using prejudice and stereotypes?
7. What did the children at school lose out on by stereotyping Lizzie? What do we lose out on in real life by stereotyping other people?

> An excellent book to use with students as a catalyst for a discussion of what it's like to live in poverty and never have what you need is *Being Poor*, by Janet Rosenberg. If your library doesn't have it, order it or borrow it on interlibrary loan—it's worth it!

## M. and S. Auto Repair _____ LA

**OBJECTIVES**   To have students recognize stereotypes based on sex.
To understand the feelings of persons who experience prejudice and discrimination because of stereotypes based on sex.

**MATERIALS**   Copies of "Worksheet: M. and S. Auto Repair," p. 107, one per student; copies of Worksheet: Roles for Marcie and Jim, p. 108, one per pair, cut in half.

**IMPLEMENTATION**   Have students read the Worksheet: M. and S. Auto Repair and answer the questions at the end. Discuss the Worksheet questions together as a class. (If your students are inexperienced with role-play, see "Role-Play Techniques," p. 56).

Now tell students that we'll do a role-play. Tell the students that five months have gone by. After much hard work and fighting opposition to their idea from many people, Marcie and Sonia have opened the M. and S. Auto Repair Shop.

Ask two students to do a sample role-play in the front of the class. Remind students they must *become* the person whose role they are playing. Even if they don't agree with the role, they should get into the feelings. Give their half of the Worksheet: Roles for Marcie and Jim to the two volunteers. After they've read it, check with them privately to make sure they understand their roles well. Tell the students since this is a sample, you will interrupt after two minutes even though the role play may not be over.

Now divide all the students into pairs, give each child a role, and begin role-playing simultaneously. After about three or four minutes stop them. Have students exchange roles.

1. Describe your feelings playing Marcie.
2. Describe your feelings playing Jim.
3. In the end did Jim leave his car or not? What arguments influenced his decision?
4. What are other stereotypes some people have about women? Let's list them on the board. How do these stereotypes hurt women?
5. What can *we* do to counteract stereotypes that hurt people because of their sex?

---

A REAL LETTER FROM A REPORT CARD

June 23, 1978

Dear Mr. and Mrs. White,
  Steven has made a lot of progress this year. He is ready for Second Grade.
  He should go to the Village Library and get books to read this summer. Boys have a way of forgetting over the long vacation. I enjoyed having Steven.

Sincerely,

---

## From Feathers to Facts _____ SS, LA, A

**OBJECTIVES**  To have students recognize stereotypes based on race, in this case, Native Americans (American Indians).
To help students understand how their stereotypes of Native Americans are incorrect and harmful.
To help students understand how stereotypes in general are harmful to those who have them and those who are stereotyped.

**MATERIALS**  Paper; pencils; drawing supplies.

**IMPLEMENTATION**  Order and read *Unlearning "Indian" Stereotypes* before doing this lesson. It will give you valuable information and ideas about teaching about Native Americans.

Students work individually. Each student draws a picture of a Native American in a setting in the United States today. This can be a school, home, or town, as long as a child the age of your students is included. Each student should write a short story about this child. Collect and post these.

Divide students into groups of four. Have each group divide a piece of paper into three columns entitled "Us," "Them," and "Both." In the first column they are to list characteristics of themselves (what they like to do, eat, play; how they feel; what they believe, and so on). In the second column they should list the same sorts of characteristics of Native American children their age. In the third column they should list characteristics they think are true of themselves and of Native American children.

Gather together as a class. Have students take turns calling out notations from their lists. Make a common list on chart-paper for all three columns. Post this with the drawings and pictures. (Save drawings for lesson in Chapter 10.)

After discussion, if possible, show the filmstrip from the Council on Interracial Books for Children, entitled "Unlearning 'Indian' Stereotypes."

**DISCUSSION**  1. What are some of the ways many of you pictured Native Americans? What did you think they looked like? In what ways are these stereotypes? (Be sure to insert correct information from your reading of *Unlearning "Indian" Stereotypes*.)
2. What did you imagine Native American children doing that was different from what you do? Where did you get these ideas?
3. How would you feel if you were a Native American child and you saw the pictures and stories in this classroom? Explain.
4. Did you, as a class, realize the very big differences in Native American life in different parts of this country? Did you realize differences between how Native Americans lived when white settlers arrived and how they live now?
5. In what ways are our stereotypes about Native Americans damaging to them?
6. In what ways are our stereotypes of Native Americans harmful to us—those who stereotype?

**GOING FURTHER** Have students collect materials which perpetuate negative stereotypes about Native Americans. (For example, packaging for foods and games, greeting cards, school dittoes.) Have them analyze them. Save for lessons in Chapter 10.

Have students look through library books and social studies textbooks which teach about Native Americans. Have them analyze those which "teach" stereotypes.

**FOLLOW-UP** "Relearning about Native Americans," p. 226; "Say It So They'll Hear It," p. 219.

---

There is nothing harmful in children dressing up to play clowns, witches, cowboys, or pilots. These are roles that can be taken on by people of any racial, religious or national group. But being a Native American is not a role. Native people are human beings with diverse cultures and distinctive national identities. . . .

When books show children doing "Indian" dances (or teachers have students do "Indian" dances) it is often insulting to Native cultures, and is frequently sacrilegious. Just as books and schools would not have children play at High Mass or Yom Kippur services, respect should be given to Native American religious ceremonies.

From *Unlearning "Indian" Stereotypes*

---

STEREOTYPERS ARE HURT TOO

Throughout the activities in this section, "Prejudice and Stereotypes," it's important to emphasize how those of us who stereotype are also hurt. We often lose out on important learnings, experiences, and friendships.

For example:
The class could have lost out on a hike because of ageist stereotyping.
Kids lose out on Renee's friendship as well as lots of learning about Filipino culture.
Kids lose out on Lizzie's company and a chance to face and potentially change their own false sense of superiority.
The residents of North Jefferson might lose out on a fine auto repair shop—and girls of the town lose out on non-traditional role models.
We lose out on a knowledge and appreciation of the Native American culture and therefore the opportunity to learn from it.

---

## We All Lose _____ R, LA

**OBJECTIVE** To have students recognize how stereotypes and prejudice have negative effects on everyone concerned.

**MATERIALS** Copies of "Worksheet: We All Lose," p. 110, two per group; copies of Situation Cards, p. 109, one set per group (cut and mount); paper; pencils; card stock; pens.

**IMPLEMENTATION** Divide students into heterogeneous groups of three to six. Give each group copies of the Situation Cards and Worksheet, paper and pencils, card stock and pens. Review definitions of prejudice and stereotypes and go over several cards as a whole class to give students the idea.

Students read cards aloud. For each one, they discuss what stereotype or prejudice it shows, why they think people might have that stereotype, and what harm it causes. Each group picks four cards and fills in the Worksheet on those. Come together as a class for the discussion questions.

After discussion, have students take the card stock and cut themselves four cards of the same size. They create new cards describing situations typical of their school or lives. For each card, they make a Worksheet entry. In that way they will have to pick a stereotype or a type of prejudice and think it through clearly.

Share these with the whole class, perhaps having each group pass its stack on to another group. Finally, as a group, discuss the new cards.

**DISCUSSION**
1. How did the person stereotyped lose in the situations? Discuss one at a time.
2. How did the person stereotyping lose out?
3. What can you do to unlearn these stereotypes and to help yourself not to learn more?

**GOING FURTHER**
Use these cards as part of a board game. Just add "lose a turn," "go back a space," or "take another turn," at the end of the card. Students can create a regular pathway game board. The theme should be connected with equality. This stack of cards can form the basis for the "luck" cards.

**FOLLOW-UP**
"From Fear to Power," p. 221.

# SECTION B    THE "ISMS"

## What Are They?—The "Isms" _____ R

**OBJECTIVES**
To define the words racism, sexism, classism, and ageism.
To understand how prejudice, when reinforced by institutional power, becomes an "ism."

**MATERIALS**
A large "ISM Chart," p. 111; Copies of "Worksheet: Find the ISM," p. 112, one for every two students.

**IMPLEMENTATION**
Explain to the students that when prejudice and stereotypes are practiced by people with more power than others or by institutions—like schools, families, government, businesses—their effect is very great. Also, prejudice and stereotypes become more powerful when imbedded in cultural attitudes and values. In these cases, people or institutions practice discrimination—they treat people or groups of people differently because of their age, race, sex, or class. The practice of such discrimination is summarized by using an "ism" word.

Post the ISM Chart and discuss each "ism" separately. (Change the key words on the chart as appropriate.) In discussing the "isms" and the examples, explain that because norms and procedures of *institutions* or prevailing attitudes and values in society reinforce "isms," they are much more powerful than prejudice and stereotypes. In addition, examples of "isms" are harder to spot because they are often "hidden" in institutions. Explain that victims of "isms" subtly learn that they are not as good or important as others, whereas those who benefit from the "isms" learn that they are normal, right, or important.

Have students work in heterogeneous pairs. Give each pair a copy of the Worksheet. One person reads the first situation aloud. Together they decide on answers and one person writes them in. They continue this procedure with other situations, deciding together who will read and write. Join as a class for discussion.

---

TO REVIEW

A *prejudice* is an unfavorable *opinion* about a person or group of people not based on knowledge.
    A *stereotype* is a *generalization* about a group of people not based on fact.
    *Isms* are prejudice and stereotypes enforced by people with more power than others, by institutions, and by cultural attitudes and values.
    Prejudice + Power = Isms.

---

**DISCUSSION**
1. What are the "isms" in the situations on the Worksheet?
2. What feelings do people have who are victims of "isms"?
3. What feelings might people have who benefit from "isms"?
4. Are there examples of "isms" in your life like those in the stories? What are they?

---

ISMS IN THE MEDIA

In 1980, 4.95% of the newspaper industry journalists were minority.

Gannet Urban Journalism Center
Northwestern University

*The New York Times* has one black editor and 18 black reporters and photographers in an editorial staff of 950.

Black Enterprise, 1980

Men make news decisions in 93% of print media (newspapers), in 95% of TV, and 89% of radio. Women hold only 232 out of 3,282 directing editorships.

Media Report to Women, 1981

---

## Me, Myself, and I _____ LA

**OBJECTIVES**
To define competitive individualism.
To give students practice recognizing it.

**MATERIALS**
Paper; pencils; copies of Worksheet: Ms. Lopez's Class (1), p. 113, one per pair. (Worksheet: Ms. Lopez's Class (2), p. 114, is optional.)

**IMPLEMENTATION**

Me or We?

PART ONE. Tell students we will be learning a new concept, "competitive individualism." Define the term. Then give out Worksheet: Ms. Lopez's Class (1) to students and have them work in pairs to complete it. As a class, discuss their responses. Then, if you wish, give out part 2 of that Worksheet for them to read with their partners. Discuss any points raised on the Worksheet that weren't already mentioned.

PART TWO. Divide students into groups of four. Each person describes one or two situations in which she thinks she'd be the winner if she and her group were to compete together. Examples: "I could ski farthest down a hill without falling"; "I could bake the most tasty fried chicken"; "I could speak the most words in Spanish." Each person then writes a sentence explaining how much time she has spent on these activities in the past, or how much experience she has had. For example: "My older sister takes me skiing in the mountains two or three times a year." Or, "I practice skiing, when it snows, at the recreation department hill in our town."

Students share their situations with their group and agree on one situation, for each person, in which they all expect that that person would win. Join together in the class for discussion.

---

Authors of the Council on Interracial Books for Children use the term, "me-first-ism" to describe individualism. Try this with students in younger grades.

---

**DISCUSSION**
1. What situations did people think of in which they expect they'd be a winner?
2. How much time and practice had been spent on these activities? How did that compare to the amount of experience of others?
3. If someone has more chances and encouragement to learn something, should they feel better if they win? Why or why not? Remind students that feeling you've won on your own merits, when in reality you've had greater opportunity, is an example of individualism.

4. When you've "lost" in competition where you didn't have a fair chance, how do you feel?
5. What are some examples of times when you shared what you knew or could do with others? How did you feel about this?
6. What are the ways in this class that we can share what we know and can do?

---

**INDIVIDUALISM OR INDIVIDUALITY?!**

Don't confuse these two! *Individualism* is very different from *individuality*, which is the growth in each person of her unique and full characteristics. Individualism in society *hinders* the growth of individuality in many people. In cooperative situations, however, people have the space and support to develop their very special individuality!

---

## Letter From Sally _____ LA, R

**OBJECTIVES**   To have students understand classism and the situation and feelings of people whose life-experiences and opportunities are affected by their class background.

**MATERIALS**   Copies of "Worksheet: Letter from Sally," p. 121; paper and pencils.

**IMPLEMENTATION**   Have students read the Worksheet. Go over difficult vocabulary words first, if necessary. Then ask students to write a letter in response to Sally as if they are Theresa. Tell them to answer the two questions at the end of Sally's letter.

When completed, discuss Sally's situation as a class, and share some of the response letters.

**DISCUSSION**
1. What are some of the feelings you would have if you were Sally? Describe the reason you'd feel that way.
2. Sally may not be able to achieve her goal because she doesn't have enough money. When have you had to give up something very important to you because of lack of money?
3. Is it fair that Sally has to think about giving up her hopes of becoming a doctor because of lack of money? Why or why not?
4. How should programs to train future doctors select students? Should the amount of money a person has matter?
5. Who remembers our definition of classism? How is Sally's case an example of classism?
6. How do all Americans lose out by this kind of classism?

Tell the students there are many Americans who have difficulties achieving their goals because they have low incomes. There are people much poorer than Sally's family who hardly have enough money to live on. Explain that you will talk more about the effect of class on people's lives as you go through the year. You'd like them to remember their feelings when they got into Sally's shoes.

**FOLLOW-UP**   "Yes, You Can Be a Doctor," p. 197.

---

**DO YOUR ATTITUDES ABOUT CLASS AFFECT STUDENT LEARNING?**

In a detailed three-year study, Roy Rist found that in the initial year of school teachers' expectations about academic potential were based almost totally on racial and socioeconomic facts about the child. These viewpoints affected student achievement and subsequent teachers' expectations.

*Harvard Education Review,* August, 1970.

# Who Will Take Care of Jamil?

**OBJECTIVES**   To better understand sexism and the situation and feelings of those people whose life and opportunities are affected by sexism.
To better understand how institutional policies and practices reinforce sexism.

**MATERIALS**   "Worksheet: Who Will Take Care of Jamil?   p. 115–16, one copy per pair.

**IMPLEMENTATION**   Tell students that they will read a story about a woman and her family, and that her situation is typical for many women in our country today. This woman is faced with sexism. Ask students if they remember the definition of sexism. If necessary, reiterate it.

Divide students into partners of mixed ability level. Pass out Worksheets and have students read either silently or aloud to each other. Students then work with their partners to answer the questions on the Worksheet. They should outline their points.

Next have two sets of partners join together to share outlines. Each pair gives new information or suggestions that might improve the other's outline.

Then, in original pairs, students write the newspaper article. You might suggest that they divide the number of paragraphs and that each person write half. Then they go over each other's paragraphs for information, spelling, and punctuation. Finally they arrange the paragraphs to make a complete article.

When articles are completed, have several pairs read theirs to the class.

**DISCUSSION**   Use the questions at the end of the Worksheet. Help students focus on the ways the institutions in this account (business and college) and also traditional family roles reinforce sexism and limit women's potential.

---

The Center for Women's Opportunities at the American Association of Community and Junior Colleges surveyed 12,000 community colleges and technical institutions and found that only 132 had child-care facilities on campus.

Campus Childcare: A Challenge for the '80's,
Women's Re-entry Project Association of
American Colleges, Washington, D.C.

---

**Ms Meg**                                    **by bulbul**

NO YOU'RE NOT CRAZY! IT'S THE "NO PAY, NO SICK LEAVE,
NO PENSION, NO APPRECIATION" HOUSEWIFE BLUES.

In 1980 there were 900,000 slots in center-based child care programs and 5.2 million slots in family-based child care programs. Thirteen million children under the age of 13 had mothers who worked full time, leaving 6.9 million families with no access to child care.

*Child Care Handbook*, Children's Defense Fund

## Health or Home? ———————————————————— SS, R

**OBJECTIVE**  To have students better understand ageism and the situation and feelings of people whose life-experiences and opportunities are affected by their age.

**MATERIALS**  Copies of "Worksheet: Can We Have our House?", p. 117, one per pair; copies of Roles—Ted and Juanita Lund, p. 118, one per pair, cut in half.

**IMPLEMENTATION**  Tell students that they will be reading about two older people, Juanita and Ted Lund. Explain that the Lund's predicament is not uncommon for many elderly people in America today.

Divide students into pairs. Mix the reading levels. Pair shy or non-assertive students with supportive, outgoing ones. Students read Worksheets with their partners.

Then tell them that they are going to role-play with their partner. One person will be Ted and the other Juanita. They will get more information about Ted and Juanita soon. Tell students that the purpose of the role-play is *not to solve the Lund's problem*. It is to understand how they would feel as Ted or Juanita. They might come up with plans for what they could do, but they don't have to. The main thing is to understand their feelings.

Give one student in each pair role-information for Ted and the other that for Juanita. They read silently. When students are ready, remind them that they are no longer themselves, but either Ted or Juanita. Tell them they are sitting together to talk about their feelings. After that they might try to decide what to do. They have five minutes for their conversation.

After the role-play students write down the feelings they had playing the role they did. They come together as a class for discussion.

Today the general population is three times as great as it was in 1900. The population of the elderly is eight times as great.

büllbül © 76

You try being serene on $120 a month.

Gran & Gramps

**DISCUSSION**

1. What were your feelings playing the role of Ted or Juanita Lund? Why did you feel this way?
2. What do *you* feel about the situation the Lunds are in?
3. What were some ways the Lunds were discriminated against because of their age? How do you feel about such discrimination?
4. Who remembers what ageism is and can define it for us? How is this account an example of ageism?
5. How did the stereotypes in the policies of the employers reinforce ageism?
6. How do we all lose out by practices that reinforce ageism?
7. Did doing the role-play help you come up with any thoughts or ideas about what could be done? Would these solutions be possible for all older Americans in a similar situation?

---

## BACKGROUND READING: *AGING IN THE U.S. FACTS AND FIGURES*

### WHAT IS AGEISM?

Ageism is any attitude, action or institutional structure which subordinates a person or group because of age OR any assignment of roles in society on the basis of age. Ageism is usually practiced against older people, but it is also practiced against young people. Ageism can be individual, cultural or institutional AND it can be intentional or unintentional.

### EXAMPLES OF AGEISM

*Individual:* "She's too old to wear jeans," or "My grandfather is too old to understand me."
*Cultural:* "You can't teach an old dog new tricks," or "There's no fool like an old fool."
*Institutional:* Compulsory retirement. Also, the expectation that older people will be volunteers rather than paid employees.

### AGEISM AND U.S. CULTURE

• *Ageism* makes it easier to ignore the frequently oppressive social and economic situation of older people in U.S. society.
• *Ageism* permits employers to retire higher-paid older workers with seniority and to replace them with lower-paid younger workers.
• *Ageism* protects younger people from thinking about things they fear (aging, illness, death).
• *Ageism* sabotages the self-image of older people and is an attack on their dignity as human beings.

### HOW MANY OLDER PEOPLE?

• In the U.S., 24.2 million citizens are over 65. This is more than 10 % of the total U.S. population of 222 million. It is predicted that by the year 2,000, one-third of the U.S. population will be over 65 and one-half will be over 60.
• Life expectancy is less for Third World people than for white people. Blacks are 12 % of the U.S. population but, because of lower life expectancy, are less than 8 % of the U.S. elderly. Most Third World males do not live long enough to be eligible for 'the benefits of Social Security.

### HOW MANY WORK?

• 10 % of those over 65 are employed full time; an additional 20 % work part time.

### WHAT IS AVERAGE INCOME OF ALL U.S. OLDER PEOPLE?

• $75 a week for a single older person.

### WHAT IS THE SOURCE OF THEIR INCOME?

• Retirement benefits: 46 %. (Social Security: 34 %; public pensions: 7 %; private pensions: 5 %)
• Earnings from employment: 29 %.
• Income from assets: 15 %.
• Public assistance: 4 %.
• Veterans benefits: 3 %.
• Other (contributions from family, etc.): 3 %.

### WHO ARE ELDERLY POOR?

• One-third of all people over 65 live at or below the poverty line set by the federal government. Most people now consider the federal government's "poverty" line ($2,717 for individuals, $3,485 for couples) outrageously low. Many experts say that a more realistic criterion is at least double the official figure and—in that case—*a majority of older people in the U.S. would be* classified as poor, most of them becoming poor after growing old.
• Of aged Blacks who live alone, 75 % are below the official poverty line. The percentage of Black widows who live in poverty is 85 %. Of aged Black females, 47 % have incomes under $1,000.

### WHERE DO OLDER PEOPLE LIVE?

• The largest concentrations are in the agricultural Midwest, in New England and in Florida. Over 60 % of older Blacks live in the South.
• Urban areas have 60 % of all persons 65 or over; non-metropolitan areas, 35 %; farms, 5 %.
• At least 30 % of people 65 or over live in substandard housing.
• Contrary to the popular myth that older people are infirm, need to be taken care of or live in nursing homes, only 5 % of those over 65 live in nursing homes or other institutions. (There are 23,000 nursing homes in the U.S., half of which can't pass basic fire inspection.) Approximately 15 % of the people over 65 live in the community with partial or total care; 80 %—the vast majority—live in the community without nursing or other kinds of physical care.

### HOW MANY ARE SUICIDES?

• 25 % of all suicides are committed by people 65 or over.

Sources for the information on this page are *Why Survive? Being Old in America* by Robert N. Butler, M.D. (Harper & Row, 1975); the Technical Bulletin Series of the National Center on Black Aged, Washington, D.C.; and *Money Income and Poverty Status of Families and Persons in the United States, 1974-1975*, Bureau of the Census, U.S. Dept. of Commerce.

Reprinted with permission from *Bulletin,* C.I.B.C., Volume 2, Number 6, 1976.

---

## Lillie's Dilemma _____ R, SS

**OBJECTIVES**    To better understand racism and the situation and feelings of those people whose life-opportunities are affected by racism.
To learn how institutional policies and practices enforce racism.
To help students see the situation and feelings of people whose life-experiences are affected simultaneously by their race, class, and sex.

**MATERIALS**    Copies of "Worksheet: Lillie's Dilemma," p. 119–20, one per pair.

**IMPLEMENTATION**   Tell students that they are about to read a true story. Divide students into pairs. Pass out a Worksheet to each pair. Have them read aloud to each other. Pair up students of different reading levels, so one can help the other. When possible, mix partners racially. Once they have finished the story, they talk about the questions, decide on the best responses, and fill those in on the Worksheet.

Then come together as a class to discuss their responses.

**DISCUSSION**
1.  Discuss the three questions on the Worksheet.
2.  How could the landlord use the power of institutions—school, the housing office, government—against Carolyn?
3.  The landlord called Carolyn a troublemaker. Do you think she was a troublemaker? Why or why not? Why are people who speak up for their rights sometimes called troublemakers?
4.  Carolyn was a poor, black woman. How did discrimination based on race, sex, and class work together to affect her?

Tell students that people can use prejudice to hurt individual people, like when the landlord called Lillie a name. They can also use the power of institutions, like schools, government, housing, to hurt. When they do this, we find an "*ism.*" The landlord threatened to use his influence, connections and power to deny Carolyn a job; this was an example of institutional discrimination based on racism, sexism and classism.

5.  Have you ever been threatened, like Carolyn, by someone with more power than you? For example: "If you don't do _____, I'll do _____." How does it feel? Share an example.

---

**DOUBLE JEOPARDY**

The impact of "double jeopardy" (the joint impact of racism and sexism on women of color in America) is indicated in these statistics about wages.

**Median Income of All People Over 15 Years, by Sex and Race, 1980**

| | | | |
|---|---|---|---|
| All Males | $12,530 | All Females | $4,920 |
| White Males | 13,328 | White Females | 4,947 |
| Black Males | 8,790 | Black Females | 4,580 |
| Hispanic Males | 9,659 | Hispanic Females | 4,405 |

**Median Income of All People Over 15 Years, Working Full Time, Year-Round, by Sex and Race, 1980**

| | | | |
|---|---|---|---|
| All Males | $19,173 | All Females | $11,591 |
| White Males | 19,720 | White Females | 11,703 |
| Black Males | 13,875 | Black Females | 10,915 |
| Hispanic Males | 13,790 | Hispanic Females | 9,887 |

U.S. Department of Commerce, 1981

---

**IN THE OLD DAYS**

One way to talk about stereotyping, "the isms," and distortions is to use "In the old days" or "People used to say." For example: "People used to say, 'Columbus discovered America.' Since Native Americans had lived here long before Columbus we *now* know to say that is racist because it presents history only from a white person's point of view." Try it!

THE "ISMS" HURT US ALL

Remind students that we *all* lose out from institutional discrimination based on race, sex, class, and age.
    For example:

Americans lose out on committed, bright doctors—like Sally Garcia could be—because of class discrimination.
We lose out on the talent, wisdom, and experience of older Americans, like Juanita Lund, because of ageism.
Marva Williams's community and employer lose out on her skills in math, and Jamil and other children lose out on the nurturing of their fathers, because of sexism.
Carolyn Raley's community loses out on a competent black teacher who could provide anti-racist education through content and example.

Worksheet:   RENEE RAMOS

> Renee is a Filipino-American.  Because the Philippines was
> a Spanish colony for almost three hundred years, Renee,
> like many other Filipinos, has a Spanish surname.  In 1849,
> the Spanish governor of the Philippines handed down an
> order which decreed what family names Filipinos should
> bear.  Many of the approved names were, of course, Spanish.
> In the U.S., this has caused confusion.  Instead of being
> properly identified as Asian-Americans, many Filipinos are
> mistakenly categorized as Hispanic.

My name is Renee Ramos.  I have six people in my family--
Ramona, Abba, Anna, my mother and father.  I am the oldest of
the children.  My mother does housework for people.  She relies
on me to help with the family chores, including baby-sitting my
sisters and brother.

I am in the fifth grade.  I go to Longfellow Elementary
School in Berkeley.  I like going to Longfellow because of my
friends.  When I play with people, I play with people who I
think are nice to play with.  They could be black, white, or
Asian.  I think the only thing that makes a friend is the
personality and not the color.

There are some things I dislike about Longfellow.  There
are people who tease me about the food that I bring to school
and because I am Asian;  they act as if these things are bad.
But I'm not ashamed of what they say because I know what I am,
and I'm proud of it!  Sometimes I say to them, "I am proud I
am," and other times I keep it to myself.  I feel better
keeping it to myself because I know not to be ashamed when
people say that.

One thing about my family is, we never leave anybody out
in what we do.  If we were in trouble, we would help each other.

My mother usually stays home and keeps house.  She is very
responsible as a mother.  She is happy when we are.  I try to
make her have the least trouble with my sisters and brother.
She is always helpful with our personal problems and I take
advice from her.

My father likes to talk.  He fights for the rights of
working people.  He goes to union meetings which concern the
liberation of farm workers and equal opportunities for jobs
and homes for Asians, blacks, and Chicanos.  I agree with him
in every way.

There are both negative and positive things that happen
because I'm an Asian-American.  A negative thing is that people
stereotype Asians by saying, "All Asians are quiet and they can't
can't do this or that."  A positive thing is that when the class
is talking about Asians, I can share my experiences with the
class.  Once on a school bus a black girl told her friend to sit
by me and the other girl said, "I don't want to sit by that
Chinese or Japanese girl."

"I WISH EVERYONE WOULD SEE ASIANS AS PEOPLE."

From Asian American Women by Yolanda Yokota and Linda Wing,
pp. 83-84.

Group Questions:  RENEE RAMOS

<u>Directions</u>:  Talk about these questions as a group and decide
upon an answer for each.  Take turns writing your answers.
Help each other with spelling.  When you are finished, all
sign the worksheet and hand it in to your teacher.


1.  Choose at least four words to describe Renee Ramos.



2.  Would you like her to be your friend?  Why or why not?



3.  What prejudices and stereotypes do some people have about
    Renee?



4.  What are some ways people treat Renee because she is
    Asian-American?



5.  How does Renee feel about being Asian-American?



                    Signed:_____


                           _____


                           _____


                           _____

Worksheet:  LIZZIE GETS OLD CLOTHES


    Most of the other kids in my class seem to like school.
They know each other.  I love learning about new things, but I
feel so different.

    When we go around the class and tell what our fathers do,
they say salesman, doctor, computer operator.  When I say farmworker, some kids laugh and whisper.

    That makes me so mad.  My father works very hard as a
farmworker.  The problem is that he can only work five months
of the year--the time of picking.  He tries and tries to work
during the other seven months, but people always say, "We don't
have any jobs."  He doesn't want to move the family all year to
follow the crops, because then I couldn't stay in one school.

    I feel left out a lot.  I hear the other kids talk about
parties.  No one ever invites me.

    But the biggest problem is clothes.  Some kids have so
many different outfits--they act so bigshot about it.  When
some of them talk about clothes, they glance at me from the
corner of their eyes.

    One day my teacher asked me to stay in by myself at recess.
She said quietly, "Lizzie, I see you've been wearing the same
clothes to school every day this week.  Don't you have anything
else?"

    I stared down at the floor.  I was wearing my only school
clothes--a pair of jeans and a red and white striped T-shirt.
I'd been given them by my older cousin.  My mother tried to
make them look nice.  She washed them every other day and
patched the places that were torn.  I guess they were so old
that nothing could make them look good anymore.  My mother also
made sure I took my bath every day, so even if my clothes were
old, I was clean.

    I didn't say anything.  The teacher asked me again, "Are
those your only clothes, dear?  I just want to help."

    I nodded my head.  She kept on talking.  "I have a good
idea.  I'll ask the other girls if they have any outgrown
school clothes they could give you.  I'm sure you'll feel much
better that way."

    I couldn't answer.  I bit my lip and kept looking down.
The teacher told me I could go out to play.  I walked out as
quickly as I could.  I felt so angry and embarrassed!  The
teacher will tell the other kids to bring in clothes for
"poor Lizzie."

    It would be okay if the girls were usually nice to me and
let me be their friend.  Then they might <u>want</u> to share their
friendship and clothes.  This way, though. . .  I wanted to
hide and never come back to school.

Three days later, my teacher asked me to see her after school. I looked down at my red and white shirt and knew what was happening.

She gave me two brown paper grocery bags with folded-up clothes in them.

"Thank you, Ms. Smyth," I said, trying hard to smile.

The next day I wore one of the outfits--green corduroy pants and a flowered blouse.

At recess that day I heard Carita whispering to Tina, "That's my old blouse Lizzie has on. I bet she'll get it all dirty and smelly. I'm sure glad I don't have to sit next to her."

Tina whispered back, "I feel bad for her. She must have lazy parents if they can't even buy her clothes for school."

If Carita and Tina had come over to me right then, I'd. . .

Worksheet:  LIZZIE GETS OLD CLOTHES  (Continued)


1.  This story ends with these words:  "If Carita and Tina had
    come over to me right then, I'd. . ."

    Write a paragraph to describe what you think Lizzie would
    have done.




2.  List three or four feelings Lizzie had.




3.  What are one or two stereotypes the other students had
    about Lizzie?




4.  The other children are prejudiced toward Lizzie because she
    is poor.  How do they show this prejudice?




5.  Now that you've been doing these lessons you might respond
    differently.  If you had been a classmate of hers, what
    would you have done or said to Lizzie?  to the other
    children?

Worksheet:   NO GRANDMOTHERS WANTED


Ms. Yung:  Last night did any of you ask your parents if they
           could go on our class hike?  Remember we need five parents
           in order to be allowed to go.

Eduardo:  I tried to get my dad to take the day off but he
          didn't think his boss could let him.

Tessy:  After both my parents said no, I called Janet, Heidi,
        and Mark and none of their parents could come either.  I
        even asked my aunt but she's got her computer class that
        day.

Ms. Yung:  We certainly have a problem.  I'd hate to see us
           cancel the hike.

Angela:  My mom's working that day but my grandma can come.
         She said she'd be really happy to.

Ms. Yung:  That was really nice of you Angela, but this is
           going to be a hard hike.  You can tell your grandma that
           we appreciate her offer, but really I don't think it's a
           hike that grandmas could do.

Angela:  You said we really need more grown-ups and Grandma
         would be fine.  She likes hiking.

Ms. Yung:  Later this year, Angela, we're going to do a baking
           project for our unit on colonial America.  Why don't you
           see if your grandma would like to help us then?

Angela:  My grandma does like to bake and she's good.  I bet
         she'd come then and also come on our hike--especially if
         she likes the class.

Ms. Yung:  No Angela, I meant the baking instead of the hike.
           Hiking isn't what grandmas do.  Tell her how kind it is
           but we'll keep trying to find parents.

Tessy:  Ms. Yung, I was at Angela's last week and her
        grandma. . . .

Worksheet:  M. AND S. AUTO REPAIR

    Marcie and Sonia are two women in their middle twenties
who live in the town of North Jefferson.  Both graduated from
high school with a strong background in science, math, and auto
mechanics.  Since then they have worked in Bob Miller's auto
repair shop.  By now they have had seven years experience on
the job.  They have excellent reputations as auto mechanics.
    Marcie and Sonia have all the skills they need to open
their own shop, M. and S. Auto Repair.  The women have saved
the money they need to get their business going.
    Sonia called the owner of a local garage to ask if it was
for rent.  The garage-owner said, "Sure, lady.  Have your husband come over any time.  I'm eager to rent."
    Sonia went to the garage-owner later that afternoon.  He
said, "Where's your husband?"  When she told him she wanted to
rent it for herself he laughed in her face.  "What?  You want
to rent the garage!  What a joke."
    "I'm not married.  I'm an auto mechanic and here is my
down payment."
    "Look, lady, I'm not renting this to you.  I'll lose money.
You'll never be able to pay your rent.  Nobody in this town
will come to a garage run by women.  Give up your pie-in-the-
sky idea."


1.  Describe how you would feel if you were Sonia.



2.  How does the garage-owner show prejudice toward Sonia?



3.  What are the stereotypes about women that the garage-owner
    has?



4.  How do these stereotypes hurt Marcie and Sonia?



5.  How will these stereotypes hurt the residents of North
    Jefferson?

Worksheet:   ROLES FOR MARCIE AND JIM

Marcie

    You are very confident in your abilities at auto repair.
You successfully fixed at least 400 cars when you worked in
your past job.  You received very few complaints.  In fact,
your boss told you that you're one of the most skilled auto
repair workers that he ever employed.

    In the role-play, try to convince the customer to leave
his car at M. and S. for you to fix.


-------------------------------------------------------------------------------


Jim

    You read about a new garage that is opening in town,
M. and S. Auto Repair.  You're so pleased, since mechanics at
the other shops have never successfully fixed your car.  You
called and made an appointment to leave the car.  When you walk
in, you see a woman.  You're shocked.  You don't want a woman
repairing your car.

    In the role-play, try to find a way to get out of leaving
your car at M. and S. Auto Repair.

Worksheet: SITUATION CARDS

1. Joe gets hit in the eye with a baseball. He starts to cry. The other guys begin to make fun of him. You feel bad for him, but chime in with the other guys and say, "Don't be a sissy."

2. You want to build a pen for your dog. The only person around tall enough to help you is Ramona. You say, "I need a boy to help me." You don't get help and the dog runs away.

3. Some Latino students ask you to join their group to do a math project. You think they're not so smart, so you join another group. Their group gets an A, yours doesn't.

4. You are a fine dancer, and would like to take up ballet. You're afraid the other guys will make fun of you. You give up your plan, lots of good exercise, and a possible career.

5. You fall and think you've broken your ankle. A black woman who is a doctor offers to look at it. You don't trust her so you refuse. You end up lying there in pain for hours before someone else comes to help you.

6. Joan's family doesn't have much money. They live in a different neighborhood than you. She invites you to her birthday party. You don't go because you think her house will be messy and dirty. You miss a great time and a spotless house.

7. You missed the bus and need a ride to school. Ms. Mendez is 82. She offered to drive you. You think she'll drive off the road. You kill your feet walking the four miles to school.

8. Your younger sister keeps calling her friend a "wild Indian." She shoots him again and again with a toy gun. You don't correct her.

Worksheet:  WE ALL LOSE

Card Number_____

Stereotype
    or
Prejudice_____

Harm caused by stereotype or prejudice to <u>each</u> person in the
situation

_____

Card Number_____

Stereotype
    or
Prejudice_____

Harm caused by stereotype or prejudice to <u>each</u> person in the
situation

_____

Card Number_____

Stereotype
    or
Prejudice_____

Harm caused by stereotype or prejudice to <u>each</u> person in the
situation

_____

Card Number_____

Stereotype
    or
Prejudice_____

Harm caused by stereotype or prejudice to <u>each</u> person in the
situation

_____

ISM CHART

_____ People are seen and treated differently
A, B, C, OR D
because of _____.
                              1
_____is/are viewed as better or
              2
more important than others and has/have more

power in society.  In our society those

people are _____.  Values and
                    3
practices of institutions (schools,

families, churches, media, etc.)  support

these inequalities.

KEY WORDS  (Fill in according to "ism" being discussed.)
A:  Racism  1) skin color;  2) one race;  3) whites.
B:  Sexism  1) being male or female;  2) one sex;  3) males.
C:  Classism  1) the amount of money a person/family has;
              2) some classes;  3) upper- and middle-class.
D:  Ageism  1) age;  2) certain ages;  3) adults (not elderly).

EXAMPLES
Racism.   Jean walks through her school and notices there is
only one picture of a black, Asian-American, or Latino person
on the bulletin boards.  The school bulletin boards show
racism.
Sexism  Laurie wants to be on the soccer team.  Applications
were only given to boys.  Laurie calls the recreation department and she's told girls aren't allowed on the boys' team
and that there is no team for girls.  The recreation department reinforces sexism.
Classism  Dominick looks through his social studies book and
realizes that most of the people who are described as "important" are people with prestige and money.  Few working-class
or poor people are emphasized, even though their hard work
built the nation.  The textbook publishing company encourages
classism.
Ageism  For a school project, Lamar did a study of televion
shows and found that only three percent of the characters were
over sixty years old, even though in real life in this country
over fifteen percent of the people are over sixty.  Lamar
concluded that the television industry reinforces ageism.

Worksheet:  FIND THE "ISM"

1.  Jobs are divided in the Wright family.  Susan must do the
    dishes and vacuum the rug.  She doesn't like these jobs!
    Peter's jobs are to mow the lawn and weed the garden.  Peter
    likes getting exercise while doing his jobs.  Susan would
    like to have some of Peter's jobs, but her parents say she
    must learn "women's work."

        Susan probably feels_____.

        Peter might feel_____.

        The Wright parents encourage_____.

2.  Laverne did a survey of her school library books.  She found
    that most characters over sixty were described as old, ill,
    or helpless.  Laverne's own grandparents are active and
    alert.

        Laverne probably feels_____.

        Her grandparents might feel_____.

        Children's book publishing
        companies reinforce_____.

3.  Ralph's father works in a factory.  He is a hard worker and
    hardly ever misses a day of work.  He makes $4 an hour, or
    $160 a week.  Ralph is an excellent student and would like
    to become a doctor.  His family can't afford it.  Even
    scholarships can't cover the $75,000 or more needed to get
    medical training.

        Ralph probably feels_____.

        Colleges and medical schools support_____.

4.  Myra and Dwayne are excited because today they are going to
    the store to buy a board game.  They walk up and down the
    aisles and notice that there is only one black child on any
    of the game boxes.

        If Myra and Dwayne are black
        they might feel_____.

        If they are white they
        might feel_____.

        Toy companies reinforce_____.

Worksheet: MS. LOPEZ'S CLASS (1)

## Definitions

Individualism - A belief that people should look out for them-
    selves first before thinking of other people.

Competition - People work against each other to get something
    for themselves.  There is a winner who is rewarded.

Add individualism and competition and stir:

Competitive individualism - A belief that competition is fair
    and that each person has an equal chance to succeed or win
    in a situation.  The individualist may feel:
    --If I win it's because of how good I am.
    --I must compete with others and win in order to feel
      successful.
    --I must feel better than others in order to feel good
      about myself.

## Ms. Lopez's Class

    Just this year, girls and boys have begun to play basket-
ball together in Davidson School.  Before, the girls didn't
play basketball at all.  The boys have played ever since third
grade.
    The boys in Ms. Lopez's sixth-grade class get more baskets
than the girls, and in general have more basketball skills.  In
gym class, the boys make negative comments about the girls.
They say such things as, "Boys are naturally better ball players.
We always knew girls are lousy athletes."  The boys call the
girls names like "spastic" and "clumsy."  Some boys say, "You
girls have an equal chance to get points and you don't--that
proves boys are the greatest athletes."

## Questions
1.  Can you tell how the story is an example of competitive
    individualism?  Discuss it with your partner and write
    down a few ideas.




2.  How could you change the story so it wasn't an example of
    competitive individualism?  Write down a few changes.

Worksheet:  MS. LOPEZ'S CLASS (2-optional)

Explanation

Here's how the story is an example of competitive individualism!

Competitive
Individualism:  The boys say everyone had an equal chance to succeed.
Reality:  Everyone didn't have an equal chance.  The boys had three years of practice and skill-building.

Competitive
Individualism:  The boys pretend they get baskets because they're naturally better than girls.
Reality:  Most girls haven't played before and haven't been encouraged by society or parents to think they can be good.  If girls had equal training and encouragement, many could be as good.

Competitive
Individualism:  The boys feel good about themselves and put the girls down because they get more points than the girls.
Reality:  Their feeling of success is not deserved--they had a head start.  They put the girls down to make themselves feel good.

Alternative

Here's what could happen to change the story so it wouldn't be an example of competitive individualism.

With the support of the teacher, the boys would cooperate with the girls by teaching them skills and strategies they've already learned.  Boys would play for a while with a slight disadvantage in order to make it a fair game.  For example they could only use one hand.  Boys would feel good about themselves for being effective teachers and helping others to learn.  They would feel pleased when girls got baskets too.  Girls would feel competent in their new skills and pleased with their friends' support.  This would be an example of cooperation, which often is an alternative to individualism.

Questions

1.  What are your thoughts and feelings about this alternative?


2.  How would you make such an alternative work?

Worksheet:  WHO WILL TAKE CARE OF JAMIL?

Marva and Tyrone Williams are the parents of a three-year-old child, Jamil.  Tyrone works as a salesman for a local business, the E.B.M. Company.  Marva had been staying home taking care of Jamil.

Before Jamil was born, Marva worked as a secretary.  She didn't like the typing too much, but she started to learn about computers.  She caught on quickly.  Her employer told her she'd be great in that area of work.

When Jamil was two, Marva decided she wanted to return to school to study math and computers.  She was nervous about it, but she wanted to try.  The local college used radio and newspaper ads to tell women to come back to school.

Last fall Marva decided to take one course.  The class met from 4:00 to 6:00.  She asked if Tyrone could get off work an hour early a few days a week to take care of Jamil.

Tyrone asked his boss if he could come to work an hour early.  Then he would get off from work an hour early to take car care of Jamil.  His boss looked surprised.  "Is baby-sitting more important than your job?"  Tyrone explained he would still work the same number of hours, just different ones.  Finally the boss agreed.

Other workers laughed at Tyrone when he'd leave at 3:30.  "Off to mind the kid!  You won't get ahead in the world like that!"  Sometimes his boss would tell Tyrone to stay at a meeting even if it went past 3:30.  This would make Marva late for school.

Tyrone was angry at his business.  It was supposed to be an "equal opportunity employer."  But it didn't help a father change his hours for child-care.  Tyrone liked taking care of Jamil very much, yet he was afraid he would be kept back for leaving work at 3:30.  At the end of her course he told Marva he wouldn't do that again.

Marva had done very well in school and she decided that she would go all day the next term.  When she went to enroll Jamil in the college's day-care center, she found out it was full.  There was only room for twenty-five children and there was a waiting list of fifty!  She was angry!  "How can you have ads to tell women to come to school when there's not enough day-care?"

Marva decided to look at day-care centers in her town. There were only three.  One was full, one was poor in quality, and the other was too expensive.

Marva was very angry.  Messages on TV, radio, and in magazines told women that they could go to school, get a job, and become active in the world.  They never said what she had learned:  "But don't try it if you have a child."

Marva decided to write an article for the newspaper on how sexism affects parents.  If you were Marva, what would you say in that article?

In your newspaper story try to tell something about the following:

1.  How do you think Marva felt?

2.  How did Tyrone, Tyrone's co-workers, and his boss support sexism?

3.  How did the college Marva goes to support sexism?

4.  How does the idea that women should have the chief responsibility for caring for children support sexism?

5.  What could the E.B.M. Company and Marva's college do to change these sexist practices?

6.  How is the Williams' problem like that of other men and women?

7.  What do others in the community lose out on by the lack of good day-care?

Worksheet:  CAN WE SAVE OUR HOUSE?


        Ted and Juanita Lund face a decision.  You will soon under-
stand how difficult their decision is.
        Ted is sixty-nine and Juanita is seventy years old.  Ted
used to work as a gardener.  He knows a great deal about plants,
flowers, and trees.  He loved his work.  His only regret was
that he was paid so little.  Juanita worked as a clerk in an
office.  She found the work boring, yet she was pleased that
she could help support the family.
        Ted and Juanita saved their money so they could buy the
house they now live in.  Over the past twenty-five years,
Juanita and Ted have made furniture and decorations for the
inside of the house so it feels like "home."  Their garden is
outstanding.  Both work hour after hour in their yard.  The
beautiful flowers and flowering bushes are admired by all who
pass by.  The Lunds get much pleasure out of their garden!
        Juanita had to retire from her full-time job at age
sixty-five.  Then she tried to get a part-time job working with
people.  She was tired of working with files and was eager to
work with children.  She applied for many jobs.  She was always
told, "We only hire people who already have had jobs working
with children.  Besides, we want someone who can work with us
for many years."  Juanita didn't feel old.  Now she had the
time to do something she always wanted to do--and she couldn't
find a job.
        Juanita was angry she couldn't get a job for another
reason--they needed the money.  It was too hard to live on the
small Social Security check they got each month.  Prices for
food and clothes kept going up.  By budgeting their money <u>very</u>
carefully, they were able to pay their bills.  Nothing was
left.
        Six months ago, Ted had a major operation.  He was in the
hospital for a month.  Now he is getting better at home.  He
still has to take a lot of medicine and visit the doctor often.
        The bills for Ted's medical care were very high.  His
insurance paid for some of it, but there are still a lot of
bills that the Lunds have to pay themselves.  They don't have
that much money in the bank.
        Juanita and Ted are faced with a painful decision.  Should
they sell their house to get money to pay their bills?  They
could move into apartments for the elderly.  Yet this is their
home.  Ted and Juanita get very sad when they think of leaving
the house that they put so much work into.  The greatest joy in
their life still comes from working in their garden.

Roles:   TED AND JUANITA LUND

## Ted Lund

You are very discouraged.  You are also angry that the hospital bills are so high and insurance doesn't cover all the costs.  You get very upset to think of leaving your house and garden.

With a sad heart, you feel that the best plan is to move.

--------------------------------------------------------------------------

## Juanita Lund

You are very angry.  You and Ted have worked very hard during your lives.  Now one major illness may take away your house.  You think it's wrong that hospital bills are so high and insurance doesn't cover all costs.

You also feel it's unfair that you couldn't get a job because of your age.  Then you could have worked and paid the bills.  You don't want to move.

You want to talk about your situation with other older people.  Maybe you all can get together and do something!

Worksheet:  LILLIE'S DILEMMA

    Lillie is eleven years old, the oldest of five children.
Lillie lives with her mother and three sisters and brother in a
rural county in Maryland.  Her father left the family when she
was eight.

    Lillie's mother, Carolyn Raley, loves her children very
much.  She's going to college in order to become a teacher.
It's not easy to raise a family and be a student in college.
Carolyn has worked hard, though, and will graduate in a month.
She hopes to join the small number of black women teachers in
the county.  Until a few years ago, the school system hadn't
hired any black teachers.

    Since Lillie's father left, the family has been on welfare.
Carolyn and her children don't like to be on welfare.  However,
this is the only way they can survive.  Carolyn is very happy
that soon she'll be a teacher so <u>she</u> can support her family.

    There is only one set of apartments in this county that
low-income people can afford.  This is where Lillie and her
family live.  About half the people living there are black.
The landlord doesn't take care of the apartments.  When their
water pipe broke, the landlord didn't have it repaired for
four days.  Lillie's family was without water the whole time.
Carolyn's many phone calls to him made no difference.  Furthermore, the landlord doesn't like black people.  When Lillie met
him once and asked him to make repairs, he replied, "Waiting a
few days won't hurt your type of people, kid."

    Last week the heat was off for three days.  Carolyn called
the landlord.  When nothing happened she called the county
housing office.  Someone said, "We'll talk to your landlord"-
but still no heat.  Carolyn was furious.  Her children were
freezing and nothing was being done.

    Carolyn decided to organize a rent strike.  This meant
that none of the people living in the apartments would pay
their rent until the landlord promised that he would make repairs on time.  Since the other people in the apartments had
problems with no heat and no water, they were all willing to
work together in the rent strike.  Carolyn was so hopeful.
"Now, maybe we can have a decent place to live after all.  The
landlord will certainly change his ways now!"

    The day before the rent strike was to start, Carolyn came
to Lillie's room.  She looked very upset.  "The landlord just
called me on the phone.  He said,'You're a rotten colored
troublemaker.  If you don't call off this rent strike, I'll
make sure you never get a teaching job in this county.  Never!'

    Lillie, I'm so angry and confused.  I want to stand up for
our rights.  We deserve to have good housing since we pay our
rent.  Everyone is so determined to finally stand up to the
landlord.  I don't want to let them down.  But, Lillie, I so
much want to be a teacher!  Worst of all, the landlord is good
friends with the superintendent of schools, the head of the
county housing office, and the mayor.  They all stick together
and have so much power in the county.  What should I do?"

Worksheet: LILLIE'S DILEMMA (continued)

1.  What are three feelings Carolyn probably felt? Why would
    she feel that way?

2.  If you were Lillie, what would you be feeling? What would
    you say to your mother?

3.  How was the landlord racist? How did he use racism to
    hurt Lillie's family?

Worksheet:  LETTER FROM SALLY


    Below is a letter from Sally to her friend Theresa.  Sally
is graduating from high school.


Dear Theresa,
    I've missed you so much since you've moved away.  I'm
very sad and discouraged this week.  I need a friend to talk
to.  I wish you were closer by!!
    Since you left, Dad got sick and had to quit his job.  He
probably won't be able to ever go back to work as a salesman.
There was no insurance plan in the small company he worked for.
All he gets is $300 a month from the government.  He's in the
hospital and may be there for a long time.
    I've told you how much I want to be a doctor.  I worked so
hard in high school to get good grades.  I got a scholarship to
an excellent college with a pre-med program, but it covers only
part of the cost.
    This year I've been helping Mom raise the four younger
kids.  Her job as a secretary only pays $160 a week.  She
doesn't get home until 5:30.  I'm here after school with them
until then.
    It's impossible for Mom to pay the rent, buy clothes, and
feed the family on her small salary and Dad's monthly check.
I'm going to have to give up my idea of college and becoming a
doctor and get a full-time job.
    Do you know how disappointed and angry I am?!  It's not
right that I work so hard in school and then have to give up
my plan to be a doctor because our family doesn't have enough
money.  Why should college and medical school be so expensive?
Another student just like me, but with parents who make more
money, will become a doctor.  I won't.
    Theresa, do you understand how I feel?  Do you think it's
fair that people with more money have more chances to become
what they want to be?
    Please write back!

                        Your friend,

                        Sally

# 6 DISCRIMINATION: PRICES AND CHOICES

> "Jimmy is in the second grade and he likes school. He pays attention in class and does well. He has an above average I.Q. and is reading slightly above grade level. Bobby is a second grader, too. Like Jimmy he is attentive in class, which he enjoys. His I.Q. and reading skills are comparable to Jimmy's. But Bobby is the son of a successful lawyer whose annual salary of more than $35,000 puts him within the top percentages of income distribution in this country. Jimmy's father, on the other hand, works from time to time as a messenger or a custodial assistant, and earns $4,800 a year. Despite the similarities in ability between the two boys, the difference in circumstances to which they were born makes it *27* times more likely that Bobby will get a job that, by the time he is in his late 40's, will pay him an income in the top tenth of all incomes in this country. Jimmy has only about one chance in eight of earning even a median income. . . ."
>
> Richard deLone in *Small Futures*, 1979.

Institutional discrimination takes a painful price from its victims. It also provides potentially powerful choices for those who benefit from it. Activities in Chapter 6 enable students to understand better these realities and opportunities.

Lessons in Section A, "Unequal Resources = Unequal Results," aim to help students examine how institutional discrimination produces inequality in both resources and opportunities for certain groups of people and how it, therefore, supports the success and achievement of other groups. Put simply, effects of the "isms" deny particular groups of people resources, thus guaranteeing unequal life-outcomes.

The powerful effect of institutional and cultural discrimination on opportunities for equality challenges the assumptions underlying competitive individualism—that "you can make it if you try," and that "everyone has an equal opportunity." The lessons in this section enable students to examine critically these assumptions. They also teach students to recognize the process of *"blaming the victim."* When people are denied equal resources through institutional discrimination, they are often blamed for their situations or their lack of success. Activities will help the students ask if the cause of inequality is in a *system* of institutional discrimination that distributes resources, opportunities, and power unequally—rather than in the deficiencies of *individuals*.

These ideas are sometimes difficult even for adults to understand, but the experiential nature of the activities will help students *feel* what it's like to be expected to achieve without equal resources and opportunities. Then, through the discussion questions, *you* can encourage them to make the connections to the effects of the "isms" on groups of people in society. More information about institutional discrimination is found in the boxes throughout this chapter and in the resources listed in the Bibliography. They provide data and examples to share with your students. Take plenty of time with the discussion questions, for making the connections between their classroom activities and the dynamics of institutional discrimination in society is a crucial element in student learning.

"Connections to Others," Section B, is comprised of lessons in which students learn to examine how the privileges of some individuals and groups are directly connected to the denial of those privileges to others. It is again through your role in assisting students to tie experiential activities to theirs and others' lives that these new ideas become meaningful. Use examples to highlight the connections between the factors that create more privileges for some people than others. For example, if a man stands to gain and a woman to lose through sexist practices in the workplace, there is a connection between the man's higher status and the woman's lower position. One's benefit is *due*, in part, to the other's loss.

Lessons will help students experience and understand the *choices* that privileged individuals or groups have in creating change. Often those of us with privilege—whether it be white skin, male sex, or middle-class status—tend to denigrate the power we have, and ignore choices that can foster greater equality by sharing resources, decision-making, and opportunities.

If your students have relatively few privileges—if they are low-income and minority—you may chose to use fewer of these activities. Nevertheless, your students can learn about male privilege, lighter-skin privilege, and their privilege of being able-bodied. Adjust processing questions accordingly.

Some activities in this chapter are "rigged," in that some students are given advantages and others not without your making this inequality explicit. The affective learning about inequality that is generated by these experiences can be very meaningful and powerful. Some teachers, however, feel uncomfortable "setting up" students in this way. Since lessons differ in degree of privilege given or withheld, your choice of lessons will depend on your feelings on this issue and your group of students. Also, if your students have difficulty handling emotionally charged situations, or if you are uncomfortable processing them, choose lessons with extra care.

In sum, students' activities will enable them to see their options, not only to share resources, but to make changes so that privilege becomes something that's shared or unnecessary. They will explore the benefits of equality to *all* people. Only when adults and students alike step back and look at unexamined choices and their consequences, can they make decisions from an "unblinded" perspective. At this point alternatives that support equality become both more conceivable and more possible.

He says, we women control the wealth.

## SECTION A  UNEQUAL RESOURCES = UNEQUAL RESULTS

### Create A Mobile _____ SS, A

**OBJECTIVES**
To allow students to experience the frustration and unfairness of a situation where some have an unfair advantage.
To help students see the connection between this specific classroom project and what happens in society when people start out with fewer resources but are still expected to achieve equally.

**MATERIALS**
Branches from trees, eighteen-gauge wire, dowel rods, thread, coat-hangers, construction paper, tissue paper, glossy paper, shells, pine cones, scissors, rulers, crayons, hole punch, toothpicks, yarn, printed wrapping paper, glue, tape, pliers, wire-cutters.

**IMPLEMENTATION**
Divide students into five groups. Explain that each group is expected to make a mobile. These will be displayed. Use a topic from one of your subject matter areas as the theme for the mobile. Groups may only use the supplies they are given; they do not have to use all of them but they may *not* use anything else. Distribute supplies as follows:

Group 1:  one coat-hanger, two sheets of brown construction paper, one spool of thread.

Group 2:  three coat-hangers, two dowel rods, assorted colors of construction paper, assorted colors of yarn, thread.

Group 3:  three coat-hangers, three dowel rods, a spool of wire, assorted colors of construction paper, assorted colors of tissue paper, scissors, glue, thread, wire-cutters.

Group 4:  three coat hangers, three dowel rods, wire, branches, crayons, pine cones, yarn, thread, construction, tissue and glossy paper, wire-cutters, pliers.

Group 5:  some of everything.

Give each group thirty to forty-five minutes to complete mobiles. During that time, take notes of group process and student comments. If students complain about the way items were distributed, be very matter-of-fact. Say something like, "That's the way life is. There will be no changes."

**DISCUSSION**
1. How did you feel while doing the project? (Give each child a chance for a short response.)
2. How did you feel when you looked over at the other groups?
3. In what ways was your project easy? hard? fun? frustrating?
4. Why do you think I set up the project this way?
5. How would you feel if we had a contest and judged the mobiles: How about if we displayed them in the hallway by the office, with your names? How would it be if we gave prizes for the best mobiles?
6. Think of a situation in school where some people start off with a greater advantage or more supplies than other people. Why does that happen? How do different people in that situation feel?

7. Think of a similar situation in your family or community. Again answer why it happens and how people feel.

8. In what ways do some people start off with more resources, money, or power—like some of you today started off with some more supplies? How does that affect what they can do for themselves? Why is it sometimes a problem?

9. What happens if we expect everyone to be able to do equally well even though they don't have the same amount of resources, money, or power? What happens if they get judged that way—the way we might judge you on these mobiles?

---

STARTING WITH ADVANTAGES

*School:* Children who have had the opportunity to go to nursery school often start off in elementary school with more skills than other children. They have a head-start in school.

*Community:* The rate of unemployment for black teenagers is over 40 percent (1980). White teenagers have many more opportunities to get jobs. They have a headstart in the job market.

---

**FOLLOW-UP**     "Using Privilege for Change," p. 239.

---

The phrase "equal opportunity employer" has become commonplace in most branches of industry and business. Yet an examination of current racial representation in virtually any American institution demonstrates that fair employment practices have not led to significant increase in black participation. Black unemployment rates remain double those of whites; within the labor force, black people are for the most part found doing blue-collar work.

The reason for the failure of the equal opportunity policy is at once clear if conditions of poor ghetto schools, lack of skilled training and union discrimination are compared with the acceptance standards of business, government and other institutions. Although it is true that a qualified lathe operator, plumber or engineer, be he black or white, can compete for any job opening, the numbers of black people in these professions have not increased. There are few lathe operator training centers serving the ghettos; few plumbers' unions willing to accept black apprentices; ghetto schools turn out a tragically small number of students prepared for a college program in engineering.

It is meaningless for an employer to say that if a black man with a Ph.D. in electrical engineering walks in the door of a technical firm he will be treated in the same manner as a white man with the same education. There is a long, unfortunate but well known history to the fact that black men with Ph.D.'s in electrical engineering do not just "walk in the door"; for all practical purposes, few such men even exist.

*From Institutional Racism in America: A Primer.*

---

## A Little Praise Goes a Long Way _____ LA, C

**OBJECTIVES**     To show students the effects of praise and support on their own and others' achievements.

To help students understand how social institutions give support and praise to some groups of people more than to others, and how this affects achievement in society.

**MATERIALS**     Copies of "Worksheet: Praise Matters," p. 142.

**IMPLEMENTATION**     Decide whether you want to let the children know what you are doing in this lesson. To let them know has the advantage of not "tricking" them. On the other hand, telling them makes the lesson less effective.

On a particular day, praise and support half the students for anything they do that is remotely good or correct and ignore all their wrong answers or unacceptable behavior. Set high expectations and encourage them to succeed. On the same day, with the rest of the class, praise nothing and criticize anything that is wrong. Set very low expectations for this group. Do this throughout the day in all your academic areas and interpersonal interactions.

Stop at least an hour before the end of school. Tell students what you've been doing. Discuss feelings briefly.

Ask students to fill out the Worksheets. Discuss the day's experience and the Worksheets as a class.

**DISCUSSION**
1. Discuss the Worksheet responses.
2. Compare the feelings of those in each group.
3. How did you do in your schoolwork? Look at your workbook pages, how quickly you worked, how many mistakes you made. Did you do better or worse than usual? Why?
4. When you are told you are doing well with something, how does that affect you? What happens to you when you are scolded or criticized?
5. Give an example of a time when someone expected you to do well and that made a difference in how you did. Give an example of a time when someone expected you to do poorly and that changed your performance.

Tell students that some institutions—like families, the media, places of employment—praise and support some people more than others. Sometimes different *expectations* are set up for different groups of people. High expectations of a person or group tend to encourage success. If a person in authority or an institution, however, has low expectations, that tends to discourage success.

6. Ask students what would happen in the following cases:
   a. If a teacher expects boys in high school to do well in chemistry, and girls not as well, what might happen?
   b. If a principal gives a lot of praise and support to black students who do well on the basketball team, but less to them when they show improvement on a test score, what might happen?
   c. *Fact:* Two-thirds of the nation's newspapers have no minority employees. How does this lack of support affect minorities' feelings about being able to achieve in journalism?
   d. *Fact:* Women hold two percent of all seats in the U.S. Senate (1982). What does this lack of institutional support do to women's feeling about achieving in government?
   e. *Fact:* Forty percent of black teenagers who want jobs can't find them (1980). How might society's lack of support for teenage employment affect their feelings about achieving in work?
7. What other examples can you think of of institutions that support some people more than others?

Explain to the students that, like individuals, *institutions* can praise, support, set high expectations by their practices and procedures. The *result* of this support or lack of support on people is similar to what they felt in this exercise.

**GOING FURTHER**
Make graphs or charts of students' normal performance compared to the performance of the two groups during this day. Put these up on a bulletin board as a reminder.

---

Individual difference in learning is an observable phenomenon which can be predicted, explained, and altered in a great variety of ways. In contrast, individual difference in learners is a more esoteric notion. It frequently obscures our efforts to deal directly with educational problems in that it searches for explanations in the person of the learner rather than in the interaction between individuals and the educational and social environments in which they have been placed.

From *Human Characteristics and School Learning*, by Benjamin Bloom.

It's Not Fair!!!

CO-OPS

## Values Auction*                                                                M

**OBJECTIVES**

To enable students to clarify values that are important to them.
To help students understand how people's relative degree of economic privilege affects their ability to acquire things they value.

**MATERIALS**

Copies of "Worksheet: Values Auction," p. 143; play money; one pair of dice for each group of four.

**IMPLEMENTATION**

This activity is designed for a class of twenty-two or fewer students. If your numbers are greater, add to the Worksheet, still leaving two blank spaces. Tell students that they will have an opportunity to decide what values are important to them in their lives. Pass out the Worksheet and ask them to rank the values from most important to least important. If this is too difficult for your students, have them check five or six most important and underline the five or six least important. They may add one or two items that are important to them but are not on the list if they wish.

Then divide students into groups of three or four and ask them to discuss their lists with each other. This gives them an opportunity to affirm their values and hear others' points of view, both important parts of values clarification. (For more on values clarification, see *Values and Teaching*, by Louis Raths, *et al.*, or *Values Clarification: A Handbook of Practical Strategies*, by Sidney Simon *et al.*)

Distribute money. Each student begins with $100. Give a pair of dice to each group. Each student rolls the dice to determine how many more dollars she gets—one dot equals $10. Those who roll a seven or more are entitled to roll one extra die as "inheritance."

Now the auction begins. Ask students who know about auctions to explain the procedure to others. One student is appointed banker to collect the money during the auction. You are the auctioneer. Auction off the list, writing on the board the name of the highest bidder and the amount bid for each item. Keep the pace brisk and use typical auction terms, such as "Going once, going twice, sold for. . . ."

**DISCUSSION**

1.  Who didn't get anything at the auction? Why not?
2.  What would you bid higher for next time?
3.  How did you feel during the auction? How do you feel now? (At this point feelings about the unequal amounts of money will surface. Be sure to allow adequate time for students to share feelings of frustration or anger.)
4.  How did the amount of money you had affect your ability to get the items you valued most?
5.  How did the amount of money you had affect your willingness to take a risk?
6.  In life, how does the amount of money or resources a group has affect their ability to get things they value most? Give examples. Some might be:
    a.  In order to become a great athlete, expensive training is necessary. This is also true for music and dance.
    b.  The more financial resources you have, the more opportunity you have to get preventive health care and quality medical care when you are sick.
    c.  The more financial resources a person has to get needed education or training for a job, the more opportunity she has both for choice of job and success.

*Adapted from *A Handbook of Personal Growth Activities for Classroom Use*, by R. and I. Hawley.

7. How was the throw of the "inheritance" die like real life? How does the privilege of inheritance affect chances to get what you value?

Now tell students they may use their remaining money to purchase items that they have written in the blank spaces. Have students decide the worth of those items compared to the price of other things they bid for and got. Ask them to share a few of these items with the group. Finally, students share some "I learned" statements from this experience.

---

### ASSUMPTIONS ABOUT EQUALITY

For some people, equality means that people are equally free to act, or to take advantage of what America has to offer. Yet this definition does not take into account people's ability to do so. For example, Jill Smoe, worker, and David Rockefeller are equally *free* to open a bank, but are they equally *able*?

Is equality possible as long as there is a disparity in wealth that allows some people access to opportunities others don't have?

---

### SHARING SKILLS

Remind students that "Equal Resources = More Equal Results." The more chances people have to gain knowledge and skills, the better chances they'll have to fulfill their potentials.

Students write down one skill or area of expertise they have that they could teach to someone else. The skill could be academic, athletic, or one learned at home.

Each student identifies one such skill and tells the class. Help students who have trouble.

Set up a system where students teach each other their skills. Set up Friday afternoons or indoor recess as special times, or build skill-sharing into the ongoing class routine. Academic skill-sharing can be a form of peer-tutoring.

---

## Blaming the Victim ———————————— LA, C, PE, SS

**OBJECTIVES**
To learn the meaning of "blaming the victim."
To help students draw parallels between these classroom experiences and our society, where some people are born with more advantages and privilege than others.
To enable students to understand that expecting everyone to reach the same goals in our society and judging them by whether they have reached them is unfair when opportunities are unequal.

**MATERIALS**
Option One: paper; pencils.
Option Two: use of a track, preferably with hurdles; stop watch.

**IMPLEMENTATION**
This lesson contains two options for students to experience and understand the idea of blaming the victim. In both cases you are asked to role-play and to blame or criticize students who don't do well, even though they were given fewer resources. In this way they can understand experientially the concept of blaming the victim. This learning can be very powerful. However, if you feel that the negative effect of such blaming, albeit temporary, will outweigh the positive learning, you may choose to omit this lesson.

OPTION ONE: IT'S ALL GREEK TO ME. Begin this as a language arts lesson. Stress the importance of the students' doing a good job since it will count heavily toward their grades.

Divide class into two groups. Call one group up into a circle. Give this group whispered directions in English:

Write at least two pages for this. Write a composition which includes in it the following items—torn curtain, a sick squirrel, five baseball bats, and a bright red potholder. Be sure there is plot in your story; something must happen.

Send those students back to their seats to begin writing. Call the rest of the class up and give them these whispered directions:

Sobe seeta hei tolk jagem. Deenty moik sewtrount trop a dwert, groalol, creth hom wert quoems. Drimt sanbred lowntoo screthmess yoxsill poltwed. Grunswix polt ou vrent.

Allow the usual time for in-class writing. Don't allow talking. If students ask questions just say, "Please do your work."

When the time is up, admonish the group who didn't finish. *Blame them* for not being able to do the task. Give them a few minutes to feel the feelings associated with being blamed. Go on to discussion questions.

---

### BLAMING THE VICTIM

The generic process of Blaming the Victim is applied to almost every American problem. The miserable health care of the poor is explained away on the grounds that the victim has poor motivation and lacks health information. The problems of slum housing are traced to the characteristics of tenants who are labeled as "Southern rural migrants" not yet "acculturated" to life in the big city. . . . From such a viewpoint, the obvious fact that poverty is primarily an absence of money is easily overlooked or set aside.

From *Blaming the Victim*, by William Ryan.

---

### OTHER EXAMPLES OF BLAMING THE VICTIM

People out of work are sometimes blamed for being lazy, not ambitious, or willing to take a handout when, in fact, there are not enough jobs for all Americans and the U.S. economy depends on a steady rate of unemployment.

Women are sometimes blamed for not being able to fix mechanical things. Yet girls haven't been taught trades or mechanical skills. Until recently they weren't allowed to take shop in school, and women are still discriminated against in many trades.

---

OPTION TWO: THE HURDLE RACE.   Take students to the playground or gym and set up hurdles or obstacles. Prepare slips of paper as follows:

  4%—"Run as fast as you can, no hurdles."
  8%—"Run as fast as you can, two hurdles."
  8%—"Run as fast as you can, four hurdles."
12%—"Run as fast as you can, four hurdles."
     (Start these people back 25 feet.)
16%—"Run as fast as you can, four hurdles."
     (Start these people back 50 feet.)
20%—"Run as fast as you can, one hurdle."
     (Tie each person's feet together.)
20%—"Run backwards as fast as you can, two hurdles."
     (Tie their feet together.)
12%—"Stay still."

If you don't have hurdles, prepare handicaps of varying degrees of difficulty, such as "Hop on one foot," or "Jump with both feet together," or "Go on hands and knees."

Prepare an appealing prize for the winner. Prepare hurdles or obstacles beforehand. Students pull slips. Give a pep talk and blow whistle to start the race. Give prize and praise to the winner. Blame the losers for their slow place, clumsiness, and lack of initiative.

---

**IT'S YOUR FAULT**

The stigma that marks the victim and accounts for his victimization is an acquired stigma, a stigma of social, rather than genetic, origin. But the stigma, the defect, the fatal difference—though derived in the past from environmental forces—is still located *within* the victim, inside his skin. With such an elegant formulation, the humanitarian can have it both ways. He can, all at the same time, concentrate his charitable interest on the defects of the victim, condemn the vague social and environmental stresses that produced the defect (some time ago), and ignore the continuing effect of victimizing social forces (right now). It is a brilliant ideology for justifying a perverse form of social action designed to change, not society, as one might expect, but rather society's victim. . . .

In defining social problems in this way, the social pathologists are, of course, ignoring a whole set of factors that ordinarily might be considered relevant—for instance, unequal distribution of income, social stratification, political struggle, ethnic and racial group conflict, and inequality of power. Their ideology concentrates almost exclusively on the failure of the deviant.

From *Blaming The Victim*, by William Ryan

---

**DISCUSSION**  Explain that you were role-playing and you *really* don't blame them. You wanted, however, for them to feel how it feels to be blamed for not achieving when you have an unfair disadvantage and *conditions* aren't equal. (Save notes from this activity for use in Chapter 10.)

1.  How did you feel if you were given an advantage in this activity?
2.  How did you feel if you were given a handicap?
3.  How did it feel to be blamed for your failure? Did you deserve it? Did achievers deserve their praise?
4.  In what ways is this like the real world? In what ways do people start out without an equal chance? Give examples.
5.  In what ways are we all expected to achieve equally even though we don't start out with equal chances?

Explain that in life people with advantages often blame those with disavantages for their problem. This is called "blaming the victim." *People*, rather than unequal *situations*, are labeled at fault.

Remind students, "I blamed the victim in this activity. What did you learn from this?

Some people and groups in society think they've succeeded "on their own." They believe that everybody has a chance to succeed if they just try hard enough. Explain that such a viewpoint doesn't take into consideration inequalities and discrimination in society. These are like the hurdles in our race. While everyone has personal hurdles, like family trouble, some people and groups face the additional hurdles that societal discrimination creates. Refer to the following box, "The Hurdles of Life."

**FOLLOW-UP**   "Removing Those Hurdles," p. 240.

> ### CASE STUDIES—THE HURDLES OF LIFE
>
> **Case study a: poor, latino female.**   Because of malnutrition of her mother during pregnancy, this child was born weak and had life-long health problems (hurdle 1). Because Spanish was spoken at home and lessons were only taught in English at school, she had academic difficulty in the early grades (hurdle 2). Facing discrimination in employment, her father was often out of work and her mother could only find low-paying factory work. She therefore had to work evenings and weekends to help support her family (hurdle 3). Since her counselor believed a female doesn't need a career, she was placed in a vocational track in high school. She was told she wasn't college material (hurdle 4).
>
> **Case study b: white, middle-class male.**   Because his mother could afford quality health care during pregnancy, this child was born healthy. School lessons were taught in his native tongue and his culture was reflected in the norms and materials of the school. He had difficulty reading and received tutoring (small hurdle). His father and mother worked to support the family and the student worked on Saturday to have spending money. He broke his leg playing football and missed a month of his junior year (small hurdle). His counselor tracked him into a college preparatory program and provided financial aid information. He got into a good college.

## Assignment: Research Paper _____ SS, S, LA

**OBJECTIVES**   To enable students to understand experientially the feelings and options of people with greater or lesser degrees of privilege in society.

To expand students' views of the choices for change that various groups have available to them.

To reinforce the understanding that expecting everyone to reach the same goals in our society, and judging them by whether they have reached those goals, is unfair when opportunities are unequal.

**MATERIALS**   Reference materials for a topic of your choice relevant to your classroom curriculum—encyclopedias, library books, newspapers, magazines; name-tags; play money; paper; pencils.

**IMPLEMENTATION**   This is an experiential activity that can catalyze strong feelings and significant learning. Read it over carefully. If you choose to do it, allow plenty of time for processing questions. They are crucial!

This is set up for a classroom of 25 students, so modify numbers accordingly. Assign the following roles and distribute name-tags and play money (students pin on name tags and keep money hidden): one police officer; two storekeepers; one welfare worker (ten 50¢ slips); one organizer; one very wealthy citizen ($20); one upper-class citizen ($15); one upper-middle-class citizen ($12); two middle-class citizens ($10 each); four lower-middle-class citizens ($6 each); four lower-class citizens ($3 each); six totally impoverished citizens (nothing).

Tell the whole class about the various roles and what people can do in those roles. Give the storekeepers the supplies necessary for preparing the research paper: all the reference materials, books, paper, writing and drawing supplies. The students playing citizens are told that they must produce research reports on the topic you have chosen. They may use only materials they obtain from the storekeepers. They may get funds in any way they can. They will have two class periods to work.

Provide guidelines for storekeepers—for example, paper, 25¢; pencils, 25¢; use of a book for fifteen minutes, $1. Storekeepers may overcharge, sell damaged merchandise, bargain, and so on. They can mistreat the poor. They can change prices at will. They can use the police officer to collect IOU's and have citizens jailed.

The police officer patrols the area, keeps a special eye on the poor and enforces "law and order" as need be. He watches for cheating and stealing and may take sides.

The welfare worker can give out fifty-cent pieces to help the poor, and can also require them to fill out long forms and wait for long periods of time. The organizer attempts to unite the poor.

Take notes of what happens, what is said, how action changes. If you have use of a video-tape camera, this is a good activity to tape. Continually stress the importance of completing the assignment. Keep reminding people they will be graded. (They will not be, of course.) As the activity is going on, praise the achievers with statements like, "Oh, what fine work; I know how intelligent you are," and blame the low achievers with statements like, "If you're not doing well, you aren't trying hard," or, "Well, I didn't expect much of you slow people anyway."

At the end of the two days, collect papers and grade as though everyone had an equal chance.

**DISCUSSION**

1. How did you feel during this activity? How did you feel toward people in other roles?
2. How do you feel about your research papers? How do you think the grade you'll get is connected to the resources you had?
3. How would you feel if someone said, "There are certain people here who are less intelligent than others, which we certainly can see by the work they've produced"?
4. How did I "blame the victim"? What did that feel like?
5. In what ways was this like real life? unlike? Give examples.
6. How did the "money" you got affect what you produced in this assignment? How did you feel about that?
7. How does the money different families have affect what they can do with their lives?
8. What did the poor people in our class do to gain more money and thus more supplies? How did that work?
9. What kinds of things can less privileged people do in life to get more of what they need? What happens when they do these things? (Note: You may add to students' comments and mention organizing, educating, boycotts, lessons in upcoming sections focus on strategies for change.)
10. What did the privileged people in the activity do? What can such people in this country do?
11. How do policies of institutions in our country—schools, government, businesses—support this unfair system? (See box below for examples.)

"We've got a lot in common—the Purple and Orange Soccer Team !!!"

---

INSTITUTIONAL POLICIES → INEQUALITIES

(a) Schools are funded in large part through local property taxes. Wealthy communities have more money to put into education, so students have more resources and special programs. Less money is spent on students in poorer districts. Sometimes it is said that poorer students are "less intelligent" and just don't do as well in school. Is it their "innate intelligence"? Remember without equal resources we can't expect equal results.

(b) It is said that females don't do as well in sports as males. It was projected that the average budget for women's athletic programs in large colleges in 1981–82 would be 27% of that for men's programs ("Sprint," Womens Equality Action League). Without equal resources, can we expect equal results?

---

An excellent example of the value of experiential learning is shown in the film, *Eye of a Storm*. Students learn about racism when they are discriminated against according to eye-color.

# SECTION B   CONNECTIONS TO OTHERS

## Team Spirit

**OBJECTIVES**
To help students see how the privileges white people get are often tied to the denial of those privileges to blacks.
To see what choices white people have to share privileges.

**MATERIALS**
If possible a copy (or several) of *Charles Drew* by Roland Bertol. (This is a strong book with one serious omission—it does not describe the institutional racism responsible for Drew's death. Drew was denied access to a "white" hospital after an auto accident, and consequently died.) Copies of "Worksheet: Team Spirit," p. 144.

**IMPLEMENTATION**
Have students read about Charles Drew or give them background information. Tell them Drew was an outstanding doctor who devised a method to dry and preserve blood plasma for transfusions. Distribute copies of Worksheets. Students read it themselves and answer the questions.

**DISCUSSION**
Discuss each question on the Worksheet. Focus on the point that when white people accept certain privileges, in this case eating at a particular hotel, they can be buying into a system that denies those privileges to others. They are, thus, very *connected* to others—in this case the black members of the team. Also stress the *choices* whites have to accept or not accept those privileges.

---

Little by little, year by year, a wall of separation is constructed in the child's mind to offer self-protection in the face of realistic guilt at unearned privilege and inherited excess. Poor people exist—so also do the rich—but there are no identifiable connections. One side does not live well *because* another side must live in pain and fear. It is a matter, rather of two things that happen to occur at the same time; side by side. The slumlord's daughter, therefore, is not forced to be unsettled, and still less tormented, by the fact that there are black and Puerto Rican families two miles distant who must pay the rent to make her luxuries conceivable . . .

To believe in victims is to believe, as well, in victimizers. It is to be forced to come into the presence of the whole idea that there must be *oppressors* in the world for there to be *oppressed*. It is to be forced, as well, to feel, and understand, that bad results too often have bad causes, that evil acts don't just "occur"—like mushrooms after rain—but have most often been initiated by the will of those who stand to profit from them.

*From The Night is Dark and I'm Far*
*From Home, by Jonathan Kozol.*

---

## Pay Day

**OBJECTIVES**
To give students the opportunity to distribute (imaginary) financial resources.
To help students understand that, with limited resources, some have more means, others have less.
To help students see that there is a connection between the privilege of some and lack of privileges of others.

**MATERIALS**
Paper; pencils; local newspapers; social studies texts about communities; chart paper; markers.

**IMPLEMENTATION**
Explain to students that, in groups, they will divide up a pretend sum of money to pay town workers. Brainstorm to come up with a list of the kinds of workers needed by a town or city. Keep the number of workers manageable.

Divide into groups of four or five students. Then tell each group that they are the town managers and have $110,000 for town salaries. They must distribute the money so that all the workers are paid.

After groups have finished, they copy their job and salary schedules on chart paper and post them in the front of the room. Go on to discuss these questions.

**DISCUSSION**
1. Did you decide to pay everyone the same salary? Why or why not?
2. If you decided to give different salaries for different jobs, what criteria did you use for this? Did the type of job matter? The amount of education? responsibility? the appeal of job?
3. Did you base your decisions on what you think really happens in a town or on what you think should happen? Why?
4. Do you think people's needs—the number of children, illnesses in the family, and so forth—should be taken into consideration in deciding salaries? Explain.
5. In a community, or society, there are limited resources, just as in your town. How fair do you think it is that some people get more than others? Why?
6. What choices do people who get more resources have?
7. What other ways can you think of to divide the resources that might be more fair?

Explain to the students that in any city (or nation) with limited resources, when some people get more, others *automatically* get less. Explain how privileged and "not-so-privileged" people are therefore *connected* to each other. One's fate affects the other's.

---

The high school senior, college freshman, university professor needs to believe his own career exists "in vacuo." He cannot dare to understand that he is there at the expense of someone else. The private patient in a pastel-painted air-conditioned room within the high-rise hospital along the river in Boston, Massachusetts, cannot bear to know that he is there at the direct expense of those who wait five, six or seven hours on a long and steamy summer afternoon within the basement of a ghetto hospital far over on the other side of town, before a hectic and unprac- ticed intern offers ten, twelve, fifteen minutes out of his long siege of eighteen desperate hours before he sends them up into a hot, unsupervised and often- times unsterile hostpial ward—or else back to the fever-ridden streets they came from. No one believes that he exploits someone else. It is more like this: "the one thing here, the other over there." It is indeed, a pity that the two things must reside together in one city. The one, however, does not "bleed" into the other. Each exists in its own private realm and separate universe. Clean steel edges: hard, explicit separations: No Connections.

From *The Night Is Dark* and *I'm Far From Home*, by Jonathan Kozol.

---

# Ice Cream Sundaes, Apples, or Raisins
SS, M

**OBJECTIVES**
To give students an experiential sense of how resources (in this case, foods) are divided among classes of people.
To help students understand the feelings of those at various economic levels, and the options open to them.
To help students understand the economic interdependence of all groups of people.
To enable students to see how the privilege of some classes of people is connected to the lack of privilege of others.

**MATERIALS**
Ice cream, toppings and nuts, for sundaes for two students; one apple each for 26 students, and one raisin each for 7 students; table cloth; two fancy cloth napkins; 26 plain paper napkins. (This is set up for 35 students; if you have a different number,

keep the proportions the same—5 percent ice cream sundaes, 75 percent apples, 20 percent raisins. Divide students randomly unless certain students can't handle certain roles.)

**IMPLEMENTATION**    Set this up some time when your students are out of the room. Place two desks together in as gracious a setting as possible for two students. You may want a table cloth, flowers, comfortable chairs—whatever gives the feeling of elegance. For another 26 students set up chairs in a circle or seats in a carpeted area. For the other 7 students, block off a bare floor area.

As the students come in, send them to their locations for this snack. First call for the two students who are getting elaborate ice cream sundaes. Read them "Privileged Citizen" from the Information Sheet (see p. 137) being sure that everyone else can hear. Let them sit down. Serve them. Then call in the apple group and read them "The Middle-Class Citizen" again so everyone can hear. Serve them one apple each. Call in the raisin group and read them the "Poor Citizen" information. Give them a plain bowl containing *one* raisin each.

Allow students to eat. Poor students must stay within their floor area. Middle-class students can go wherever they want. Note what students do and say. Allow the activity to go on until students get restless or until it becomes potentially destructive. Then gather for discussion. Be sure to talk about the feelings, so that students don't retaliate against those who had the sundaes.

---

We tried this at camp over the summer with a group of people eight to thirty years old. It was very powerful, but manageable. Initially feelings were very strong and some were directed against those running the activity. As the discussion proceeded, the children, including some of the young ones, were able to draw parallels to our country. They began to see the interdependence, to see what privilege meant. This became a good reference point throughout the summer, as we often thought back on the activity and saw our actions in terms of it.

Ellen Davidson

---

**DISCUSSION**    1.  How did you feel about where you were when you first came in? How did you feel as the activity went on?
2.  What did you do? Was there anything else you wanted to do but didn't do? Why didn't you do it?
3.  How do you think people in the other two groups felt? What did they do? How do you feel about what they did? Would you have done anything differently in the circumstances?
4.  Those people getting sundaes, how did you feel? What benefits would there have been for you to share sundaes? (If students didn't.)
5.  In terms of our nation, what group are you in in real life? What do you do in terms of people in the other groups? What could you do?
6.  You didn't get to decide on your group in this activity. Do people get to decide that in life? What can people do about the group they are born into? What *can't* they do?
7.  What do you think it would be like to be hungry and to know that others are well fed?
8.  In the United States, how are people who have plenty of food connected to people who are hungry? What should be done about this?

    Define *interdependent* for children.

9.  How are all people in the United States interdependent? What responsibility does a person who is interdependent have?
10. In what ways do people with more benefit by sharing food or redistributing resources?

BENEFITS OF EQUALITY TO *ALL*

Throughout this section, help students explore the potential benefits that would come to *all* by distributing resources and opportunities based on equality.

For example: White team members might have benefited by acting against racism and keeping Drew on their team. Sundae eaters might have felt better about themselves, and avoided anger, resentment and hard feelings, by sharing.

Most of us feel better about ourselves when we *act* on our beliefs. When we say we believe in equality but don't act, we often feel guilty or compromised. These feelings don't help us change things. Sharing power and redistributing opportunity also lessen tension, anger and hostility between those with more and those with less. Help students see these benefits for themselves even when they have more resources, in working for equality.

---

INFORMATION SHEET

*Privileged Citizen*
You are a privileged citizen of this country. Welcome. Your group makes up 5 percent of the nation's population. You have almost unlimited enjoyment of the nation's goods. You enjoy good health, education, and many other opportunities.

*Middle-Class Citizen*
You are a middle-class citizen of this nation. Your group makes up 75 percent of the nation's people. You have some education, adequate health, and enough food to live.

*Poor Citizen*
You are a poor citizen of the United States. You are part of 20 percent of the nation's population. Your health is poor and you don't have enough food. You don't get to travel. You have to be creative and resourceful if you are to survive.

See *Small Futures: Children, Inequality and the Limits of Liberal Reform*, by Richard deLone and the Carnegie Council on Children for sources of these statistics and a powerful account of the effect of economic inequality on children's lives and future options.

# Up and Over We Go

**OBJECTIVES**    To have students understand the advantages of cooperative work within groups.
To have students examine the choices those with privileges have to see or not to see their connectedness to others, both in the activity and in society.
To help students examine the choices those with privileges have to use or not to use the benefit of those privileges to create change, both in activity and in society.

**MATERIALS**    A wall about nine feet high. (If you can't find one, make imaginative use of playground equipment.)

**IMPLEMENTATION**    Divide students into groups of about six to ten. Have three groups in all. One group should be the tallest third of the students, one group the shortest third and one group the "middles." (If you have fewer than eighteen students, have only two groups—a tall one and a short one. With more than thirty students, make more groups, using height distinctions.)

Have students cluster in groups. Tell them "Your task is to get everyone in the group over the wall. You may not use any props that you don't now have on you." Spot carefully for safety. Don't suggest cooperation but allow it within a group or between groups, if they think of it. Give each group a turn, encouraging the others to observe carefully.

**DISCUSSION**
1. How did you feel when you saw how the groups were divided?
2. How did your group "solve" the task? How well did you work together to reach a decision and to carry it out?
3. How did you feel about the other groups? Was the task easier or harder for them? Why? How much of that depended on their sizes and how much on the way they did the task?
4. What are some times when a size difference makes a difference in how you can do a task? an age difference? a sex difference? a race difference? What are some things you can do to make that difference less of a problem?
5. I said, "The task is to get everyone in the group over the wall." How did you define "group"? You had a *choice* to think of "group" as a small group or as the whole class. Why did you make the choice you did?
6. In this activity being tall was a privilege that made the task easier. The tall group had a *choice* to use the privilege for themselves or to share the benefits with others. What did the tall group do with the benefits that their privilege gave them?
7. Did the members of the tall group "earn" their privilege?
8. What are examples in society of individuals and groups who have privileges that make doing certain tasks, or getting ahead in society, easier for them?

---

### PRIVILEGE

Some privileges we're born with. One example is being born white. That's a privilege in the United States today because whites don't have to face racism in institutions and culture like minorities do.

Other privileges come from circumstances we're born into—like the resources our family has or the amount of money our community spends on education, recreation or health care. These circumstances are privileges because they give some people, more than others, opportunities to develop skills and abilities to their fullest potentials.

People with privilege can choose to try to change the "rules of the game," so that *all* people have equal access to resources and opportunities. For example, men who work in predominantly male jobs, like plumbers or electricians, or their unions, can change their union practices or training programs to include more women in their profession. Such actions get at the *causes* of inequality.

In the wall activity, our lives, or society look to find out *why* inequality exists—why some people have more opportunities than others—and work together with others to change the causes.

9. In what ways can groups with privilege in society choose to share the benefit of those privileges with others?
10. How could the wall activity have been more fair?
11. Did anybody think of changing the members of the teams, or asking me if the teams could be mixed more equally? Why or why not?

---

**EXAMPLES IN SOCIETY WHERE PEOPLE WORK TOGETHER SO EVERYBODY WINS**

(1.) In some schools, students work together in small groups to help each other learn material for a lesson. They cooperate by tutoring and quizzing each other. When they are evaluated by their teacher they know *everyone* will do better. Instead of feeling proud because they know more than someone else (or feeling lousy because they didn't know as much) students feel proud because they helped each other learn! Everybody wins!

(2.) In some work places, people work cooperatively to make products and share the profits equally. One example is a woman-run factory, McCaysville Industries, in Georgia. The women who started McCaysville had previously worked in a huge factory where they were pushed to work fast. No-one got a bonus unless, as an individual, she produced a specified amount. Women were under great pressure because they knew only *some* people could "make production." The profits from the factory went to other people—owners and stockholders.

At McCaysville, women wanted to work together to try to "make production" as a group. They would help each other and encourage each other. If the workers *as a group* met their quota, they would get a bonus. They would no longer compete, but cooperate with each other. Here the workers shared the profits the company makes.

(3.) In a food co-op, individuals or families join the cooperative and give a few hours a month of work. Food is bought wholesale at a cheaper price than each member could buy it in the grocery store. By pooling their resources, all win!

---

## Can I Get In?            PE, C

**OBJECTIVES**  To experience being part of a dominant group, or being excluded.
To learn the options people in a majority group have for including or excluding those in the minority.

**IMPLEMENTATION**  Tell students you will be doing an activity in which all but one volunteer will hold hands and form a circle. Form the circle. When everyone is ready, tell the volunteer—who is on the outside—to try to get in.

Many things can happen. Usually people in the circle form a tight bond. Outsiders often try to squeeze in between people, go under legs, and on occasion try to convince someone to let them in. Sometimes outsiders try to force their way in. If anyone gets too rough, or the outsider gets too frustrated, call a halt. The activity usually ends when the outsider either gets in or gives up.

**DISCUSSION**
1. Outsider, how do you feel now?
2. How did it feel being on the outside of the circle?
3. How did it feel being on the inside of the circle?
4. What strategies did the outsider use to try to get into the circle?
5. Did any of the insiders feel badly for the outsider? How, if at all, did you act on those feelings? What did you tell yourself that convinced you to keep the outsider out?
6. Did the people in the circle talk to each other? If so, about what? If not, why not?

Now let's compare what happened in the activity to what happens in society.

7. What are some groups of people in society that are the more powerful groups? Which groups are on the outside?
8. In society the circle might represent access to power, privileges, jobs, money, and so on. How are some of the strategies the outsider used (or might have used), like the strategies people in minority positions in society use to try to get opportunities?

---

STRATEGIES TO GAIN EQUALITY

In this activity, the outsider could have: asked politely; used an assertive strategy like giving the group a "talking to" or crawling between legs; been creative—for example, tickled; or used force—for example, tried to break the insiders' hands apart.

There are many societal comparisons. If a girl wanted to be in an all boys' baseball league she might use a variety of approaches to get in: ask; petition; get so good "they" wanted her; stage a sit-in on the baseball field.

During the civil rights movement in this country, black people originally asked for equal rights and later used assertive tactics, including mass marches and strategies like freedom rides, to gain national publicity

---

9. Let's focus on the majority of people on the inside of the circle: How do people with power and privilege in society keep that power and privilege from others? What do they do? What arguments do they use? How is this like what you did in this activity?

---

HOW PEOPLE HOLD ONTO POWER

In this activity people might have thought to themselves: "I like being on the inside, it feels good"; "Everybody else is keeping the outsider out, I'd better not be different"; "The outsider might feel bad, but it's only a game."

Take the societal examples cited above. The boys on the baseball team might say: "Girls aren't as good as boys, so they can't play"; "If I want girls to play, my friends will call me a 'girl-lover' or 'sissy'"; "Girls might feel bad, but it's only a game."

During the civil rights movement, white people might have thought or said: "If blacks get some rights, I'll lose mine"; "I support equal rights, but I don't want to get involved"; "If I actively support civil rights I might lose my friends."

---

10. What other choices did you have in the activity for including the outsider? What choices do people in powerful positions in society have for including those in a minority position?

---

**EQUAL RESOURCES, MORE EQUAL RESULTS**

Use your classroom as the setting for putting the "equal resources" maxim into practice. Think of any resource that might not get distributed to children equally. With students, develop a creative way to make things fairer.

For example, because of their class-background, some children are able to order more reading books from the book clubs than others. Talk with the class about setting a class goal—for example, everyone ordering at least three books. Then devise a creative way for raising money or gathering resources.

If your school is in an economically diverse neighborhood, a car-wash, bake-sale, or raffle could be effective. Many local businesses donate items for raffles in exchange for publicity.

Students have fun with such a project, and all have more equal resources with which to order books!

---

## Ms Meg                    by bulbul

IF MEN HAD THE BABIES CHILD CARE WOULD BE FUNDED
....LIKE THE PENTAGON IS FUNDED!

Worksheet:   PRAISE MATTERS

1.  Which group were you in_____?
                                   praised, criticized

2.  How did you feel when you came to school this morning?

3.  How did you feel in the middle of the morning?

4.  How did you feel at lunchtime?

5.  How did you feel in the middle of the afternoon?

6.  How did you feel right before our end-of-day discussion?

7.  How did you do in each subject compared to how you usually
    do?

    Math_____     Reading_____

    Language Arts_____     Social Studies_____

    Science_____     Others_____

8.  What do you think happens to students who never get praised
    or supported by adults?  What could be done to change this?

9.  What do you think happens to groups of people in society
    who get more criticism than praise for reasons they can't
    control--like their skin color?

Worksheet:  VALUES AUCTION

| your order | item |
|---|---|
| _____ | 1.  great athletic ability |
| _____ | 2.  ability to make a few close friends |
| _____ | 3.  happy family life |
| _____ | 4.  ability to lead others |
| _____ | 5.  artistic skills and success |
| _____ | 6.  love of learning |
| _____ | 7.  good health |
| _____ | 8.  chances for adventure |
| _____ | 9.  lots of money |
| _____ | 10.  ability to do very well in school |
| _____ | 11.  success in the job of your choice |
| _____ | 12.  good looks |
| _____ | 13.  power over things--fix cars, computers build houses |
| _____ | 14.  being important |
| _____ | 15.  musical talent |
| _____ | 16.  ability to bounce back |
| _____ | 17.  ability to give love to others |
| _____ | 18.  ability to help other people |
| _____ | 19.  ability to make many friends |
| _____ | 20.  success at changing the world to make it a better place |
| _____ | 21.  parents who trust you |
| _____ | 22.  chance to travel wherever you want |
| _____ | 23._____ |
| _____ | 24._____ |

Worksheet:  TEAM SPIRIT


    Then one day the track team went to Brown University for
an important meet.
    After the game the coach talked to Charlie and the other
black members of the team.  He said that blacks weren't
allowed in the Narragansett Hotel, where the team was going to
eat dinner.
    "But then where is the team going to eat?" asked Charlie.
    "Why don't you boys eat in a cafeteria?" answered the
coach.  "The rest of us will go to the hotel."
    "A team is supposed to stick together," snapped Charlie,
but the coach just walked away.
    Late that night the team returned to Amherst College.
Charlie shut himself up in his room to think.
    When I score points for the team, everyone cheers, he
told himself.  But when the game is over, I'm just another
Negro.  I don't want to be an athlete anymore, Charlie decided.

                From Charles Drew, by Roland Bertol, p. 10.


1.  Cite two examples of racism in this account.


2.  How did the coach's racism harm Charles and the other
    black team members?  How was it harmful for the whole team?


3.  How was the privilege that the white team members got tied
    to the denial of privilege to the black members?


4.  List three things the white team members could have done.


5.  What would you have done?  Why?


6.  What benefits would the white athletes have got if they had
    acted against racism?

# 7 INVESTIGATING YOUR ENVIRONMENT _____

Chapters 7 and 8 contain activities in which students examine their environment for personal and institutional discrimination. In this chapter, they explore their classroom, school and home. In the next, they examine the media, their community, and then assess how their environment has affected them.

The intent of the activities is to educate students, and those with whom they come in contact with while doing these tasks, and not to criticize. Students investigate their environment, not for purposes of "putting down" people or finding fault with institutions, but to discover examples of inequality. Only when people become aware of discrimination, can changes happen. Reinforce the educational purpose of these activities constantly, so all involved perceive them as the learning experiences that they are.

It's important to reiterate that all of us discriminate, or have done so. Often this is unintentional. For example, we do so by accepting and following the norms of a sexist institution. Encourage learning rather than guilt when students find examples of discrimination close to home. Point out also, however, that much institutional discrimination is intentional, and serves to keep opportunities and power in the hands of some persons and groups and away from others. Intentional or unintentional, stereotyping and institutional discrimination reinforce inequality.

Some of the students' investigation involves interviewing parents, teachers, and community members. Let these persons know the educational purpose of the activities, so as to alleviate potential misunderstanding. When appropriate, students can share results of these activities with interested persons to heighten their awareness of inequality. Use your judgment about what's workable for your community and school.

## SECTION A  EXPLORING YOUR CLASSROOM AND SCHOOL

### Stop and Look Carefully _____ M, LA

**OBJECTIVE**  To have students look more critically at school bulletin boards for stereotypes, omissions, and "isms."

**MATERIALS**  A chance to roam around the school; paper and pencils.

**IMPLEMENTATION**  Divide students into small heterogeneous groups. Each group takes an area of the school and notes hallway bulletin boards and those in classrooms, if permission can be secured from teachers. It is helpful to have each bulletin board seen by two groups for comparison.

First, brainstorm as a group for things to note. Make a list. Examples might be:

1) number of men and number of women; 2) roles and occupations of men and women; 3) number of minorities compared to whites, and their roles; 4) the ages of people and what they are doing; 5) family and job situations and what these reflect in terms of class; 6) number of people cooperating compared to those competing, or achieving individually.

When the groups come back they prepare a presentation for the class. The teacher, or a student recorder, tallies the results. (Save the information for use in lessons in Chapter 10.)

**DISCUSSION**

1. Was there a difference in how frequently women and men were portrayed and the roles they were in?
2. What was the representation of different racial groups?
3. How were elderly people portrayed, compared to younger people?
4. What was the difference in numbers of people cooperating, compared to those competing or achieving individually?
5. Were bulletin boards geared to certain social and economic groups? If so, how?
6. When companies produce bulletin board materials with omissions, stereotypes, and "isms," what does this do to students' thinking and view of the world?

**GOING FURTHER**

Have students prepare a bulletin board that counters some of the stereotypes and omissions commonly found.

Have students prepare a helpful critique of bulletin boards and circulate it to interested teachers.

**FOLLOW-UP**

"Let Me Tell You What I Think," p. 234.

> Chapters 9 and 10 contain follow-up lessons that provide ideas and strategies for changing any inequities students find in their environment. You can choose to do those later when your class is focusing on making changes. If, however, students are very involved in these lessons and want to take immediate action, you could choose to do the follow-up lessons right away.

# Why Are We Off From School Today?

LA, SS, M

**OBJECTIVES**

To have students understand how racism and sexism can be institutionalized through school holidays.

To have students understand how this affects their thinking, learning, and experiences.

**MATERIALS**

School calendar; calendars from alternative groups—women's groups, Latino groups, Afro-American groups; paper; pencils; rulers.

**IMPLEMENTATION**

Students meet in small groups and go through the school calendar to list all the holidays. They add any holidays which are not vacation days but which are celebrated. Then each group labels every item on its list as to the race and sex of the person being commemorated or the culture being reinforced.

Each group creates a bar graph with numbers on the vertical axis and the following groups listed on the horizontal: white men, white women, minority men and minority women. They share these graphs. Then, in small groups, they look through the alternative calendars. They list any holidays that the schools neglect that should be celebrated. They can also use any other information they have to think of important people who are being neglected, or events which should be commemorated.

**DISCUSSION**  1. What groups of people are recognized in our schools? Why? Who makes the decisions about this?
2. What groups get neglected? Why? What does this tell you about what you are being taught?
3. How do you feel about this if you are a member of the group being acknowledged frequently? How about if you are part of one of the neglected groups?
4. In what ways is this damaging for all students?

**FOLLOW-UP**  "Calendars," p. 223.

---

CONGRESS REJECTS KING HOLIDAY

In December of 1980 Congress voted against a bill to make Martin Luther King's birthday a national holiday.

Designating January 15 a paid national holiday would cost too much and would damage U.S. productivity, opponents argued.

Backers of the national holiday pointed out that no one had proposed eliminating any of the nine existing federal holidays because they hurt productivity or wasted taxpayer's money.

One foe of the King measure said "It is time we draw a line because the next holiday would be one to honor a lady who was very active in the women's liberation movement."

*The Guardian,* (New York, December 5, 1980).

---

## Our Textbooks: Are They Fair? _____ LA,M

**OBJECTIVES**  To have students examine their textbooks for racism, sexism, class bias, ageism and competitive individualism.
To see how texts influence students' expectations of certain groups of people and of themselves.

**MATERIALS**  Texts you currently use (and for a longer project, those your school or district uses) in social studies, science, math and reading. (For a lesson on analyzing fiction, look at "Read Me a Story," p. 156.

**IMPLEMENTATION**  Textbooks are one of the most powerful reinforcers of equality or inequality. If students learn to examine their texts for the "isms" they will have an important critical skill that they can use again and again. If, for budget reasons, you must use texts that are not ideal, students can nevertheless sharpen their critical thinking by analyzing them for inequality.

We strongly urge that you order and read *Guidelines for Selecting Bias-Free Textbooks and Story Books* and *Stereotypes, Distortions, and Omissions in U.S. History Textbooks* from the Council on Interracial Books for Children. These are excellent resources that will enable you to teach this lesson and upcoming ones in the most informed way.

There are various options for implementing this activity, depending on the amount of time you allot. For all options, divide students into heterogeneous groups of four or five. In all cases, when groups are finished have them report their findings to the whole class and follow this with discussion. You or your students can make checklists with the specific items that students should look for while analyzing texts. Do this once you have decided on the subject area (science, math, social studies, reading) and *category* (race, sex, class, age, competitive individualism). (Save all your information for lessons in Chapter 10.)

| | |
|---|---|
| **Options for Organizing the Lesson** | 1. Choose one subject area and one category. Each group analyzes the same text.<br>2. Choose one subject area. Each group analyzes the same book for a different category.<br>3. Choose one category. The groups analyze books from different subject areas. |
| **Timing** | For a *short-term project* have students |

1. Analyze illustrations.
2. Examine content. Choose a small section of a book to examine (for example, math problems on pages 21–35), or use a portion of a text students have studied that year (for example, science text, chapters 1 to 4).
3. Record findings orally, in charts, graphs, or reports.

For a *longer-term project* have students

1. Analyze whole texts used in your classroom.
2. Compare different texts used in your school or district.
3. Write comprehensive reports on their findings and distribute them to other classes.

**Categories**   Suggestions for focus

1. *Racism*
   a. How many white people compared to minority persons are presented?
   b. What specific racial groups—black, Latino, Native American, Asian-American—are presented?
   c. Is there a difference in the roles people of different races play? e.g., Do people of color have less responsibility than whites?
2. *Sexism*
   a. How many males compared to females are presented?
   b. Are there differences in the roles they play? e.g., Are females helping and men acting?
3. *Classism*
   a. How many people are at least middle-class compared to people who are poor or working-class?
   b. Are there differences in how people from different classes are presented? e.g., Are poor or working people shown as less important in the world than people of the middle class or above?
4. *Ageism*
   a. How many older people, compared to others, are presented?
   b. Are there differences in how older people are depicted? e.g., Are older persons more sick, forgetful, and in passive roles?
5. *Competitive Individualism*
   a. How many people do things individually compared to working together?
   b. Are successful people or leaders those who made it on their own, or those who work with, and for, others?

**Subject Areas**   Suggestions for focus

1. Science. Look especially at pictures; examine scientists who are chosen as role models.
2. Math. Examine word problems and pictures.
3. Social Studies. Look at the contributions of different groups of people; examine the perspective from which the subject is presented; look for omissions, distortions.
4. Reading. Analyze the story line and characterization.

**DISCUSSION**
1. What did each group find from their study?
2. What stereotypes or "isms" were present?
3. Who was omitted?
4. How does that textbook tell students about which groups of people are leaders and achievers?

5. What influence could these textbooks have on students?
6. What can we do about textbooks that aren't fair?

**FOLLOW-UP** "Find That Class(ic) Bias," p. 150; "Read Me A Story," p. 156; "Textbook Alert," p. 230; "Finding Better Books," p. 230; "And We Wrote Them Ourselves," p. 231; "Change That Class(ic) Bias," p. 232.

---

### THE IDEAL AND REALITY

To present positive role models for all children, and to reflect the population distribution of our society, textbooks would have to portray 50 percent females in active leadership positions; 20 percent minority people; 10 percent older people [and 40 percent working-class or poor people]. . . . In reality, white males between the ages of 20 and 65 control over 80 percent of active leadership positions, even though they are roughly 20 percent of the population. So the dilemma is whether to "tell it like it is" or to present the ideal society we envision.

Both the reality and the ideal must appear in textbooks. There actually are some female, minority, and older . . . people in leadership positions. Such portrayals do not reflect an impossibility; besides, they help to destroy stereotypes and they create much needed role models. On the other hand, we do children a disservice if we instill illusions which leave them ill-prepared for reality when they leave school. Young people should learn of the societal roadblocks that must be surmounted before equity is achieved. They should learn why and how to create the social changes necessary to achieve equity. . . .

All of this requires that textbook content must become more respectful of children's capacity to recognize social injustice, and it must display confidence that children can be critical of the way our society operates without losing faith in their country and its future.

Jeana Wirtenberg, *Guidelines for Selecting Bias-Free Textbooks and Story Books*

---

## Find That Class(ic) Bias

**OBJECTIVES**  To learn to pinpoint examples of class bias in reading books.
To see how reading books influence students' viewpoints about class.

**MATERIALS**  Reading books at reading level; copies of Worksheet: Class Viewpoint, p. 158.

**IMPLEMENTATION**  Because class is an unfamiliar concept to most students, this lesson gives them a chance to analyze their books for this factor alone.

Remind students that because of the different amounts of money that people have inherited or earned, they have various degrees of choice available to them. Tell children that people's treatment of each other may be affected by class differences. As a reminder, you might distinguish between people who have more than they need to live on—sometimes called upper- or upper-middle-class; people who have enough money to live on—sometimes called middle-class; people who don't have enough money to live adequately—sometimes called lower-class; and people who are barely surviving . . . people in poverty. Stress that it is usually not a family's responsibility but the result of a combination of circumstances, including discrimination, that determines class status.

Choose a number of story books that are easy for your students to read. Divide students into heterogeneous groups of three or four and give each group a pile of books. (See suggestions in Bibliography for books without class bias.) Have students pick one book and analyze it together using the questions on the Worksheet. Once they get the idea, have them each analyze other books and answer the questions for each Worksheet. When completed, the group makes a composite Worksheet that represents its total findings. (Save this information for lessons in Chapter 10.)

**DISCUSSION**
1. What classes of people are most stories written about?
2. How did you decide which classes families or people were from?
3. What kinds of concerns and problems do people or families from different class backgrounds have, according to each author?
4. How are upper-class, middle-class, lower-class and poor persons or families described by the authors? What are their opinions about them? How can you tell? How are these the same or different from yours?
5. If you were a middle-class student how would you feel reading these books? a lower-income or poor student? an upper-class student?

> The Council on Interracial Books for Children's *Human and Anti-Human Values in Children's Books* provides a fine set of criteria for examining children's books. It also analyzes books at all levels according to those criteria.
>   These are a few books that are free of class bias:
>
> *Last Night I Saw Andromeda* by Charlotte Anker
> *Song to the Trees* by Mildred Taylor
> *New Life: New Room* by June Jordan

## Who's Who In Our School. . . .

**OBJECTIVE**  To have students understand how sexism and racism are reflected in the division of labor in their school.

**MATERIALS**  Paper, pencils, graph paper, markers or crayons.

**IMPLEMENTATION**  Divide students into groups of four or five. Each group should be assigned a different category of school personnel to count. Categories can include: teachers, custodians, secretaries, cafeteria workers, administrators. Each group counts the number of people in its area by sex and race.

When the groups return, add the totals to find how many staff you are considering. If your students can handle percentages, have each group figure the percentage of men, women, whites, and third world personnel within each category. Then calculate these in terms of the total staff. Graph. Compare to the pupil population. For younger students use picture graphs. Come together as a class. Each group shares its findings.

**DISCUSSION**
1. In what areas did you find racial balance? sexual balance? What areas were very unbalanced racially or sexually?
2. Brainstorm on reasons for these differences.
3. Compare the ratio of black and white teachers to black and white pupils. What reasons can you find if these are not proportionate?
4. Does the assignment of various jobs in our school reflect racism and sexism? If so, how?

**GOING FURTHER**
Your district's administration or affirmative action office should have district-wide figures for school-system personnel in all jobs by race and sex and the salary range in each job category. Try to obtain these, simplify information, and distribute to students. Have students compare the numbers of men and women, minorities and whites, in jobs throughout the district. Have them compare salaries. Discuss the ways, if any, that the school system encourages racism and sexism.

---

Only 3 percent of the nation's high school principals are women.

> American Association of School
> Administrators, 1981

Women represent one percent of school superintendents.

> American Association of School
> Administrators, 1981

The proportion of women on college faculties has hovered around 25 percent since 1960—a lower share than women held in 1930.

> *On Campus with Women, 1981*

---

# . . . And How Do They Feel About It? _____ LA

**OBJECTIVE**
To better understand how racism and sexism may have affected opportunities for, and choices of, jobs.

**MATERIALS**
Paper and pencils.

**IMPLEMENTATION**
Review interviewing skills with students (p. 62). Then divide students into pairs. Each pair interviews one or more than one member of the school staff, as time permits. Try to see that all staff categories are covered. Students will want to find out about people's job opportunities and choices, and their feelings about them. Here are some possible questions:

1. Do you like being a _____?
2. Did you plan to be a _____ as a child? At what point did you make the decision to be a _____?
3. What did your mother do? Your father?
4. Did your parents or teachers influence your expectations of future jobs? If so, how?
5. Did your race affect your job opportunities or job choice? If so, how?

6. Did your sex affect your job opportunities or job choice? If so, how?
7. Do you think your job opportunities would have been different if you were the opposite sex? another race? If so, how?
8. If you could be anything at all now, what would you choose to be? Why?
9. What do you like about your job? What don't you like?

Have students write up their interviews. Post these on a bulletin board and have students read all interviews. Then have students work in small groups to answer some of the following questions:

1. Did racism influence people's job opportunities? If so, how?
2. Did sexism influence people's job opportunities? If so, how?
3. Employees with which types of jobs are most satisfied? What do they like? Employees with which types of jobs are most dissatisfied? What are their reasons?
4. Do the same for groups of employees by sex and race.

**DISCUSSION** Come together as a class and discuss the four questions above.

**GOING FURTHER** Have students do the same interview with their parents or community people in various occupations. Write these up for the bulletin board display.

> A black woman teacher applied for a job in a town in Westchester County, New York. She was told that the school children, all white, were only accustomed to black women as maids. The interviewers told her that if she were hired she would have trouble with discipline since the children wouldn't be able to see her as a "teacher." She was not offered a job.

There's no need for that here. The girls in this office are very happy.

## Listen Carefully _____ M, LA

**OBJECTIVES** To encourage awareness of the subtle ways in which teachers, other school personnel, parents, and students perpetuate stereotypes and expectations based on race, sex, class, age, and individualism.
To understand the impact of these "isms."

**MATERIALS**   Paper and pencils.

**IMPLEMENTATION**   Secure permission from teachers, secretaries, recess aides, parents and so forth for students to listen to their conversations. Explain that the purpose is to learn how people, often *unintentionally*, reinforce stereotypes. Explain that students will be happy to share their findings with them if they wish. (It might be more revealing to do this without permission, but that would have unfortunate overtones of spying.)

"FIREFIGHTER"

Explain to students that many adults and children reinforce unfair expectations based on race, sex, class, and age in their daily conversation. Their ability to notice this can help them do it less themselves, and view it more analytically when others do so.

Have students work in pairs over a couple of days. Tell them to listen to adults and other students. They station themselves with paper and pencils in the back of classrooms, in the office, outside on steps for recess, at home, in the park, and so on. They should note all remarks that might have to do with someone's sex, age, class, race. Give some examples: "Big boys don't cry when they're hurt"; "Nice little girls don't make so much noise"; "She's so pokey, just like an old lady"; "You're acting like a bunch of wild Indians"; "They behave like wild animals" (referring to a group of black students). Also ask students to listen for examples of "me-first" statements: "Ha, ha, I beat you"; "Don't help Tom, do your own work"; "What, you don't have a ten-speed"? "If people work hard, they'll get ahead in this country—anyone can make it."

Have students relist these by age, class, sex, and race. Have them share their findings with the large group.

**DISCUSSION**
1. Using the students' findings, come up with a list of expectations people have for each race, sex, class, or age.
2. What examples of "me-first" statements did you find?
3. What were your emotional reactions to the comments you heard?
4. Which remarks were said most often? Can you think why?
5. What do these expectations and stereotypes teach us about whites and minorities, females and males, older people and younger people, middle-class people and lower-class people, competition and cooperation?
6. Where do people learn these expectations? Are you learning them? Can you do anything about that?

**GOING FURTHER**   Depending on the situation, the students may want to share their findings with the people to whom they listened.

If parents agree, the students can take one kind of expectation and remind them every time they unconsciously say it. They can ask if parents are willing to change that expectation to something which will leave more choices open.

Students can be aware of what they say to younger brothers and sisters. Are they teaching them some of these same things? Can they change that?

# Me or We _____ LA

**OBJECTIVE**   To give students practice finding examples of competitive individualism in their environment.

**MATERIALS**   Chart paper, magic markers, paper, pencils.

**IMPLEMENTATION**   Review the definition of individualism with the students.

Post the beginnings of a large chart with two headings: "Me First" and "Cooperation." This poster will describe individualistic behavior as contrasted to cooperative behavior. List several items yourself and then ask students to suggest more. For example:

| ME FIRST | COOPERATION |
|---|---|
| Trying to beat or do better than other people. | Helping others to learn things. |
| Keeping information or ideas to self. | Sharing information and ideas. |
| Putting a person down. | Telling someone something positive about herself. |

Divide students into heterogeneous pairs. Each pair makes a small chart with the two headings. They work together to observe behavior in all areas of the school. As they see examples of "me first" behavior and cooperative behavior, they add these examples to their charts. Give a few examples to get people started:

A group of kids on the playground wouldn't let another play kickball because he wasn't "good enough."
Janie helped Yvonne catch up with the work she missed when she was out sick.

After a couple of days of observation discuss the findings. In the discussion don't allow students to "blame" others. You can keep the reporting objective by not using people's names and only describing behavior.

**DISCUSSION**
1. What examples of "me first" behavior did you find in our school?
2. How do you feel when you give "me first" statements or act in "me first" ways? How do you feel when you're on the receiving end of those statements and behaviors?
3. What are examples of cooperative behavior that you found?
4. How do you feel when you cooperate and share?
5. Why do we get into "me first" behaviors and statements? How can we change some of these behaviors to cooperative behaviors in our school?

---

LISTENING, ANYBODY?

Have you used the strategies for improving listening that students learned earlier? See the Worksheet: "Listening" (p. 36), try "Listening-Checking" (p. 27). All are applicable to many lessons in *Open Minds to Equality*.

---

# SECTION B  WHAT ABOUT YOUR HOME?

## But I'd Rather Take Out the Garbage
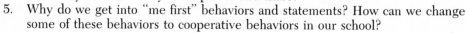
SS, LA

**OBJECTIVES**
To encourage students to look carefully at how home chores for both adults and children are allotted.
To have them understand why these are allotted as they are, and the different options that are available.

**IMPLEMENTATION**
As a class, students brainstorm on the chores they do at home. List these on the board by sex. Is there a pattern? Discuss. Then they brainstorm on what chores adults do at home. Identify those chores by sex, too. Discuss. Students rank each chore, on a scale of one to five, according to how much they like or don't like doing it. They pick, from the entire list, which chores they would prefer. How do these compare to the actual chores done? How much of the difference (if there is one) is because chores are assigned on some basis other than appeal?

Now students go home and discuss with their parent or parents why they have been assigned certain chores. If they live with two parents, they ask why the parents have split their home chores the way they have.

1. Did sex determine what chores children do? What adults do?
2. Did people like their own chores best, or would they prefer others? Would they prefer more variety in what they do?
3. Are sex roles more of a factor in adult chores or children's chores?
4. Why have adults decided to split chores in certain ways?
5. How did adults learn these distinctions? Are they satisfied? What happens when there is a single parent in the home?
6. Are chores consistent among families? Do most have the same patterns?
7. What, besides the home, reinforces who does certain chores? (For example, roles on TV shows, in stories, in magazine advertisements.)

**GOING FURTHER**   Have the family sit down and everyone decide what chores she or he would like best. Try those for a week. Reevaluate and make necessary changes.

Have all the girls go home and ask if they can do traditionally male jobs, and the boys do female jobs. How did adults react? If they agreed and the students tried it, how did it go?

Have students who live with two parents try to have parents switch traditional chores. How did they react to the idea? If they did it, how did they react to the experiment?

**FOLLOW-UP**   "Job Sharing or Who's the Cook Tonight?" p. 194.

---

What does it mean to be a father? A lot of responsibility and a good job to keep your family. And you also need a lot of patience and time. You have to love a wife and children. You have to baby-sit when your wife has to work.

What does it mean to be a mother? It means to cook supper every evening and to wash dishes until midnight. And to have a fight with your husband. And have children every few years and get older and older.

Rhonda, age 11.

---

## Presents I've Received ——————————————— LA

**OBJECTIVE**   To help students understand the effects of family expectations about sex roles and competition, as shown in gifts.

**MATERIALS**   Copies of Worksheet: Presents I've Received, p. 161.

**IMPLEMENTATION**   Give out the Worksheets to the students. They can take them home to complete them, or fill them out in class.

**DISCUSSION**   1. What kinds of presents have you been given?
2. Group them into types—"board games," "sports," "home-making toys," "war toys," "crafts," and so forth.
3. How do these compare to presents which have been given to your brothers or sisters?
4. Can you tell what kind of interests your family expects you to have?
5. What kinds of behavior and action do these interests and presents encourage?
6. What would you have liked to have been given that was different from what you were given? In what ways might that have changed the way you are?

---

Can you imagine the look on your child's face if he or she found this fabulous assortment of toys under the tree on Christmas day? If Daddy or Grandpa are handy, get them started now on the wood projects. While they work, you can knit the bathrobe-slipper set. . . .

From "Christmas Crafts," *Family Circle*, November, 1979.

7. How do adults' sex-role expectations influence their children?
8. In how many of the games do you have to compete to win? In how many do you have to cooperate to win?
9. What do games teach us about winning?

---

CLASS DIFFERENCES, HURT FEELINGS

Be sensitive to the potential bad feelings that could emerge from class differences in doing this lesson. If students come from a variety of class backgrounds, why not have students write down small presents rather than "big" (expensive) presents, like bikes or record players. In this way children whose families can't afford expensive presents won't feel badly.

---

## Read Me a Story _____ R, LA

**OBJECTIVES**  To make students and parents alert to racism, sexism, classism, individualism, and ageism in the books they read at home.
To have them understand the effects their reading has on the way they view the world.

**MATERIALS**  Books at home; copies of Worksheet: Review on Books, 1 *or* 2, pp. 159–60.

**IMPLEMENTATION**  Explain to students that this is an activity they can do with their parents. Parents and students can work together to look at the personal or library books that the students have at home. Fairy tales and nursery rhymes are particularly good. Discuss how what we read is enjoyable, but also has an effect in terms of how we think.

Introduce the lesson with a brief review of stereotypes of various groups of people. Choose the Worksheet that you feel will be more effective. Go over the worksheet and answer any questions the students may have.

When children bring in their results, they work in small groups to discuss and share them. (Save this information for lessons in Chapter 10.)

---

ME-FIRST FICTION

Do you need an example of "Me-First Fiction"? Read students this summary of *The Great Brain Does It Again*, by John Fitzgerald:
Tom is an eleven year old boy who calls himself the "Great Brain." He makes up tricks to play on his friends and family. The purpose of playing these tricks is to make money. He leaves every boy in town sadder and poorer. Tom thinks his tricks are very funny. Other people don't.

---

**DISCUSSION**  1. Go over each question on the checklist with students and discuss what they found. Then generalize from the findings.
2. What are the similarities in the books' presentations of minorities and whites, females and males, upper, middle and lower-class persons, and older persons and adults or children?
3. What stereotypes were most common?
4. What did these books teach us about whose values and ideas are right?
5. Which students would feel best about themselves by reading these books?
6. Did these books encourage competitive individualism or cooperation? Give examples. How can this influence our behavior?
7. List the books that showed none or few of these problems. In what ways did these books help fight stereotypes?
8. List some of the books with many of the problems. Give examples from the books of each of these problems.
9. How did your parents feel about doing this?

**GOING FURTHER**  Using the same system, work in small groups and consider three story books from the school library.

**FOLLOW-UP**  "Finding Better Books," p. 230.

> *Guidelines for Selecting Bias-Free Textbooks and Storybooks* is an invaluable resource that will aid you in preparation of this lesson! Order from the Council on Interracial Books for Children—deliveries are speedy!

Grandma, how come you don't sit around in your rocking chair?

Worksheet:  CLASS VIEWPOINT

| Name of story | 1a. | b. | c. | 2 | 3 | 4 | 5 |
|---|---|---|---|---|---|---|---|
| | | | | | | | |
| | | | | | | | |
| | | | | | | | |

1a. How many people or families were upper class?

b. How many people or families were middle class?

c. How many people or families were lower class or poor?

2. Pick the 2 or 3 most important characters.  What class background were they?

3. What information in the story did you use to decide on class background?

4. Choose one adjective to describe each of the 2 or 3 main characters, from the author's point of view.

5. Choose an adjective to describe each of the 2 or 3 main characters, from your point of view.

158

Worksheet: REVIEW ON BOOKS  (1)

Title_____

Author_____

Checkers_____


1.  Illustrations.  Are minority people shown?  If so, in
varied roles or stereotypic ones?  Are minorities and whites,
males and females, middle-class and lower-class people included?
In what proportion?


2.  Story Line.  Do people succeed through competition or
cooperation?  Do they work for goals for themselves or to
change situations to help many people?


3.  Life Styles.  Are different races and classes shown?  Is
everyone judged by white, middle-class standards?  If not, how
are people judged?


4.  Relationships.  Who has power?  What sexes are they?  what
races?  what classes?  How are families shown?  Are all ethnic
groups shown with the same family patterns?  Are all families
the standard nuclear family or are alternatives shown?


5.  Heroes.  Are the standards the same for men and women?  for
different races?  for different classes of people?  Who takes
leadership and makes decisions?


6.  Loaded Words.  Are there insulting words for certain groups
of people?  If so, do these words label certain groups in
stereotypic ways?


7.  Older People.  Are they in the story?  If so, are they
shown in varied ways or stereotypic ones?

Worksheet: REVIEW ON BOOKS (2)

Title_____     Name of Checker(s)_____

Author_____     _____

| | RACE | | | | | SEX | | AGE | | | CLASS | | |
|---|---|---|---|---|---|---|---|---|---|---|---|---|---|
| | Latino | Asian-American | Native American | White | Black | Male | Female | Children | Adults Under 65 | Older People | Poor or lower-class | Middle-class | Upper-class |
| 1. Write the number of people in illustrations. | | | | | | | | | | | | | |
| 2. Write the number of people in each category present in the story. | | | | | | | | | | | | | |
| 3. Check any people who are stereotyped in pictures. Give a word that describes that stereotype. | | | | | | | | | | | | | |
| 4. Check any people who are stereotyped in the story. | | | | | | | | | | | | | |
| 5. Check those people who give leadership, solve problems, make decisions. | | | | | | | | | | | | | |
| 6. Check those people whose values/ideas are presented as right. | | | | | | | | | | | | | |
| 7. Whose positive self-image would this story reinforce? | | | | | | | | | | | | | |

8. Do main characters work for goals for themselves, or work to change situations to benefit many people? Give example(s).

9. Other Comments.

160

Worksheet:  PRESENTS I'VE RECEIVED

Can you remember what kind of presents you've been given for
your birthday or other holidays?  If not, ask your parent or
parents to help you.  List only two or three presents each year.

_____

As a baby

_____

1 year old

_____

2 years old

_____

3 years old

_____

4 years old

_____

5 years old

_____

6 years old

_____

7 years old

_____

8 years old

_____

9 years old

_____

10 years old

_____

# 8 MORE ENVIRONMENTAL INFLUENCES AND THEIR EFFECT _____

Students have an opportunity in Sections A and B to examine both the media and their community for messages that influence assumptions, beliefs, and behaviors. As in Chapter Seven, they use active investigation and data-gathering techniques to examine inequalities in insitutions they know, like the family and school. In Section C, students examine how the bias they found may have affected *them*.

It is important to reiterate that persons they live with and learn from—teachers, parents, friends—haven't necessarily tried to limit their experiences. Instead, it's by living in biased institutions that we come to see the world in a particular way, and believe that way is the right way. Through the activities in the final section of this chapter, students can come to understand how *their own* lives may have been affected by such inequality. They may then want to discover alternatives.

## SECTION A EXAMINE THE MEDIA

### Black Lies and White Lies _____ R

**OBJECTIVE** To help students understand how connotations in our language perpetuate racism.

**MATERIALS** Dictionaries, paper, pencils, chart paper, markers.

**IMPLEMENTATION** Tell students they will work on an activity to examine language. Teach the term "connotation." Divide students into groups of five. Give each group a large sheet of paper. They list all the words or phrases they can think of that have the word "white" or "black" in them. For example, "black lies," "black eye," "white as snow." After ten minutes the groups mark their lists as follows: "+" for a phrase with a positive connotation, "−" for one with a negative connotation, and "0" for one with a neutral connotation. Groups then look up the words "white" and "black" in their dictionaries and write down the definitions. It is helpful if different groups have different dictionaries. Use dictionaries as advanced as they can handle.

The class joins together. Appoint a recorder to stand at the front of the room. Starting with "black," each group calls out a word or phrase with "black" in it. Record these along with the markings of "+", "−", and "0." Go around in turns until all the groups have their ideas listed. Then do the same for "white." Similarly, list dictionary definitions. (Save these lists for lesson in Chapter 10.)

**DISCUSSION** 1. How many "black" words have positive connotations? How about "white" words? How many of each have negative connotations?
2. What reactions do you have as you look at this list?
3. How might black people feel hearing these words and phrases all the time? How about white people?

4. Many of our ideas are formed through language. Our feelings about ourselves often come from words we hear. What does our language imply about white people? about black people?

FOLLOW-UP   "Say It So They'll Hear It," p. 219; "New Words Help Us," p. 229.

---

A NOTE FROM ELLEN

I was in the fabric store in early December. The two women who work there were hanging cloth ornaments they had made. I commented that I like the Vogue pattern from a few years ago and have especially enjoyed making sets of angels, one black and one white. One of the women said, "Is that so one can represent the devil?"

---

WORD CHOICE CHALLENGES RACISM

While word meanings don't change, students and teachers can be careful of *how* they use the terms black and white.

For example, don't create a hero named Colonel White and a villain named Captain Black, as a popular TV show did. When you put on a play dress the forces of good in black and those of evil in white—or avoid color symbolism entirely. Raise others' consciousness!

---

## Are They Advertising More Than The Product?                                    SS, C

OBJECTIVE   To help students understand how advertising reinforces racism, sexism, classism, and ageism.

MATERIALS   Access to television; props as necessary.

IMPLEMENTATION   STEP 1.   Divide students into groups of two to six. Each group picks a television advertisement that all members are familiar with. These should have the right number of parts for group members. Students tell the teacher so as to avoid repeats. The children then go home and, if possible, watch shows in which these advertisements appear.

The next day, groups act out their advertisements. After the presentations, the class as a whole discusses the following questions.

DISCUSSION   1. How was each person in the advertisement portrayed?
2. How do these portrayals teach us to see men and women, old people, blacks and whites, middle-class and poor people in certain ways?
3. Were the advertisements meant to be funny? Were they funny? Why or why not?
4. How did you feel about the advertisements?

STEP 2.   Now divide students into eight groups. Have two groups look at each of the following areas: racism, sexism, classism, ageism. Ask everyone to watch for examples of individualism.

Have students who have TV's watch for at least one-half hour a night for a week. See if students who don't have TV's can visit a friend or neighbor. Students make notes on each commercial they watch according to the following guidelines:

*Racism.* Number of whites, blacks, Hispanics, Native Americans, Asian-Americans? What is each person doing or saying? What are they advertising?
*Sexism.* Number of men, women? What is each person doing or saying? What are they advertising?

*Ageism.* Number of people who look over sixty-five? What is each person doing or saying? What are they advertising?

*Classism.* Number of middle-class people? Number of lower-class or poor people? What are they advertising?

*Individualism.* Number of people competing, or wanting to have the "best" of something? Number of people cooperating, sharing, and working together? Give examples.

After a week of observing, groups compile their findings.

**DISCUSSION**
1. What was the number of _____ compared to _____ in the advertisements? (For example, middle-class compared to lower-class people.)
2. How would you feel as a _____ watching these advertisements? (For example, black person, white person, low-income person, middle-class person.)
3. How would you feel over a long period of time, seeing these advertisements again and again?
4. How do advertising companies use TV to reinforce race, sex, class and age stereotypes?
5. How many people were competing or wanting the "best" of something? How many were cooperating? Give examples.
6. How does advertising affect our view of cooperation and competition?

**GOING FURTHER**
Have students ask their parents if they see the stereotypes in advertisements, and if they are offended? Encourage more awareness of this during family TV time.

**FOLLOW-UP**
"TV Turnabouts," p. 233.

---

JUMPING AROUND?

Are you like many teachers, who love to "jump around" when using resource books? Restrain yourself! Concepts build upon each other. Are you moving sequentially through chapters and chapter sections? While it's not necessary to teach each lesson in each chapter section, it *is* important to move from one section to the next in order to teach at least one or two lessons. Build concepts sequentially!

---

## 2,912 Hours a Year                                        LA, M

**OBJECTIVES**
To encourage critical watching of television so that students think about how it reflects the real world and what segments of the real world, and in what ways it is a distortion.
To have students understand how TV shows perpetuate discrimination.

**MATERIALS**
Copies of Worksheet: 2,912 Hours a Year, p. 178.

**IMPLEMENTATION**
Give students the statistics on the number of hours the average American child watches TV (see title). Compare to the number of hours children do other things. Discuss the effect of television on the way they see the world. Give out worksheets and review the terminology. Have them decide who will watch which program. They may want to have at least two children watch any one program for comparison, or they may want to aim for as wide a variety as possible.

After they have all had a chance to watch their programs and complete the worksheets, divide students into groups. Each group goes through the worksheets, looking for commonalities, and prepares a short presentation which it shares with the class.

**DISCUSSION**
1. What did you learn about TV families' or people's economic situations? How does that compare to this country as a whole? Why is it different? (See box.)

We can do it —
TOGETHER!!!

2. What did you learn about people of color (Afro-American, Asian-American, Native American, Latino) on TV? How was their portrayal realistic? stereotyped?
3. What characteristics did old people have? Is this real or stereotypic?
4. What are the roles and qualities of women and men on the shows? How are they realistic or stereotypic?
5. How do people in TV families solve their problems? How does your family solve its problems? If there are differences, make some guesses at why.
6. What are the goals of the main characters? Are they for themselves or for others? If they are "heroes," what does TV teach about the qualities of heroes?
7. How do TV programs influence the way people think about themselves? If a person is less well-off than TV families, how would it make her feel? How about if she is equally well off? How would a Native American feel if TV shows always showed "wild Indians"? How would that make white people feel?
8. As you watch TV, keep alert. Do you see stereotypes and omissions of people of different races, sexes, classes, ages? Are you letting them affect you? What can you do to change this?

---

CLASS IN AMERICA

Experts disagree about the percentages of the U.S. population that fall into various class categories. The following broad outline would be accepted by most sociologists.

Upper class—1%
Upper middle class—10%
Lower middle class—about 30%
Working class—about 40%
Poor—about 20%

from Ian Roberston *Sociology*,
1981

The top five percent of the population owns 53 percent of the total personal wealth. The top one percent of the population owns 80 percent of the total corporate stock. If personal wealth was distributed equally, the average family of four would have an estimate of $160,000.

"Notes on Wealth, Power, and Poverty in America,"
Dr. Barbara Scott, S.U.N.Y. New Paltz, 1982

---

## Sell, Sell, Sell, Buy, Buy, Buy ————————————— R, LA, A

**OBJECTIVE**    To increase students' awareness of the messages in magazine and newspaper advertisements, how these influence them, and why they are the way they are.

**MATERIALS**    Magazines, newspapers, construction paper, scissors, glue, pencils, paper.

**IMPLEMENTATION**    Explain to the class that, since people buy products at least partly according to what they see advertised, advertisements influence many of our choices. Many advertisements are sexist, racist, ageist, or classist. Some are obviously so. Others are so by omission—for example, only young people are shown using certain products; only middle-class homes and neighborhoods are pictured; black athletes are featured more than blacks in other professions.

Students work individually or in small groups. Everyone gets several magazines or newspapers, scissors, glue, and construction paper. Some groups cut advertisements out which reinforce a particular stereotype, mount these on paper, and label their posters "racist," "sexist," "ageist," or "classist" as appropriate. Other groups make posters, "Who's Missing Here," to point out typical omissions. When done, display these around the room. (Save for lessons in Chapter 10.)

**DISCUSSION**

1. Did you find more advertisements that were racist, sexist, ageist, or classist? Try to think of reasons why. Talk to adults of different ages to see if this has changed in their lifetimes.
2. How do you feel when you read an advertisement in which you are a member of the group omitted or stereotyped? How about when you are in the power group?
3. Why would advertisers make advertisements which put down women (or any other group)? Where do they get the idea? How does it serve them?
4. How would you feel if you couldn't afford most products advertised? How do advertisers teach us it's "normal" to want all these products? How does this serve them?
5. How might things change if advertisers changed their policies? Think of as many differences as you can in what people would value, would buy, and would do.

**GOING FURTHER**    Prepare a display for a school showcase or bulletin board about what was learned. Or prepare an audio-visual presentation: take slides of the advertisements and make a tape-recording of the text. Ask questions on the tape. Take it to other classes.

**FOLLOW-UP**    "Let Me Tell You What I Think," p. 234.

---

CONSISTENT COOPERATION

Are your students forgetting some of the keys to cooperative group process? Why not use methods they learned in the "Learning Cooperative Skills" section of Chapter 3. The "No Interrupting" activity, "Do's and Don'ts of Helping" checklist, and "Consensus Guidelines" can be used with many lessons. Student skills need refreshing now and again!

---

DADDY, HOW COME BOYS GROW UP TO BE MEN AND GIRLS GROW UP TO BE GIRLS?

# SECTION B  LOOK AT YOUR COMMUNITY

## Please Buy Me One _____ LA, M

**OBJECTIVES**    To help students understand how producers of toys and games influence their ideas about what is appropriate, and thus their purchases.
To help them learn how racism and sexism can be perpetuated by game companies.

**MATERIALS**    Paper and pencils; access to stores; copies of "Worksheet: Inventory of Games and Toys," p. 179.

**IMPLEMENTATION**    Explain to students that most games available in stores are produced by major companies whose goal is to sell their products. Have students try to recall illustra-

167

tions on the boxes of games and toys that they or their siblings have. They should describe the cover pictures as to the race and sex of the people depicted.

Each student then completes the Worksheet. If they can get to a store, they work in pairs or groups of three. If not, they should examine games and toys in their homes.

After the Worksheets are done, a class tally is made. Make a large copy of the Worksheet on chart paper and list all the games investigated—don't repeat any. The class as a whole can create circle graphs, one for race and one for sex.

Interview answers are written in narrative form. (Save work for follow up lesson in chapter 10.)

**DISCUSSION**
1. What are your reactions to our survey? Was it what you expected? If you were surprised, in what ways were you surprised?
2. Look at your two circle graphs. Are companies today portraying a better mix of races or of sexes? How could you explain that?
3. What types of toys and games have primarily girls on the packages? What do these teach us about what girls are "supposed" to do?
4. Which ones have primarily boys? What do these teach us?
5. How did your parents react? How did people in stores react?
6. What changes need to be made in toy and game boxes? Think of reasons why these changes are important. Why are they likely to happen? Why unlikely?

**GOING FURTHER**
Have students look at products for adults. What are the race and sex roles on these packages?
Have students tell their parents or other adults what the class discovered, and ask them their feelings.

**FOLLOW UP**
"Let Me Tell You What I Think," p. 234; "We Can Design Them Ourselves," p. 236.

Do you have a doll that plays like Billie Jean King, thinks like Margaret Mead and speaks out like Barbara Jordan?

## A Firefighter, Not a Fireman _____ LA

**OBJECTIVES**
To increase student awareness of the sexism of many of the occupational terms in our language.
To have them notice how these influence our images of people in these roles and the expectations they set for themselves.

**MATERIALS**
Chart paper and markers; children's books and magazines.

**IMPLEMENTATION**
Discuss sexism in occupational terms with the whole class. Give examples of sexist and non-sexist terms, for example, fireman, firefighter; mailman, mail carrier (see box).

Divide students into groups. Groups list on chart paper as many occupation terms as they can think of. They list both the traditional term and the newer, nonsexist, one if they can think of both. Occupation terms which are not sex-role-based are listed on a separate page. Students can look in books and magazines for ideas.

Join together, post the lists, and discuss their findings. (Save student work for follow up lesson in Chapter 10.)

**DISCUSSION**
1. When you think of a _____, do you think of a woman or a man or both? (Use a sexist term.) Why? Discuss several terms.
2. What happens when you think of a _____? (Use a nonsexist term here.) Discuss several terms.
3. How has our language affected people's thinking about what they can be? How has it affected you?

---

**OLD AND NEW JOB TITLES**

| OLD | NEW |
|-----|-----|
| mailman | mail carrier |
| fireman | firefighter |
| garbage man | garbage collector |
| housewife | homemaker |
| chairman | chair or chairperson |
| bell boy | porter |

---

**GOING FURTHER**
Have students use the new words as their spelling words. Have them use the words as part of an assignment for a story in language arts.
Have older or more advanced students look up these words in other languages. Are they sex-role-based? In which languages? What might that tell us about a culture?

**FOLLOW-UP**
"Let Me Tell You What I Think," p. 234.

## Guess What, Our Dentist is a Woman! _____ M, LA

**OBJECTIVES**
To have students recognize how the division of labor in community jobs reinforce race and sex bias.
To encourage them to think critically about these roles and be aware of the institutional discrimination involved.

**MATERIALS**
Copies of "Worksheet: Neighborhood Tally," p. 180; paper, pencils.

**IMPLEMENTATION**
Give each student a copy of the Worksheet and go over it together. Explain that we make assumptions based on the people we see doing certain jobs. For example, if every time we have our teeth seen to we are treated by a man, we generally begin to think of dentists as men. Students take the Worksheet home to fill out.

After students return with completed sheets, make a class tally. Individual tally sheets can be posted, and copies of interviews can be rewritten carefully and posted on bulletin boards.

**DISCUSSION**
1. What percentage of the people on your tally sheet were white? minority? What percentage were male? female?
2. Were you surprised by these results? If so, why? What had you expected?
3. If you are used to people in certain jobs being a certain race or sex how does that influence your thinking about those jobs, and what you can be?
4. How are opportunities for jobs and positions of power influenced by racism and sexism? What can be done about this?
5. Are institutional sexism and racism evident in your community? How? What can be done about this?

**GOING FURTHER**
Invite speakers of different occupations to your classroom. Try for a wide range of occupations. Try for some people in jobs not traditional to their sex or race. Encour-

age students to ask questions about how sexism and racism influenced these people's job opportunities.

## The Message in the Package _____ LA

**OBJECTIVES**
To better understand how the packaging of products influences buying and how it helps perpetuate stereotypes.

To understand how images of some people (whites, middle-class, young) in advertising reinforce a positive self-concept and sense of being "normal."

To see how the paucity of images of some people (people of color, lower-class, older) reinforces inferiority.

**MATERIALS**
Access to supermarket; paper and pencils; large bags for collecting items; copies of "Worksheet: Supermarket," p. 183.

**IMPLEMENTATION**
Brainstorm as a class on the types of food, toiletries, and so on that are sold prepacked in illustrated containers—cookies, cereals, syrups, canned juices, frozen desserts, and so on. List these on the board. Have students volunteer to take a category or two, depending on how many you list. Each child takes a copy of the Worksheet to the supermarket and takes notes of what illustrations are on the packages. If these are products that the family buys, empty containers can be brought to class.

Students work in small groups to note and compare findings and make a group report. Discuss the project with the whole class. (Save packages and student work for "Sharing Results" in Chapter 10.)

**DISCUSSION**
1. What kinds of products have only males on the package? which have only females? What messages is the advertiser giving you?
2. What products use pictures of people of color? Which use white people? Why do you think they do? If you were a minority person how would this make you feel? if you were white?
3. Which products show middle-class families? Which show lower-class or poor families? If you were middle-class how would this make you feel? if you were lower-class?
4. What products have older people, adults, or children? What is the message the advertiser is giving?
5. Does the sex, race, age or class of the person in the illustration make a difference to you in considering buying a product? If so, how?
6. What does the advertising industry teach us about ourselves? Others?

**FOLLOW UP**
"Sharing Results," p. 235.

---

**HOW'S THAT PROCESS?**

How effectively are your students working together in groups? Have you recently used the group process observation methods they learned in Chapter 2? The more students *process* their own groups, the more productive their groups will be! See worksheets pages 36 and 38.

---

**WHITE IS RIGHT**

If white people see disproportionally numerous positive images of themselves in advertising, the media, and our culture in general, they develop the feeling that to be white is to be "right" or "normal." Without any positive images, feelings of inferiority can be reinforced in people of color. So, too, middle-class people's sense of well-being and normality is perpetuated while poor people's is further undermined.

Preston Wilcox in *White Is,*
© 1970 by Grove Press and Preston Wilcox

## On the Horns of a Dilemma _____

**OBJECTIVES**  To make students more aware of how classism, sexism, ageism, and racism influence people's expectations of others.
To understand how these affect opportunities in life.

**MATERIALS**  Copies of "Worksheet: On the Horns of a Dilemma," p. 181–82 (one story with two parts for each student pair); paper and pencils.

**IMPLEMENTATION**  Divide students into pairs. Each pair interviews one adult in the school—other teachers, secretaries, aides, custodians, administrators. (Get permission first.) In addition, each pair interviews at least two other students, and each student interviews at least one adult at home.

Each pair takes one of the four stories, with its two parts. (Be sure the four stories are divided among all students in class.) Students tell each person *either* story a *or* b. They do an even number of each. They write down a summary of each response and the reasoning. After the interviewing, students form small groups and tally the responses to story a and those to b. Through discussion, students will learn responses to all stories.

**DISCUSSION**  Discuss each story set separately.

1. What solutions did people give for each dilemma?
2. What reasons did they give for their solutions?
3. Did Beena's and Sean's sex affect what people thought should happen to them? If so, how? Is this fair? (Similarly: Julia's and Hillary's races; Louise's and Lucy's ages; Adam's and Aaron's class backgrounds.)
4. How can the "isms" affect people's expectations of others?
5. How do those expectations adults hold affect your views of the world? How comfortable are you with this?

> History has shown that value systems, like social systems, are not static. Human values change when society changes, and because society changes.
>
> *Human and Anti-Human Values in*
> *Children's Books* (New York, CIBC) 1976, p. 3.

# SECTION C   HOW HAS THIS AFFECTED ME?

## More to It Than Just Calculating _____

**OBJECTIVES**  To enable students to see how racism, sexism, classism, and ageism can influence their thinking and perceptions.
To encourage them to see how omitting people is a way to reinforce these "isms."

**MATERIALS**  Paper, pencils.

**IMPLEMENTATION**  Divide students into small groups. Choose math skills the class is working on. Each group writes five math problems to be given to another group to solve. Tell them to write problems that include people *doing things*.

Groups trade and solve the problems. Then groups examine the problems for racism, classism, sexism, ageism. Here are some possible questions.

Can you tell if any black, Asian-American, Native American, or Latino people were included in the problem?

Do the problems deal with the experiences of all people—or only one group of people?

Do females do stereotyped "female" things? Do males perform "male" roles?

Are any older people included in the problems?

**DISCUSSION**
1. Share responses to the questions.
2. What groups, if any, were stereotyped in our problems?
3. What groups, if any, were omitted?
4. Why did we omit the people we did?
5. What does this teach us about the effect of the "isms" on our view of the world?

**GOING FURTHER**
Have original groups rewrite their problems so that they include a variety of people of all ages, races, classes in positive, non-stereotyped roles.

---

EXAMPLES OF MATH PROBLEMS THAT REINFORCE EQUALITY

1. Tabitha and her grandfather were baking cookies for the church supper. If they made 5 dozen peanut-butter-banana cookies and one and a half dozen gingerbread-chocolate-chip cookies and Tabitha's younger brother Carlos and their dog Maypo ate 2 dozen, how many cookies did they take to the church supper?

2. Jimmy and Erica were helping their mother move into their new apartment. The apartment was on the fifth floor. They counted the steps each time they carried boxes up. They didn't bother counting going down because it was too much fun to run and jump and see how many steps they could skip. If they made 13 trips and altogether each went up 1495 steps, how many steps is it up to the fifth floor?

3. Meiko wanted to make her friend Kenji a present. She decided he would like a lamp. She went to a few stores to ask prices for materials. She found out that the wood for the base would cost $3.89. The electrical parts would cost $2.60. She found an old frame for a shade at a yard sale for 35¢. She wanted to macramé a new one and the cord would cost $1.80. She had saved $10. How much did she spend for the supplies for Kenji's lamp?

---

# Traits People Have                                                                          R

**OBJECTIVES**
To discover some assumptions students have about race, sex, and class as these pertain primarily to personality traits.
To consider the origin of these assumptions.

**MATERIALS**
Copies of "Worksheet: Traits People Have," p. 184, one per student; pencils.

**IMPLEMENTATION**
Hand out Worksheets. Students check those characteristics they think are generally true of each group. (Go through the list with the children beforehand for vocabulary, if necessary.) Collect the Worksheets and prepare a group tally before redistributing them.

**DISCUSSION**
This activity has validity both as a personal inventory for each student, as well as a group inventory of attitudes and beliefs.

STEP ONE.    Each child looks at his own list.

1. What characteristics did you check for all six groups?
2. What characteristics did you check for just women? Just men? Just minorities? Just whites? Just middle class people? Just lower income people?

3. Did you check according to people you have met? According to what you have seen on TV? According to what you have been told by adults? By other children? In school?

STEP TWO.  Children look at the group tally.

1. What were the characteristics that most people thought were true of each group? Do you agree with these? What experiences have you had that might make you feel the same or different from other people?
2. What characteristics were true of all groups? Of none?
3. In what ways do our lists show stereotyping? Which group was stereotyped most?
4. Did any of you refuse to classify people in this way? Why were you willing to do this?
5. Think back to what we've learned so far. How does racism, sexism, and class bias affect our thinking? How can we change stereotyped thinking in ourselves and others?

---

DRAW IT

Give each student one piece of paper to fold in half horizontally. On one half he draws a black woman doing something and on the other half a white woman doing something. When finished he writes or dictates a sentence about each picture. Repeat the next day, drawing black and white men. Process this activity with the "Traits People Have" lesson asking questions that point out stereotypes.

---

## Unfinished Adventures _____ R, LA, A

**OBJECTIVE**  To see how racism, sexism, and ageism affect expectations of people's behavior in a stress situation.

**MATERIALS**  Copies of Worksheets: A Moving Day, p. 185, and A Sunday Surprise, p. 186. Extra writing paper, pencils; picture cards for each story, p. 177; drawing paper and crayons (alternative).

**IMPLEMENTATION**  Give each student a copy of the Worksheet: A Sunday Surprise.

Read it aloud, holding up the illustration card. (The card has been drawn to clearly show the race of the family, but *not* to show any defined sex roles.) When you finish, the students continue the story by following the directions on the top of the page. (Alternatively, have students draw the conclusion of the story and explain their drawings.) Another day, do the Worksheet: A Moving Day, in the same manner.

Either read aloud a number of the students' conclusions to the stories, or pass them around the room and give students time to read them to themselves. Then join together for discussion.

**DISCUSSION**  1. How did the men in your stories act? Were most of them scared? Calm? Helpful? Bossy? Efficient? Comforting? Decisive? Were there many exceptions to what the majority of you wrote? How close is this to the stereotype of how men should be?
2. How did the women in the stories act? Were most of them scared? Calm? Helpful? Bossy? Efficient? Comforting? Decisive? Were there many exceptions to this? Is this the way women you know act?
3. Did it matter whether the people in the story were white or minority? Did that affect how you decided they should act?
4. Now think about the children in your stories. Was it important that they were young, or did it matter more whether they were girls or boys? black or white?
5. Think about the grandmother. Did she act differently because she was older?

6. Who took the leader's role in each story? An adult or a child? A man or a woman? Was it different for minorities and whites?
7. How does racism, sexism, and ageism influence the way we think people act? How can we make our assumptions more fair and realistic?

---

WATCH ASSUMPTIONS ABOUT "FAMILY"

Remember that only about 40 percent of the children in this country live in traditional nuclear families. Be careful to use language and examples that don't exclude children from single-parent, divorced, or alternative families. For example, say "parent or parents," and preface questions about families with something like, "If you live with both your parents. . . ." Help all students feel okay about their living situation!

---

## What If It Hurts? _____ LA, C

**OBJECTIVES** To examine ways that males and females are conditioned to react to hurt.
To think about what this does to people.

**IMPLEMENTATION** Discuss with the whole class that there are very different ways people react when they are hurt—either physically or emotionally. Explain that they will do several role-plays to help them examine this. (Use "Role-Play Guidelines and Techniques," p. 56, to refresh memories.)

*Role-Play One*. Four girls are playing soccer. One accidentally kicks another in the ankle instead of kicking the ball. She kicks her very hard.

*Role-Play Two*. Same as above, but have four boys.

*Role-Play Three*. Same as above but have a boy kick a girl; the other two players can be either sex.

*Role-Play Four*. Same as Three, but have a girl kick a boy.

*Role-Play Five*. Jacob is having a party. He puts invitations on all the desks except Wilbur's. Role-play is at recess with Wilbur, Rodney and Buffy.

*Role-Play Six*. Do the above with Tamayia having a party and not inviting Penelope.

*Role-Play Seven*. Three girls are at the water fountain. Sumi pushes Yolanda roughly out of the way because she wants a drink first. Yolanda's friend, Bessie, is there, too.

*Role-Play Eight*. Same as above, but with Leroy, Josh, and Xavier.

*Role-Play Nine*. Same as above but with Chris, Terry, and Pat. (That's right, those names are androgynous.)

**DISCUSSION**
1. The first four role-plays were about being hurt physically, by mistake. The next two were about being hurt emotionally. The last three were about being hurt physically, when someone meant to hurt. Which seemed most real to you? Which seemed as though they wouldn't happen? Explain your answers.
2. In which role-plays do people cry? Why? Why didn't they cry in the others? Was crying related to how badly someone was hurt? If not, what was it related to?
3. In which role-plays did people react by hurting back? Why? Discuss whether that was what would really happen. What makes people decide whether or not to fight back? Was there a difference between males and females?
4. Did anyone have any strategies for making a situation less angry? If so, what? Were these more common among boys or girls, or didn't that matter?
5. What have we learned from these activities about how boys are expected to react to hurt in our society? girls? What alternatives do you have?

**GOING FURTHER**   Ask the students to keep a record of actual times when people get hurt. You can set up a shoe box with slips of paper by it. They could fill these out for themselves or others, anonymously. Go through the box every few days for a while and discuss how a situation was handled. Use it as a chance for the students to find sex-role related behavior and see if they can become more open to a variety of reactions.

## What I Want to Be _____ LA, A

**OBJECTIVE**   To help children see in what ways their future occupational aspirations are influenced by racism, sexism, and classism.

**MATERIALS**   For Option One: lined chart paper and magic markers.
For Option Two: thin cardboard, assorted fabrics, scissors, glue.

**IMPLEMENTATION**   Students complete the sentence, "When I grow up I want to be a. . . ." Then the boys complete the sentence, "If I were a girl, I would want to be a. . . ." The girls complete the sentence, "If I were a boy, I would want to be a. . . ." Then the white students can complete the sentence, "If I were a person of color I would want to be a. . . ." And the students of color complete the sentence, "If I were white, I would want to be a. . . ." All students then complete the following sentences: "If my family had plenty of money, I would hope to be a. . . ." and "If my family had very little money, I would hope to be a. . . ."

For Option One, students print their sentences on chart paper which then can be posted for the discussion. For Option Two, they cut out cardboard portraits of themselves doing whatever it is they have chosen. They can then clothe these figures. They do the same for one of the two alternatives—being the opposite sex, or being a different race.

**DISCUSSION**   1.   What did you say that you want to be when you grow up? Tell us about that.
2.   Did you change your choice when you pretended to change sex? race? Why or why not?
3.   Did you choose something that others usually expect people of your sex and race to be?
4.   What kinds of hopes and jobs did you list for a middle-class family? A low-income family? Why? What similarities and differences are there?
5.   How does what class our family is from influence our hopes for ourselves? How fair is this? What can we do to change it?
6.   How do racism, sexism, and classism influence what we think we can do or become?
7.   What are some things to be that people usually don't expect of someone of your race, sex, or class? Would you like to be that? If so, how can you make that happen?

# Put-Downs LA

**OBJECTIVES**  To develop sensitivity to stereotyped put-downs, understand their sources and their effect on both people involved.
To see how they reinforce racism, sexism, classism, ageism, and individualism.

**MATERIALS**  Chart paper and markers.

**IMPLEMENTATION**  Start this as a group project. Ask students to think of put-downs they hear that stereotype people. Brainstorm either as a whole class or in small groups. Here are some examples, if you need them to get going.

"You faggot," "Retard," "Indian-giver," "You're a sissy," "Dumb nigger," "You're just a baby, I won't play with you," "That's for girls only," "Dumbie," "Oh, he's a _____ [last name of a poor family], I'm not gonna sit next to him," "Four-eyes."

Be very insistent that students understand that these put-downs do reinforce stereotypes. This activity hits very close to home, and many times students will deny the power of these put-downs with statements like, "Everyone says that, it doesn't mean anything."

Help students see that by using such language, no matter how it is intended or what is "accepted," they are still using race, class, sex, or age to put someone down. Even if, for example, black students call each other "nigger," they are accepting and reinforcing a negative, powerless image of themselves and other black people. For this reason it's crucial for you to insist on "no put-downs" in a classroom based on equality.

**DISCUSSION**
1. How does (put-down) reinforce a (racist, sexist, etc.) stereotype? How do put-downs reinforce "me-first" thinking?
2. How do you feel when you say one of these to someone? How do you feel when someone says it to you?
3. Where do you learn these phrases?
4. Why do people say things like this?
5. What other ways can we express the same emotions?
6. How comfortable are you about reinforcing stereotypes and the "isms" in this way? What do you want to do about it?

---

**DEALING WITH PUT-DOWNS OF HOMOSEXUALS**

The terms "faggot," "sissy," "dyke," are commonly used as put-downs and thereby reinforce strict sex-defined behavior and norms. What boy will dare be gentle if he risks the label "faggot"! Furthermore they perpetuate negative images of homosexuality.

Talk to students about how these put-downs hurt people. Remind them it's okay for boys to be sensitive and girls strong. If you feel comfortable, discuss how these put-downs enforce homophobia, the fear of homosexuality. Explain that their expression of friendship and affection toward people they care about—no matter what their sex—is part of being human, and okay!

---

THE GRINCHES

--------------------------------------------------------------------------

THE GARNER FAMILY

Worksheet:  2,912 HOUR A YEAR

1.  Name of TV program_____

2.  What class are people in the show--well-to-do, middle-class,
    poor?_____
    Describe the qualities of the characters._____
    _____

3.  What races are people in the show?_____
    Describe the qualities of the characters._____
    _____

4.  What roles do males and females play in the show?_____
    _____
    Describe the qualities of the men and women._____
    _____

5.  What roles do older people play in the show?_____
    _____
    Describe their qualities._____
    _____

6.  What problem is presented?  How do people handle it?
    _____
    _____

7.  What are the goals of the main characters?_____
    _____
    To get ahead, be best, be "heroes"_____
    To work together to make changes for lots of people_____
    _____

Worksheet:  INVENTORY OF GAMES AND TOYS

Name of store_____

    or

Name of your family_____

1)  List three young children's toys.  Next to each, list the
    sexes and races of the children depicted on the package.



2)  List young children's toys whose packages mix races and
    sexes.



3)  List three board games.  Note races and sexes of children
    on packages.



4)  List games whose packages mix races and sexes.



5)  List three toys for older children.  Note races and sexes
    of children on packages.



6)  List toys for older children whose packages mix races
    and sexes.



7)  If you are in a store, talk with three people shopping
    there.  Share your findings with each.  Describe these
    people and their reactions.  If you do this at home, share
    your findings with an adult there.  Describe that person's
    reactions.

Worksheet:  NEIGHBORHOOD TALLY

|  | black | white | Hispanic | Asian-American | Native American | female | male |
|---|---|---|---|---|---|---|---|
| 1. I am | | | | | | | |
| 2. My neighborhood is | | | | | | | |
| 3. My school is | | | | | | | |
| 4. My friends are | | | | | | | |
| 5. People who come to my house are | | | | | | | |
| 6. My teacher is | | | | | | | |
| 7. Our principal is | | | | | | | |
| 8. The doctor I visited last was | | | | | | | |
| 9. The dentist I visited last was | | | | | | | |
| 10. We shop at a store run by | | | | | | | |
| 11. The cashiers are | | | | | | | |
| 12. Our mayor is | | | | | | | |
| 13. Our town council is mostly | | | | | | | |
| 14. The bank manager is | | | | | | | |
| 15. Most police officers are | | | | | | | |
| 16. Our mail carrier is | | | | | | | |
| 17. Our repair people are | | | | | | | |

Now interview one of these people about how he got the job
and how he feels about it.  Ask how racism and/or sexism might
affect others trying to move into that job.

Worksheet:  ON THE HORNS OF A DILEMMA

   Story 1a:   Beena is an excellent speed skater.  She wants
to train for the Olympics.  Her family lives sixty-five miles
from the nearest large outdoor rink.  Her father has a job in a
local shoe factory.  Her mother works for the telephone company.
If they go on living where they are, they will have major gas
costs in transporting Beena to skating.  One would have to work
an evening shift in order to be free to drive.  If they move to
the town with the rink, they will have to find new jobs there.
If they do neither of those, Beena will never be able to become
a well-trained speed skater.  What should they do?
-------------------------------------------------------------------
   Story 1b:   Sean is an excellent speed skater.  He wants to
train for the Olympics.  His family lives sixty-five miles from
the nearest large outdoor rink.  His father has a job in a
local shoe factory.  His mother works for the telephone company.
If they go on living where they are, they will have major gas
costs in transporting Sean to skating.  One would have to work
an evening shift in order to be free to drive.  If they move to
the town with the rink, they will have to find new jobs there.
If they do neither of those, Sean will never be able to become
a well-trained speed skater.  What should they do?

_____

   Story 2a:   Julia's family is thinking of moving from their
Puerto Rican neighborhood into a new neighborhood.  The neighborhood and school would be part Puerto Rican, part black, and
part white.  Julia is happy in her school and is getting good
grades.  Julia's mother wants to move so she will be closer to
work.  Should Julia object?
-------------------------------------------------------------------
   Story 2b:   Hillary's family is thinking of moving from an
all white neighborhood into a new neighborhood.  The neighborhood and school would be part Puerto Rican, part black, and
part white.  Hillary is happy in her school and is getting good
grades.  Hillary's mother wants to move so she will be closer o
to work.  Should Hillary object?

Story 3a:  Maia and Jordana's parents just died in a car accident.  Their seventy-five-year-old grandmother, Louise, has offered to have them live with her.  They have only met her once since she lives 2,000 miles away and their parents didn't like to travel.  They are worried about leaving all their friends.  They will be put in a foster home in their town if they don't go.  What should they do?

------------------------------------------------------------------

Story 3b:  Maia and Jordana's parents just died in a car accident.  Their mother's thirty-five-year-old sister, Lucy, has offered to have them live with her.  They have only met her once since she lives 2,000 miles away and their parents didn't like to travel.  They are worried about leaving all their friends.  They will be put in a foster home in their town if they don't go.  What should they do?

------------------------------------------------------------------

Story 4a:  Adam hasn't been doing his homework.  His teacher must decide today if he should move Adam into the lowest reading group or give him another chance to improve.  His teacher knows Adam's family is poor and Adam's mother never graduated from high school.  Adam is very busy after school doing odd jobs in order to earn money to help support his family.  What should the teacher do?

------------------------------------------------------------------

Story 4b:  Aaron hasn't been doing his homework.  His teacher must decide today if he should move Aaron into the lowest reading group or give him another chance to improve.  His teacher knows Aaron comes from a well-educated family.  His father is a doctor and his mother is a teacher.  Aaron is very busy with many after-school activities.  What should the teacher do?

Worksheet:  SUPERMARKET


Number of products observed_____

Number of Sex:        men_____        women_____

Race:        whites_____        blacks_____        Hispanics_____

             Native Americans_____        Asian-Americans_____

Class:        middle-class_____        working-class
                                                 or poor  _____

Age:        adults over 65_____        adults under 65_____

            children_____




What were people doing?




What kinds of jobs did people seem to have?




What stereotypes did you find, if any?

Worksheet:  TRAITS PEOPLE HAVE

| BLACK BOYS OR MEN | BLACK GIRLS OR WOMEN | LOW-INCOME PEOPLE |
|---|---|---|
| ___kind | ___kind | ___kind |
| ___get into fights | ___get into fights | ___get into fights |
| ___artistic | ___artistic | ___artistic |
| ___dumb | ___dumb | ___dumb |
| ___friendly | ___friendly | ___friendly |
| ___good at fixing things | ___good at fixing things | ___good at fixing things |
| ___slow | ___slow | ___slow |
| ___shy | ___shy | ___shy |
| ___good at sports | ___good at sports | ___good at sports |
| ___clean | ___clean | ___clean |
| ___loud | ___loud | ___loud |
| ___good-looking | ___good-looking | ___good-looking |
| ___cry a lot | ___cry a lot | ___cry a lot |
| ___helpful | ___helpful | ___helpful |
| ___musical | ___musical | ___musical |
| ___sloppy | ___sloppy | ___sloppy |
| ___good sense of humor | ___good sense of humor | ___good sense of humor |
| ___cuddly | ___cuddly | ___cuddly |
| ___smart aleck | ___smart aleck | ___smart aleck |
| ___good at cleaning | ___good at cleaning | ___good at cleaning |
| ___strong | ___strong | ___strong |
| ___talkative | ___talkative | ___talkative |

| WHITE BOYS OR MEN | WHITE GIRLS OR WOMEN | LOW-INCOME PEOPLE |
|---|---|---|
| ___kind | ___kind | ___kind |
| ___get into fights | ___get into fights | ___get into fights |
| ___artistic | ___artistic | ___artistic |
| ___dumb | ___dumb | ___dumb |
| ___friendly | ___friendly | ___friendly |
| ___good at fixing things | ___good at fixing things | ___good at fixing things |
| ___slow | ___slow | ___slow |
| ___shy | ___shy | ___shy |
| ___good at sports | ___good at sports | ___good at sports |
| ___clean | ___clean | ___clean |
| ___loud | ___loud | ___loud |
| ___good-looking | ___good-looking | ___good-looking |
| ___cry a lot | ___cry a lot | ___cry a lot |
| ___helpful | ___helpful | ___helpful |
| ___musical | ___musical | ___musical |
| ___sloppy | ___sloppy | ___sloppy |
| ___good sense of humor | ___good sense of humor | ___good sense of humor |
| ___cuddly | ___cuddly | ___cuddly |
| ___smart aleck | ___smart aleck | ___smart aleck |
| ___good at cleaning | ___good at cleaning | ___good at cleaning |
| ___strong | ___strong | ___strong |
| ___talkative | ___talkative | ___talkative |

Worksheet:  A MOVING DAY

Finish this story by explaining what each member of the
family did and how each felt.

The Garner family was moving.  For ten years they had
lived in the city.  The younger two children, Barry and Katie,
had never lived anywhere else.  Kristine and Jon, who were
older, hardly remembered the country home they had lived in as
babies.  Their mother and stepfather had grown up on farms and
were eager to move out of the city.

It took them weeks to pack.  They had rented a truck.
After driving for seven hours, everyone was tired.  However,
not wanting to leave their belongings in the truck, they spent
several more hours carrying all 131 boxes into the house.
Finally they had a supper of peanut-butter and tomato sandwiches and all fell asleep.

About 3 a.m., Barry and Kristine woke up.  They heard a
knocking at the door.  It got louder.  It changed to banging
and thumping.  Then...

_____

_____

_____

_____

_____

_____

_____

_____

_____

_____

_____

_____

Worksheet:  A SUNDAY SURPRISE

    Finish this story by explaining what each member of the
family did and how each felt.


    The Grinch family--Becky, Neal, Mr. Grinch, Grandmother
Grinch--was going on a Sunday trip.  They'd packed a picnic
lunch.  While they were in the car, Becky and Neal played
Dictionary Fictionary with their father and grandmother.  Often
they would stop and all get out of the car.  They took photos
or sketched pictures.  They also played catch or frisbee.
    They had been driving for an hour when the sky started to
get dark.  They listened to the radio.  Tornado warnings!!
What can they do?  Just then they saw a tree fly by.
    "Help, help!  I'm scared!"

_____

_____

_____

_____

_____

_____

_____

_____

_____

_____

_____

# 9 THINGS CAN BE DIFFERENT

People have more energy and commitment to make changes when they know that things can be different. When we see that more equal personal and societal relations aren't "pie-in-the-sky" fantasies, but can and do exist in the real world, this provides motivation for change.

In the first group of activities, *People Making Change: From Then to Now*, students learn about individuals who have struggled for equality. They examine the varied strategies for change and think about ways they can be applied today.

*Creating Alternatives: Envisioning the Future* contains lessons with concrete examples of egalitarian living, working, or learning situations. From job-sharing in the home to equal access to medical education, these lessons give students practical examples of the creation of more equal structures for interaction. They are encouraged to discuss the application of the various approaches to their communities.

A vision of a just and equal society is essential if people are to maintain the courage and perseverance necessary for what will be a protracted social transformation. Students too, need to have a vision of *what can be*. Some lessons, therefore, include an image of a very different, and more equal, society. Especially since that society won't appear tomorrow, it's important that students can envision and hold on to a picture of a more equal future!

---

Anthropologist Ruth Benedict discovered, in comparing many different societies, that aggression is lowest in those social orders in which "the individual by the same act and at the same time serves his own advantage and that of the group." That is, some societies are organized so that the group values and rewards the individual for doing what benefits the group. For example, in one Eskimo society, a man proves his prowess by hunting and bringing back seals, which are then distributed equally to all members of the group for food. Thus the society benefits from the same act that benefits the individual.

From *Developing Effective Classroom Groups*, by Gene Stanford.

---

## SECTION A PEOPLE MAKING CHANGES: FROM THEN TO NOW

### Here's What Some People Did

R, SS, S, LA

**OBJECTIVES**
To give students information about people in history and society who have brought about change.

To give students a realistic idea of the problems and the satisfactions of fostering change.

To get students excited about the possibilities for change.

**MATERIALS**    A collection of library books about people who have brought about change. (See Bibliography under heading "Biographies.") Task Cards: People and Change, p. 205.

**IMPLEMENTATION**    Ask each student to pick and read a book from your selection. Then students choose and complete one or more task cards. Students can do this lesson individually, or in small groups if they read the same book. Share in groups, with the whole class, or via a bulletin board.

**DISCUSSION**
1. What are some feelings you have about the person you read about?
2. How did the person in your book bring about change?
3. What obstacles did that person face?
4. What satisfaction did the person get?
5. What kinds of support did that person get?
6. What difference did the person make in the world?

---

An excellent book to use for this lesson, or to read aloud to your students, is *Fannie Lou Hamer*, by June Jordon. This courageous black woman worked for voter registration during the Civil Rights Movement, joined in forming the Mississippi Democratic Party, and founded the Freedom Farm Cooperative in rural Mississippi.

While easy to read, this Crowell biography is moving and powerful.

---

## Sojourner Truth Puppet Show _____ C, LA, A, SS

**OBJECTIVES**    To give students a role-model of a black woman who chose to challenge the racism and sexism of her day.
To give students the opportunity to work cooperatively and creatively to design a product which they can share with their peers.

**MATERIALS**    Copies of one, or more than one, of the following: *Sojourner Truth* by Helen Stone Paterson, (second-grade reading level); *Sojourner Truth*, by Julian May (fourth-grade); *Sojourner Truth*, by Victoria Ortiz, (sixth-grade). Lined paper, large newsprint, pencils, scrap fabric of all sorts, felt, embroidery thread, yarn, socks (brown, black, tan), stuffing, needles, thread, cardboard.

**IMPLEMENTATION**   You will need to make at least five puppets, and can make up to ten. Decide size of student groups. Each group makes one or more puppets. Make Sojourner Truth in three outfits—as Belle, the slave child; as Belle the free woman worker and mother; and as Sojourner Truth the preacher. Make at least one slave owner, and at least one of the people who later helped her. When possible, make Sojourner's son, whose freedom she won in court; slave owners in two stages of her life; women associates in the suffrage movement; Lincoln. Students work cooperatively to make the puppets. (See Bibliography for books on puppet-making.)

Make a puppet stage—a large box, the type appliances are shipped in, serves well. Cut out an open area. When students kneel down and hold their puppets up, the bottoms of the outfits should be level with the lower part of the opening.

Before students write scripts, see that your entire class becomes familiar with the story of Sojourner Truth. Use some of your read-aloud time or social studies class time to read from one of the three books listed above, or use the books with reading groups.

As a class, brainstorm on the scenes needed and list them on the blackboard. Then students work in groups of three or four to write the scripts. Groups which finish their scripts, and correct them with you, can make more puppets, if these are needed. Make one cast of puppets first, however, since this provides motivation for the academic work, script writing.

Small groups switch scripts and critique each others'. Gather as a class and read scripts aloud. Make changes when appropriate.

Students rehearse in small groups, then perform before the class. Send invitations to parents to come to a performance. Make arrangements with other classes to see your show. Have discussions with the visiting classes.

**DISCUSSION**   1.  How did you decide which incidents in Sojourner Truth's life were particularly important? Give a reason for each incident you chose.
2.  How did Sojourner Truth work with others to make changes? Give examples.
3.  What strengths did she have as a person which made this possible? How can you develop these strengths?
4.  In what ways did you like making a puppet with other classmates as compared to doing so on your own? In what ways did you dislike that?

---

The man over there says that women need to be helped into carriages and lifted over ditches, and to have the best place everywhere. Nobody ever helps me into carriages or over puddles or give me the best place . . . and ain't I a woman? Look at my arm! I have ploughed and planted and gathered into barns, and no man could head me—and ain't I a woman? I could work as much and eat as much as a man—when I could get it—and bear the lash as well . . . and ain't I a woman? I have borne thirteen children, and seen most of 'em sold into slav'ry, and when I cried out with my mother's grief, none but Jesus heard me . . . and ain't I a woman?

Sojourner Truth, 1851.

---

## Stop! Don't Take It for Granted _____   S, SS, M, LA

**OBJECTIVES**   To teach children about the life of a black man who invented several items which improved the safety of life.
To learn that individuals can make changes that improve many people's lives through their work.

**MATERIALS**   Copies of Worksheet: Garrett Morgan, p. 201; Task Cards: Garrett Morgan, p. 202, one card per group; paper, pencils.

**IMPLEMENTATION**   Divide students into heterogeneous groups of three or four. Each group reads aloud the Worksheet. Answer any questions on information or vocabulary. Then either have each group pick one of the task cards, or assign them.

After the work is completed, gather together as a class and have groups share their work. Make a display, if you like.

**DISCUSSION**
1. What impresses you most about Garrett Morgan's life? Why?
2. What surprises you most? Why?
3. We tend to forget that every useful invention was thought up by *someone*. Why does that happen? Is there anything bad about that? If so what could we do differently?
4. Can you think of other women or minority people who have improved the conditions of life for all through their work?

---

> Who invented the cotten gin? No, not Eli Whitney. Catherine Greene, a female friend of Whitney's, gave him the plans because women were unable to obtain patents.

---

## Alone and Together _____ SS, R

**OBJECTIVES**
To learn about the role of Rosa Parks and others involved in the Montgomery bus boycott.
To understand the power one person can have in fostering change.
To understand a variety of strategies people can use together to bring about equality.

**MATERIALS**
Copies of poem, "I Am Only One Person," p. 203; a copy of *Rosa Parks* by Eloise Greenfield or "Rosa Parks," (Stories for Free Children Series) *Ms. Magazine*, August, 1974. (If your local library doesn't have either of these, they are easily available on interlibrary loan. Many interlibrary loan systems will send copies of magazine articles free. Allow several weeks for delivery.) Copies of Question Cards: Rosa Parks, p. 204, one set for each group.

**IMPLEMENTATION**
PART ONE.  Tell students they are going to study what people, both alone and together, can do to foster equality. Explain that you will begin with a poem about what one woman did to challenge segregation. Discuss this word with the class. Then distribute a copy of the poem to each student. While you read it, have them follow along, or do a reading in unison.

**DISCUSSION**
1. Who was Rosa Parks?
2. What did she do?
3. Why was what she did so important?
4. Have you ever said to yourself something like, "I am only one person, what can one person do?" If so, when?
5. What does the account of Rosa Parks teach us?

Ask students to put copies of their poem in a safe place because they'll be using them again. (If necessary collect, to redistribute later.) Tell students they will now learn more about Rosa Parks and the beginning of the Civil Rights Movement.

PART TWO.  Divide students into heterogeneous groups of four. They will use the "jigsaw method" to learn more about Rosa Parks. In this method, each person in a group will get part of the story of Rosa Parks. Each person will be telling part of the story to the others, and will be answering questions, so each must study carefully.

If you have the *Ms. Magazine* article about Rosa Parks, make one copy for each group. Otherwise, write a synopsis of the book for the students. Divide the account into four parts, so that each student has a part of the account to read. Divide amount of reading unevenly if skill levels vary greatly. Once students have read their material, they teach the others in their group. You may wish to distribute question cards at this time, if you want students to be selective in what they teach each other. Each student "teacher" should check to be confident that the others in the group understand the material.

Copy the questions (p. 204) on 3 × 5 cards, having one deck for each group. Students shuffle the deck and draw cards until all are taken. The students write their questions, followed by the answers, on their papers.

Next, students take turns reading one of their questions and the answer to the group. Group members should agree that the answer is correct. Continue around the group until all questions are read. Then students make whatever changes are needed on their papers. The answers are handed in and the group is evaluated as a whole on its responses.

**DISCUSSION**
1. What are some feelings Rosa Parks probably had in fighting for her rights?
2. How did Rosa Parks give other people courage?
3. A "boycott" is a strategy for change. People collectively refuse to use or buy a certain service or product in order to put pressure on a business or group to change its policies. Can you think of a recent boycott?
4. Civil disobedience is a strategy for change. People don't obey a law that they feel supports inequality. Rosa Parks used that strategy in 1955. Can you think of an example today?
5. Do you think boycotts and civil disobedience are effective strategies for change? In what ways are they effective? ineffective?
6. How is the account of Rosa Parks an example of people working alone and together to bring about equality?

"Yo creo que..."

---

**BOYCOTTS AND CIVIL DISOBEDIENCE**

The United Farm Workers Union used a very successful national boycott of non-union grapes and lettuce to win contracts from California growers.

A nationwide boycott of products made by the J.P. Stevens Company, known for its repressive labor practices, helped support workers struggling to win union recognition.

People who oppose nuclear power have practiced civil disobedience while sitting-in at nuclear power plants. They refuse to obey police officers' orders to move. They believe the dangers of nuclear power threaten the lives of thousands of people.

---

## Chicanos Strike at Farah* _____ R, LA

**OBJECTIVES**
To learn about issues involved in the strike of Chicano garment workers in the Southwest.
To examine the strike as a strategy for change.

**MATERIALS**
Copies of Worksheet: Chicanos Strike at Farah* (1), pp. 206–207; and (2), p. 208; dictionaries.

**IMPLEMENTATION**
Tell students that they will examine the strike, another strategy that can be used to bring about equality. Explain that they will first read about a strike by Chicano garment workers in the Southwest.

Students may work individually or in groups to read and answer the questions on the Worksheets. After students have completed the Worksheets, join together as a large group and discuss the answers. Then go on with the following discussion questions.

**DISCUSSION**
1. In the case of the Farah workers, what were the advantages in using the strike as a strategy to bring about more fair working conditions? What were the disadvantages?
2. Can you think of other times when the strike was/is used as a method for bringing about equality?

---

*Summarized from "La Chicana Curriculum" by Susan Groves and Clementine Duran, Berkeley, California Public Schools.

3. What are the advantages of using strikes? the disadvantages?
4. There have been student strikes in many schools and colleges. For what issues do you believe it is appropriate for students to strike?

**GOING FURTHER**

Assign students to read the local newspapers, listen to local radio programs, and talk to their friends and relatives to find out if there is currently a strike in their community. If so, assign some students to try to interview workers who are striking. Assign others to try to talk with the management, or at least learn the management's point of view from local papers. Have both groups report the issues to class.

> We must begin to see our work as having value and meaning in and of itself, not just in terms of what it will produce or what it will enable us to consume. We need to begin perceiving our work as an end in and of itself, not just a means (be that a means to profit for the companies, or a means to more leisure time, another car or whatever for ourselves). Work can be so much more once we begin demanding and exercising control over it and striving to make it a positive experience in which we labor with others in a co-operative and just community to create the kinds of goods and services which we value. We have a right to decent work and to a say over both how we'll work and to what ends we'll work. We have a right to struggle towards changing the nature of work.
>
> From "Work Liberation" by Vocations for Social Change, 1975

## Affirmative Action
## Before and After _____ SS, R, LA

**OBJECTIVES**

To have students learn about a concrete example where providing equal access and resources produced more equal results.

To examine affirmative action policies as one way to change institutional discrimination.

To see how the results of such affirmative action changes affect individual women.

**MATERIALS**

Five copies of Longshore Workers Interview, p. 209; copies of Worksheet; Sabra's Letter, p. 210; two or three copies of Task Cards: Affirmative Action, p. 213; paper and pencils.

**IMPLEMENTATION**

Introduce this lesson by reiterating that people and social institutions sometimes blame the victims for their problems. Remind them of what they learned in Chapter 6, that only with equal resources and opportunities can we expect more equal results. This lesson shows how changing institutional discrimination brought greater job equity to women workers.

STEP 1.   Get together with a group of five students during a free period of time. Review the Longshore Workers Interview, so that they are sure of all the words and meanings; have them practice so that they can read it aloud to the class as a play.

   Present this interview sequence to the whole class. Check that the words were understood. Then discuss the first set of questions.

**DISCUSSION**
1. Why do women want longshore work? What is the major benefit?
2. Why didn't the employers want to hire women? Try to think of at least several reasons.
3. In what way did the National Organization for Women help these women?
4. How was what the women did an example of anti-racism as well as of fighting sex discrimination?
5. Why were women given heavy physical labor jobs in factories during World War II? Why were these taken away from them after the war?
6. What is affirmative action?

STEP 2.   Hand out Worksheet: Sabra's Letter to all students. Before they start reading go over vocabulary. You may need to answer some questions as they read.

   Divide students into heterogenous pairs. Each pair chooses one of the Task Cards, and completes the work. After all pairs have finished, get back together as a group. Have each pair share its results with the whole class. Then go on to discussion questions, below.

**DISCUSSION**
1. In what ways has affirmative action helped Sabra find a job which is good for her?
2. Why do you think it had been harder for Sabra's friend Jaconda to support herself and her family than it would have been if Jaconda's husband had earned the family money and Jaconda done the child care?
3. The unions might not have had the training program if it were not for affirmative action. Why?
4. How might affirmative action change the job distribution in your school?
5. How might it effect jobs in your community? Give some specific examples.
6. Why do we need affirmative action as a program, rather than just letting people apply for whatever jobs they want?

## THE LAW

We live in a democracy.

So <u>why</u> do we need sex equality laws???

If they're so important

...how come nobody thought 'em up before???

I like the good old days better.

When equality was more unequal.

— donovan 1978

## SECTION B   CREATING ALTERNATIVES: ENVISIONING THE FUTURE

### Job-Sharing or Who's the Cook Tonight?

M, LA

**OBJECTIVES**

To learn about one example of a way of allocating household jobs that is not sexist or ageist.

To consider implications of this system.

**MATERIALS**

Copies of Worksheet: Job-Sharing, pp. 211–12.

**IMPLEMENTATION**

Divide students into trios and have them quietly read the Worksheet to each other. One takes the role of Dave, another Noelle, and a third the interviewer.

When they've finished reading, divide into pairs. Students write down three questions they want to ask their partners regarding that person's feelings, thoughts, or questions about the job-sharing plan. (The questions and responses will be handed in at the end of the lesson.) Students then interview their partners and summarize their partners' responses in writing. (You may want to review skills for summarizing material.)

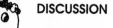

**DISCUSSION**

1. What are your feelings about the Porter family job-sharing plan?
2. What do you see as the strengths and weaknesses?
3. This is an anti-sexist plan. Why is that so?
4. What do the males gain by cooking, which people used to think of as "women's work"?
5. This is an anti-ageist plan. How and why is that so?
6. In what ways could a job-sharing plan work for your family?

Explain that sometimes people argue that equality is a good idea, but it can't be put into practice. Tell students that in fact there are many examples of equality that *do* work. This is one example that has worked very well in a family situation.

**GOING FURTHER**

Have students take the Worksheet home. Suggest that they, together with others in the family, make a list of the jobs their family needs to do, and develop a chart for equal job-sharing. Report family responses to the class.

# Inuit*

**OBJECTIVES**
To have students learn about a culture in American society that is without class distinction and discrimination, and where cooperation is a norm.

To encourage students to think about how their lives would be different in a more cooperative culture and what they could do to achieve that.

**MATERIALS**
Copies of Worksheet: Inuit, p. 214; one or more books in Bibliography on Alaskan Eskimos; encyclopedias on Alaskan Eskimos; chart paper and markers.

**IMPLEMENTATION**
STEP ONE.   Hand out copies of the Worksheet to students. Divide into heterogenous groups of three or four. Have students read the passage aloud to other group members. Answer questions on word-meanings. Each group then writes down any questions they have about traditional Alaskan Eskimo life. Get together as a class and, using information from books or encyclopedias, find answers to these questions. Encourage students to look up information and share with the class.

Put up two large sheets of chart paper. Title them "Inuit." Students brainstorm on the advantages of cooperation and lack of class distinction for Alaskan Eskimos. List these. Then students brainstorm on problems traditional Alaskan Eskimos would have if they lived in a more competitive society. List these and leave lists up.

STEP TWO.   Put up two more sheets of chart paper. Title them "Our Culture." You may have a number of charts in a multicultural classroom. Again brainstorm, this time on the advantages of cooperation in our culture and on the problems caused by competition and classism. Use the discussion questions to compare these lists.

STEP THREE.   Brainstorm on situations in your community and school which are now competitive or classist. List these with enough description so students will remember what was said. Get enough workable situations so there will be one for every group of three to five students.

Each group discusses what is competitive or classist about its situation and what problems that causes. Then groups take the perspective of people in a cooperative, non-classist culture and think of ways to handle the situation. Each group shares its ideas with the whole class. Encourage suggestions and revisions. Then each group designs a skit to demonstrate the current competitive or classist way the situation is handled and its new, cooperative way.

Present skits to other classes, first explaining about the cooperative nature of the Alaskan Eskimo way of life. Follow by discussion questions.

**DISCUSSION**
1.   Give examples of the cooperative basis of traditional Alaskan Eskimo culture.
2.   Why does traditional Alaskan Eskimo culture not have the same class structure that we do?
3.   In terms of cooperation and lack of classism, what would you like about the Eskimo way of life? What would you not like? Why?
4.   What might a traditional Alaskan Eskimo child say about your competitive way of life if she were to visit your family and school?
5.   Why might it be harder for you to do things more cooperatively in your family, school, or community than it is for a traditional Alaskan Eskimo child to do in his? What can you do to make it easier?

> At camp, we have campers of many different income levels. We don't want to have some campers able to buy candy, soda, and souvenirs and others not able to buy anything. Therefore there is no canteen or store within camp. No one is allowed to bring any spending money. The camp puts in $10 a person into "cabin money" for each cabin. Whenever a group goes on a trip, all are given the same amount of money, with the chance to spend it in whatever way they want.

*The Eskimos' name for themselves. It means "the real people."

## The Children's Place _____

**OBJECTIVES**      To learn about an example of an employer-sponsored day-care center.
To consider how availability of quality day-care can change institutional sexism.

**MATERIALS**      Copies of Worksheet: Children's Place, p. 215.

**IMPLEMENTATION**      DAY ONE.   Begin with this five-minute discussion and homework assignment. Ask students to share what they remember about the lesson, "Who Will Take Care of Jamil?" p. 115–16. Tell them they will now read about a day-care center that is sponsored by the workers' employer.

Pass out the Worksheet. For homework have students read the information about this New York State-sponsored day-care center. Have them interview two working parents with young children concerning their opinions of the Children's Place.

DAY TWO.   Ask students to get out the Worksheet and come together.

**DISCUSSION**      1.   How do you feel about the Children's Place? What makes you feel the way you do?
2.   How did the persons you interviewed feel about the Children's Place? Did they want to have such a day-care center at their place of work? Why or why not?
3.   Think back to the lesson, "Who Will Take Care of Jamil?" How would the Children's Place help Marva and Tyrone Williams? How could it help other men and women who are parents?
4.   How do employers gain by providing day-care at their places of work?
5.   Name at least two ways day-care centers at peoples' places of work help change sexism in society.

**GOING FURTHER**      Write to major employers in your area. Describe the Children's Place and ask if they would start such a program. Discuss their responses.

Call or write representatives of parents' groups or women's groups in your community. Tell them about the Children's Place. Ask them if they would be willing to advocate such a center in your community. Discuss their responses.

Take away our child care centers , will ya! We'll lower your expectations.

# Yes, You Can Be a Doctor _____ LA, SS

**OBJECTIVES**   To show students an economic system different from our own, which better meets the needs of citizens of different ages, races, and classes.

To encourage students to compare this system to that of the United States and to hypothesize what its effects might be in this country.

**MATERIALS**   Copies of Worksheet: Asmund and Kirsten's Letter, p. 216; paper, pencils; possibly stationery, stamps, photographs, and addresses.

**IMPLEMENTATION**   Explain to students that not all countries have the same economic system as the United States does. Some countries have more government programs to help people and some have fewer. The example in this lesson comes from Norway, a Scandinavian country. If you have not studied Norway in school, you may want to give students background information.

Divide students into pairs. Give each pair two copies of the Worksheet. Answer any questions about vocabulary or content. Each pair writes an answer to Asmund and Kirsten. They give their reactions to what the Norwegian students have said about Norway, and they explain how the medical system works in this country. If they have done "Letter from Sally" (p. 121), ask them to remember what they learned. If not, review it yourself.

Many more people want to be doctors than go to medical school in the U.S. Many of these can't afford the $75,000 (1982) needed for training; for others, there aren't enough places in medical schools. Most people who become doctors go into private practice in areas where they want to live rather than give service to the country in areas where they are needed. Have students get up-to-date information on current costs of medical training and medical care in the U.S. today.

Students proofread and correct their answers, then trade off with two other groups so everyone has read three letters. Post letters on a bulletin board so students see even more reactions.

**DISCUSSION**   1.   What did you think of what Kirsten and Asmund had to say about medical training in Norway? In what ways would you like to see that system in this country? In what ways would you not like that?

2.   What are some advantages in the Norwegian medical system as compared to the American one? If we had that system here what positive changes would it mean in our medical care? in chances to become a doctor?

3.   State how the structure of medical training in Norway is an example of providing equality for people of all classes. Think back to the lesson, "Letter from Sally." Compare this to Sally's situation.

**GOING FURTHER**   Your class might enjoy writing to pen-pals in other countries, especially ones with different economic or political systems.

---

MEDICAL TRAINING AND CARE IN THE U.S.

1. Access to medical training depends very much on a person's class background. For example, 64% of medical students come from families where the father is a physician, professional, owner, or manager (1978).
2. Minority access to medical training has been limited. Twelve percent of the U.S. population is black, yet only 2 percent of physicians are black (1980).

Statistics from "Fact Sheet on Institutional Racism," C.I.B.C.

3. Availability of doctors varies greatly. Poor people usually have limited access to medical care. Twenty million Americans receive inadequate medical care or NO care at all. Fifty thousand more physicians are needed.

"Notes on Wealth, Power, and
Poverty in America,"
Dr. Barbara Scott, 1982

## Youth and Age in Action _____ LA, R

**OBJECTIVE**  To have students learn about the Gray Panthers, an activist group dedicated to securing equality, particularly for older Americans.
To learn about a different vision of what society could be.

**MATERIALS**  Copies of Worksheets: Gray Panthers (1), p. 217 and Gray Panthers (2), p. 218, one set per group; dictionaries.

**IMPLEMENTATION**  Tell students they will be studying ways older people in our communities are active in creating changes.

STEP ONE.   Divide students into heterogenous groups of five and give several dictionaries to each group. Cut up pages of Worksheet (1) and give each person in each group one "news item."

Tell students to imagine that they are all coming from different parts of the country and are meeting for the first time. They have all read a short news item about the organization the Gray Panthers in their hometown newspapers before they came.

Students look up underlined vocabulary words and write down the definitions. Then each summarizes to the whole group what she has learned about the Gray Panthers from her news item. Based on everyone's information, the group writes a short article, "The Gray Panthers: Who They Are and What They Do." Encourage students to summarize what they've learned. Ask them to use at least four new vocabulary words in their article. Share articles with the whole class.

STEP TWO.   Cut Worksheet (2) into sections, and distribute to the groups. Explain to students that the Gray Panthers have a vision of a new society. Tell them if they compile all the information they have just been given, they will get a picture of that society. Students read their own pieces of information, look up vocabulary words, and then summarize to each other.

Next, the group writes a cooperative story about a person who lives in the new society, as the Gray Panthers would like it. The story describes a typical day in that person's life. It should tell how the person contributes to or is affected by jobs, health care, and so on. At least four new vocabulary words should be used.

When stories are completed, students read them to the class.

**DISCUSSION**  1.  How do you think the older people in the story you wrote about feel about themselves? about being older?
2.  How would you compare their feelings to those of older persons today?
3.  How does the society the Gray Panthers want compare to ours today?
4.  What are your feelings and opinions about the society the Gray Panthers foresee?
5.  Think back to the lesson "Health or Home" p. 97, and remember the situation of Ted and Juanita Lund. How would they feel about the society the Gray Panthers want?

FOR HOMEWORK: Describe the society the Gray Panthers foresee to an older person you know. Write down that person's opinions about it.

Look through newspapers and magazines and talk with parents, relatives and friends. Bring in information about older people who are acting for change in your community.

STEP THREE (SEVERAL DAYS LATER). Choose one or two elders who are active in working for changes in your community and invite them to speak with your class.

The day before, students generate questions to ask. Examples: How are you working for change in our community? How is it different being an older person working for change? How do you deal with any discrimination against older persons that you face? What kinds of changes do you feel need to be made to make life for older people in America more equal? We learned about the Gray Panthers—how do you feel about their ideas? What groups or organizations are working on behalf of older people in our community? How do you think younger people can work together with older people to bring changes? What projects could we get involved with in our community now?

AT YOUR AGE YOU MUST EXPECT TO FEEL LOUSY

**GOING FURTHER**     Obtain the film *Wrinkled Radical*, a thirty-minute documentary about Maggie Kuhn and the Gray Panthers. It is an inexpensive film available through many library film networks.

Help children get involved with a community project that your visitor suggested. If appropriate, make it a class project.

## Atalanta or Cinderella? _____ LA, A

**OBJECTIVES**     To have students see the possibility that a fairy-tale-type story does not have the traditional characterization, sex roles, or ending.
To provide students with a vision of an alternative to a sexist society.

**MATERIALS**     "Atalanta" from the book or the record *Free To Be You and Me;* paint brushes, paper, pencils.

**IMPLEMENTATION**     Either read "Atalanta" aloud to the class or play the story on the record. Discuss the story as a class.

**DISCUSSION**
1. In what ways, if any, did you like "Atalanta" better than traditional fairy tales? Why?
2. In what ways, if any, did you like "Atalanta" less well? Why?
3. What parts of "Atalanta" did you like best? Why? what parts least? why?
4. How did you feel about the ending? How did it compare to endings in most fairy-tales?
5. Did you find "Atalanta" more or less "realistic" than traditional fairy-tales? Explain your reasons. In what ways do you like or not like that?
6. The story of Atalanta presents a vision of people living in a world free of sexism. How would you and others be different in such a world?

Next, have the class list aloud parts of the story which can be illustrated. If you get as many topics as there are students, great. If not, several students can paint each episode. Have them write several sentences about the pictures. Arrange the pictures and captions in order and put them on a hallway bulletin board.

Divide students into groups of four or five. Each group lists several questions about sex-roles which it feels would be good for other students in the school, viewing the bulletin board, to ask themselves about Atalanta and about fairy-tales. Gather as a class and share questions. Finally, discuss the project with the class.

**DISCUSSION**
1. What parts of the story did the class want to illustrate? What parts were not wanted? What does this tell you?
2. How many people painted Atalanta as white? as Afro-American? as a member of another race? Did people make her their own race or another? why? What about the other characters?
3. How hard or easy was it to come up with different bulletin board questions? Why?
4. How do you expect students who have not been studying equality to feel about the questions? Which will seem difficult to them? Why? Which will be easy? Why?

---

*X: A Fabulous Child's Story,* by Lois Gould, is an excellent book for your school library to buy and for you to use in class. Creative and thought-provoking, it helps children see what life might be like without sex-role stereotyping. Read it to students, discuss the ideas, and have them create skits to present to others!

---

Worksheet:  GARRETT MORGAN


    Garrett Morgan was a black man born in Kentucky or
Tennessee in 1875.  As is often the case for people of color
at that time, historical records are incomplete, so different
resource books give different information.

    In 1901, Garrett Morgan created his first invention--a
safe belt-cover for sewing machines.  At that time, sewing
machine belts were in the open and dangerous to people's hands.

    Garrett Morgan continued to invent equipment to make
people's lives more safe.  In 1914, he invented a breathing
helmet for rescuers who were entering areas filled with smoke
or gas.  Two years later he demonstrated the importance of
this in rescuing trapped workers in a smoke filled tunnel
under Lake Erie.  He received a Gold Medal for that from the
City of Cleveland.  People were impressed and, at first, his
invention sold rapidly.  Then it became known that the helmet
was invented by a black man.  People were so prejudiced that,
even though it saved lives, they wouldn't use it.

    Garrett Morgan continued to invent more safety items.  In
1923 he invented the automatic traffic light.  Today we take
this for granted.  Yet when he introduced the idea, traffic
lights did not seem valuable to people.  He couldn't sell his
idea.  Finally, years later, General Electric bought his idea
and paid him $40,000 for it.  ($40,000 sounds like quite a lot
of money, but it doesn't sound as much when you realize that in
1981 a single traffic light cost $2500.)

Task Cards:  GARRETT MORGAN

---

Call your city traffic department and ask about the cost of
various types of traffic lights.  If you live in a town with no
traffic lights, call a nearby city.  Then calculate the cost of
any traffic lights between where you live and the school.
Calculate how many traffic lights could be bought for the
amount that G.E. paid Garrett Morgan.

---

In pairs, stand on a street corner where there is a traffic
light.  Using the skills you have learned about interviewing,
ask passersby if they know who invented the traffic light.
Record reactions.  Do so until you have talked to at least ten
people.

---

Interview five adults you know about the importance of traffic
lights.  Ask them if they have ever stopped to think about
what would be different if we didn't have traffic lights.

---

Look up information about another inventor who was a woman or a
member of a minority group.  Write a description of the person's
life and invention(s).  Send it to your school or town paper.

---

Write an article for your school newspaper or a letter to your
town newspaper about the advantages and importance of Garrett
Morgan's safety inventions.

---

Write a newspaper article that might have appeared in 1923 when
people first saw a traffic light and didn't realize how important it would turn out to be.  Write a letter back to the newspaper from someone who was better at imagining the future,
explaining why it would be helpful.

---

It is 1918.  Write a letter to the newspaper complaining about
people not using the safety breathing helmet just because it was
invented by a black man.  Explain why you think people are
making a bad choice.

Worksheet:  I AM ONLY ONE PERSON

I am only one person.
What can one person do?


Rosa Parks
Was just one person.
She said one word.
She said it on December 1, 1955.


One person
Said
One word.
She said it on a bus.
She said it to the bus driver.
On the Cleveland Street Bus
In Montgomery.


The bus driver said,
'Stand up, Nigger woman,
And give up your seat
To that white man!'


Rosa Parks,
One person
Said one word.
The word was 'No!'


One woman
Said one word
And a nation
blushed!


One woman
Said one word
And a world talked!


One woman
Said one word
And the Supreme Court
Acted!


One woman
Said one word
And the buses were
Desegregated.


I am only one person.
What can one person do?


They put her in jail,
Because she didn't 'know her
place,'
Because she didn't 'stay in
her place,'
Because she was an 'uppity
Nigger.'


It was a Thursday
When she said
That One Word.


On Monday morning
The buses ran.
The Negroes walked.
Each white man had two seats.
Empty seats.
Symbols of a people,
Moved to walk,
Moved to march
Moved to act
By the sound of
One woman's
One word,
'No!'


One woman
Said one word
And a nation
blushed!


Author unknown

Question Cards:  ROSA PARKS

1.  What did the Ku Klux
    Klan do to black people
    in the South?

2.  How were black people
    and white people treat-
    ed differently in the
    South?

3.  What did Rosa Parks
    learn from her mother?

4.  What is the NAACP and
    what did it do?

5.  What was the Montgomery
    Voters League and what
    did it do?

6.  What did black people
    have to do when they
    rode the bus?

7.  What did Rosa do that
    got her arrested?

8.  What did black people
    decide to do to protest
    the bus company policy?

9.  How were leaflets used in
    organizing people?

10. How were the churches used
    in organizing people?

11. After Rosa was arrested
    what happened to her at
    her job?

12. What was the Montgomery
    Improvement Association
    and what did it do?

13. How long did black people
    have to walk before the
    end of the Montgomery bus
    boycott?

14. What is the Supreme Court
    and what did it decide?

15. Why is Rosa Parks called
    the Mother of the Civil
    Rights Movement?

Task Cards:  PEOPLE AND CHANGE

Pretend you could spend a day with the main person in your book.
Describe that day.  What would you ask?  What answers would you
get?  What would you do together?  How would you feel about it?

---

Suppose the main person came to your school.  What would he or
she like?  Dislike?  Try to change?  Give specific reasons for
your answers, using examples from the person's life.

---

Take one scene from the book.  Write what you think the person
was thinking and feeling.  Pick a scene where the author
doesn't tell this.

---

Write a correspondence between yourself and the person in your
book.  Write at least four letters together.

---

Write the person's name at the top of a page.  Divide the page
in half.  On one half, list at least five obstacles the person
had to overcome.  On the other, list the strengths the person
had and support he or she got.

---

What do you and the person in the book have in common?  List
some words that describe both of you.  List some skills you
both have.  List some problems you both have.  List some differences.  List some ways you would like to be more like that
person.

---

Write a radio advertisement that would take two minutes for the
announcer to read, which tells people why they should read this
book and what it will tell them about change.

Worksheet:   CHICANOS STRIKE AT FARAH   (1)

In May of 1972, 4,000 Chicano factory workers went on
strike.  A strike is when a group of people refuse to work
until certain conditions are met.  These people worked for the
Farah Company, which makes men's and boys' pants.

They had many good reasons for striking:

1.   They made very little money.  They got $70 a week.  In
     1972, the average worker in the U.S. got $150.

2.   The factory didn't want to pay pensions to people when
     they got too old to work and had to retire.  So work-
     ers were fired when they got older.

3.   Almost every worker was Chicano but none of the super-
     visors were Chicano.

4.   Most of the workers were women, but none of the super-
     visors were women.

5.   When a woman left to have a baby, the factory would
     not save her job for her.

6.   If they gave women their jobs back after having babies,
     they were paid much less than before they left.

7.   The factory used a "speed-up" system.  That means that
     they kept wanting people to do more work each day in
     the same time.  The very fastest workers got the most
     money.

There was so much that was bad about working for Farah that
the workers wanted a union.  A union is like a club for people
who work at the same place.  They have meetings about what is
bad for them about working at a place and organize to get that
changed.  Many of the workers at the Farah factory met to talk
about setting up a union.
   Some of the bosses at the factory took pictures at the
meeting.  The next day, some of the workers who had been at the
meeting were fired.  More workers got mad.  They went on strike.
Workers in other Farah factories got angry too and went on
strike.

Here is what Virgie Delgado, one of the workers said:

But I had to think about it before I walked out, because
there are nine kids in my family, and me and my sisters
work at Farah to support our family.  I had to go home and
tell my Mom what I was going to do.  She said to do what I
thought was right.
   The next morning I got my girlfriends together and
said we were going to walk out.  I got all their purses.

We started in the very back and started calling to the
other workers to walk out with us.  My legs were shaking
the whole time.  We were really scared because we didn't
know what was going to happen.  My three sisters joined us.
All these people followed us.  By the time we got to the
front door I looked back and saw 150 people behind me.

The strike lasted for a year and a half.  During that time
the workers didn't get paid any money.  That was very hard on
them.  But the factory was losing a lot of money.  Finally, the
bosses said they would agree to some of the workers' demands.
The workers got better pay and better working conditions.

Most of the strikers were Chicanas, Mexican-American women.
They had not had practice working with a union before.  They
worked hard and became good at organizing.  They went on trips
to speak about the union.  The men had to learn to let the
women do this kind of work.  They got better at understanding
that.  They knew that the work that the women were doing would
help everyone.  Julia Aquilar, who was a worker, said:

We women are much more on the go now than before.  Because
we were women, we were staying behind.  Now, we just bring
out children to our meetings, and we bring them to the
picket lines.  Sometimes they ask, "Are we going to the
picket today, Mommy?"

When all working people work together, they get better
lives.

Worksheet:  CHICANOS STRIKE AT FARAH (2)

1.  List three reasons why the Farah workers went on strike.




2.  Cite an example of sexism.




    Cite an example of racism.




3.  Explain why The Farah Company wanted to run non-union plants.




4.  How did the strike change the role of the Chicanos?

Interview:  LONGSHORE WORKERS

Interviewer:  We are going to meet with some women today who have
    fought to be longshore workers, people who load cargo on boats
    into New York harbor.  Why did you have to fight for these jobs?
Jane Silver:  No women have yet been accepted as dock workers in this
    area.
Interviewer:  Why do women want such strenuous work?
Mary Baffi:  Let me explain.  I'm a divorced mother of three children.
    I've been working for the minimum wage at the telephone company.
    It's almost impossible to provide for my children on a salary of
    $6,000 a year.  I need a better-paying job.
Interviewer:  How much can you make working on the docks?
Mary:  We will be able to make between $18,000 and $22,000 a year.
Interviewer:  Tell us what happened when you went to apply for the
    jobs.
Jackie O'Shaughnessy:  There were six of us who went, three black
    women, one Hispanic woman and two white women.  Three represent-
    atives of the National Organization of Women went with us.  We
    said we wanted to apply for the job of cargo checkers and were
    told there were no applications available.
Debra Brown:  We asked what companies were hiring pier guards and
    warehouse men.  The clerk at the Waterfront Commission told us he
    couldn't give us their names.
Jackie:  When we were leaving a male employee called out, "Hey Al,
    you should have asked one of them for a date."
Debra:  It was after this that we filed discrimination charges and
    began a lawsuit against the Waterfront Commission.
Interviewer:  Why is this effort so important?
Jane:  Many women coming to our Job Development Program are on welfare
    or are below the poverty level.  If women can get these jobs, they
    will be able to get off welfare.
Jackie:  Also we're excited because we're a group of black, white and
    Hispanic women working together.  Once we get working on the docks,
    we'll have to support and help each other, since some men don't
    want us on the docks.  We know we can do it!
Interviewer:  How do you know you women can do heavy physical labor?
    Aren't you too weak?
Debra:  I'd like to remind you of your American history.  During
    World War II when the men were in Europe fighting, women worked in
    the factories making tanks, planes, and battleships.  They worked
    at the blast furnaces.  They rivetted huge metal work.  They loaded
    cargo on and off ships.  Women have proven that they have the
    strength.
Interviewer:  What does all this have to do with affirmative action?
Jane:  Affirmative action means that employers must give women and
    minorities equal chances for jobs.  In many cases, women have been
    kept out of these jobs because of discrimination.
Debra:  We're fighting for affirmative action for longshore workers on
    the docks.  We're fighting together for a better chance.

> Adapted from "Rocking the Docks:  Women
> on the Waterfront" by Constance Pohl.

Worksheet:   SABRA'S LETTER

Dear Ellen,

      Remember how I've been wanting to learn a trade?  I needed
to be able to do my music and also earn a living.  I've found a
solution!  The trade unions in this area needed to have more
women in order to meet federal laws.  They decided they wanted
to train women so that the jobs would be done the way the
unions wanted.
      I got into a training program in Lowell, Massachusetts.
There were thirty women in my group.  Only a few of them were
married.  More than half had children they were supporting.
Most of them had been doing factory work before they got into
this program.  Factory work doesn't pay very well.  These women
thought that construction would be more interesting and it does
pay much more.
      We spent the first three weeks with a chance to decide
what we wanted to learn.  We did carpentry for one week,
masonry for another, and painting for another.  I was very
lucky that we had a woman counselor who did lots
to help us decide which we liked best.  I decided on painting.
Carpentry was much too noisy.  I knew I couldn't stand it.  I
did best being a "bricky" (that's working in masonry) but I
knew that the bad weather wouldn't be good for me and I didn't
want to be on my knees so much.  I know now I made the right
choice.  There are some bad things, like the dust from sanding,
but there's lots that I like about painting.
      We had fifteen weeks of training in our fields.  Then we
became apprentices.  As an apprentice, you earn less than what
a journeyperson earns.  Journeypersons are the regular trained
workers.  In painting we work as apprentices for about
three years;  the brickies and carpenters spend four years as
apprentices.  The first year you earn about half of a journeyperson's salary.  Then every six months or so you go up.  If
you learn fast and you're lucky, your pay goes up faster.
      You've probably heard that apprentices get all the worst
jobs.  That's true.  But still, even at the beginning, there's
more independence than working in a factory.  We all feel like
we have real skills and that makes us feel better about ourselves.  Sometimes it's scary, like when I was walking on a
plank at least forty-five feet up in the air and it slipped.
Sometimes it's very good, like now I'm getting the right wrist
movements and can really do the things I've been watching the
experienced painters do.  There's a real rhythm to taping,
sanding, and painting.  The best part is that I can sing while
I work.  I love how strong my body has become.
      You'd be interested in my friend Jaconda.  She was one of
the few married woman and has two kids.  Her husband would
much rather stay home with the children.  She needed to find a
job that would support all of them.  She became a mason and
now they've all moved to Maine where she's working.

                          Love,
                          Sabra

Worksheet:  JOB-SHARING


       Dave and Noelle Porter, their father, and stepmother have
developed an equal way to share jobs in their household.  They
began their system about six years ago, when Dave was eleven
and Noelle was eight.  As it's been a success, they've continued it ever since.

Interviewer:  Please tell us about your job-sharing plan.
Dave:  The first step in our job-sharing plan is to get every-
       body to sit down together and make a list of all the jobs
       that need to be done each day and another list of the
       jobs needed to be done each week.
Noelle:  Our daily chart has these jobs;  cook, set the table,
       wash dishes, clear the table, and dry dishes.
Dave:  This only applies to dinner.  All of us get our own
       breakfast and wash our dishes.  On weekends, the same
       applies to lunch.
Interviewer:  What about the weekly jobs?
Noelle:  Our weekly chart has these jobs;  clean the kitchen,
       living room, bathroom, and dining room.  Each person
       cleans his or her own room.
Dave:  Once we list the jobs we make two charts.  The weekly
       chart is easy, because each person gets one job.  We
       must each do our jobs on Friday night or Saturday morning.
Noelle:  We post the jobs on the refrigerator.  If we forget
       our job, we can be sure there are people to remind us!!
Interviewer:  How does the daily job chart work?
Noelle:  For the daily jobs, we make a bigger chart with a
       column for each day of the week and rows for each job.
       One person chooses one job and Dave and I fill it in on
       the chart.  Then the next person chooses, and we continue
       until the chart is full.
Dave:  The fact that there are seven days in the week and
       four of us causes a small problem.  One person gets the
       most time-consuming job--cooking--only once a week.
       Usually that person gets the hardest weekly job--like
       cleaning the kitchen.
Interviewer:  How do you feel about this system?
Dave:  Having a definite schedule posted allows me to make my
       plans around jobs I know about.  I don't have to worry
       about someone asking me to do something at the last
       minute.
Noelle:  The adults think the system's terrific!  They don't
       have time to fix complicated meals, but they can often
       count on Dave or me to fix something special.  We've
       become great cooks.
Interviewer:  Do either of you feel angry that you have to do
       these jobs?
Noelle:  Sometimes I go "yuk."  But then I remind myself that
       many people don't like to do jobs and this is certainly
       the fairest way.

Dave: I think the job-sharing system brings a feeling of
    equality and unity to all of us.  It's a more positive
    experience to tell yourself you have to do something than
    to have some "superior" reminding you all the time.  It
    makes me feel a lot freer, because I'm not being bossed
    around.  The adults become people on the same level and
    having the same responsibilities as the kids;  not more,
    not less.
Interviewer:  What are some problems with this system?
Noelle:  One cook is very messy to clean up after!
Dave:  Some unfairness comes because on certain days it's more
    common to have company.  This can usually be evened out
    by rotating the scedule every few months.
Interviewer:  What recommendations do you give to others who
    might want to try a system like this?
Dave:  Do it!  But don't worry about copying ours exactly.
    Find a system that works for your family.
Interviewer:  Do you have any final thoughts or feelings about
    job-sharing?
Noelle:  Yes, kids and adults who come over notice our schedule
    and are very interested in it and eager to try it.
Dave:  I never feel embarrassed about our job-sharing system.
    In fact, I'm pretty proud of my cooking ability which the
    responsibility has encouraged me to develop.
Both:  Try job-sharing!

Task Cards:  AFFIRMATIVE ACTION

1. Write an article for your school newspaper about women becoming longshore workers.

2. Write an editorial for your school newspaper supporting affirmative action and explaining exactly why you think it should be the law.

3. Write a dinner-table conversation in your household with you doing your best to argue for affirmative action.  Use both the interview and the letter for information in support of what you say.  Have your family members say what you think they actually would say.

4. Write a letter to Sabra asking her questions about her job and about women in construction work.

5. Write a list of at least five reasons why working as a painter is a good choice for Sabra.

6. Pick a job that you would like that is not usually associated with your sex.  Write down as many reasons as you can why you would enjoy and do well in that job.  Write down as many reasons as you can why an employer should hire you.

7. Pick an area in your school where most, or all, of the workers are of the same sex, race, or age.  Write down why the school should go out of its way to hire workers of different sexes, ages, or races.  How would that benefit the people hired?  the school?  the community?

8. Pick an area in your community where most, or all, of the workers are of the same sex, race, or age.  Write down why the employer should go out of his way to hire workers of different sexes, ages, or races.  How would that benefit the people hired?  the employer?  the community?

9. Make a list of reasons present employees in a job might be against affirmative action.  Why might they want to keep things the way they are?  Then give some ideas of what could be done to meet those concerns.

Worksheet:  INUIT


        The Eskimos presently living in Alaska migrated there at
least 10,000 and perhaps 28,000 years ago.  Eskimos learned to
get food, clothing, and shelter from their frozen land.
        Eskimos have had to make frequent choices about how to
survive.  For example, with only a small supply of fat (in the
form of blubber from seals and whales) they discovered they
could live longer by eating it than by burning it.
        Eskimos developed a cooperative lifestyle in order to
survive.  It was impossible for an Eskimo to hunt alone, kill
game, and bring it back alone.  Cooperation, in order to win
life from the land, was necessary.  Eskimos realized that they
did not, and could not, control their natural world.  Hard
work was admired, but it was also understood that a certain
amount of what happened was luck.  Those who worked hard and
did not hunt successfully were never looked at as though they
did anything wrong.
        Children learned that they must help in order to receive
help and attention.  Family members were dependent on each
other for comfort and for survival.  There was only free time
for play if all those in the family first worked to see that
their basic needs were met.
        If a man inherited a boat and already had one, he could
choose which to keep for his family.  The other would go to
a family in need of a boat.  Land was never owned by anyone.
        Sharing is a natural way of life for Eskimos.  There is
no need to thank someone for shared food, or to give a gift
in return.  The belief is that the time will come when the
receiver will be able to be the giver and that, in all, it
evens out.  When an Eskimo or group of Eskimos kills an
animal in a hunt, the food and skins are shared with the whole
community.  No hunter would hoard food for his family while
others in the community were hungry.

Worksheet:  CHILDREN'S PLACE

The Children's Place is a special kind of day-care center.
It is a center that New York State has set up for the children
of its workers.

The Children's Place is in the government office buildings
in Albany, New York.  Admitting children from eight weeks to
four years of age allows parents to return to work soon after
their child is born.  Parents work close to the Children's
Place.  They spend lunch hours with their children and can
attend to their children's illnesses.  Mothers can nurse their
infants at the center.

The center has had a positive effect on the government
workplaces.  Supervisors have not minded when parents have to
leave to attend to a sick child.  In fact, morale among parents
and nonparents has improved since the center opened.

Molly Hardy, the director of the Children's Place, said,
"Workers are also parents and New York State has shown they
understood this with the opening of the center."

Interview Questions

1.  How do you feel about the Children's Place?

2.  Would you like to have such a day-care center at your place
    of work?  Why or why not?

Worksheet:  ÅSMUND AND KIRSTEN'S LETTER

Kjære Venner,

    That means "Dear Friends" in our language.  We are glad you
want to know more about our country.  We hope you will want to
write back and tell us about your country.  We go to school in
Bergen, Norway's third-biggest city.  It is on the Atlantic
coast.

    Our father is a doctor and our mother is a teacher.  In
Norway it is not expensive to get an education.  We understand
that that is different in your country.  Both our parents went
to college and graduate school without paying any money.  In
fact, the government gave them money to live on while they were
going to school.  That is true for all Norwegians, it doesn't
matter how much money your family earns.  After they finish all
their training, people are expected to do service to pay back
our country.  This is especially true of doctors.  That is how
our country gets good medical care even way out in the country,
on islands far away from the coast, or way up north far away
from anything.

    Since all doctors do this service after getting trained,
we can have good medical care all over.  Sometimes, though,
sick people need to come into cities to specialists.  When they
have to do that, the government pays all their transportation.
Our government really does believe that all our citizens should
have good medical care and that all our doctors should help
provide it.  We believe that anyone who is interested enough
and smart enough to be a doctor should get to be one, not just
those from families with money.

    When our family is on vacation, we go cross-country ski-
ing to our mountain cabin.  Some of the kids we know there come
from doctor's families, but others come from families where
their fathers work in the post office, or their mothers work in
stores.

    Tell us about medical care in your country.  We look for-
ward to hearing from you.

                          Beste hilsen,
                          Kirsten and Åsmund

Worksheet:  GRAY PANTHERS  (1)

News Item:
     The motto of the Gray Panthers is "Age and Youth in
Action."  The main purpose of the Gray Panthers is to fight for
the rights of the <u>elderly</u>, but the Gray Panthers also struggle
for a better life for everyone.

---

News Item:
     Gray Panthers' leader Maggie Kuhn gave her support yester-
day to forces fighting to stop the <u>demolition</u> of the Poletown
area of Detroit by General Motors Corporation.  The Corporation
wants the site for a new Cadillac plant.
     Ms. Kuhn, a national <u>advocate</u> of the rights for the
elderly, said she believes the plant can be built without
wiping out the neighborhood.
     "People here are not receiving the kind of <u>consideration</u>
from General Motors and government <u>officials</u> that <u>civic</u>
<u>responsibility</u> in a democracy needs," she told the audience.
                              <u>Detroit News</u>, March 9, 1981

---

News Item:
     Naomi Howard, a Gray Panther in Arizona, <u>testified</u> at a
public meeting to protest constantly rising electric rates in
that state.
     It's as if the Valley of the Sun has had an <u>epidemic</u> of
rate increases.  Low-income people are at rock-bottom now.  If
they have to pay more for utilities, that means they don't eat,
they don't get their medicine, or they change their housing
situation."

---

News Item:
     In Austin, Texas, Gray Panthers have supported <u>alternative</u>
housing and day-care for the elderly.
     In the "cooperative living center," a dozen older people
live in a group of apartments with a recreation room in common
and someone on call.
     There are three adult day-care centers in Austin with fees
on a <u>sliding</u> <u>scale</u>.  These centers are used by people who live
with a family but can't stay alone during the day.

---

News Item:
     Maggie Kuhn says, "We older Gray Panthers can raise our
voices because we don't have much to lose.  That is the beauty
of older activists.  We have the time to spend all day in
legislative meetings.
                              <u>Houston Chronicle</u>, March 9, 1981

Worksheet:  GRAY PANTHERS  (2)

## Jobs

The right to a job must become the most basic of civil
rights.  Otherwise generations will be pitted against each
other for paid employment.

## Service to America

In our vision there will be a United States Unarmed
Services (USUS) which will recruit people of all ages to
provide basic health care and to work on conservation projects.
The USUS will be strong on equality of the sexes and opposed
to any age bias.

## Politics

Political parties will be replaced by regional councils.
The rise of neighborhood block organizations will make
officials far more sensitive to local citizens.

## Health Care

Health care will be turned on its head, with preventive
care and health education becoming top priorities.  The
"healthy block" will become the cornerstone of neighborhood
organization.  People will help each other with basic care for
minor sickness and injuries.  Health care, like employment,
must be considered a basic human right.

## Teaching

Older people, often discarded now, will become teachers
in the Elder Training Program.  Elders can settle fights, be
counselors, advocates, and historians, telling about the past
and helping with the management of children.

## Family

The idea of family will grow to include two or more
persons who share resources, goals, and values over time.
Intergenerational cooperatives will develop, inhabited by
families.

From Maggie Kuhn and Tish Sommers, Gray Panther Network,
January/February, 1981.

# 10 WE CAN MAKE CHANGES

"We Can Make Changes" is an exciting chapter. The activities here provide chances for students to act to make a difference.

These lessons are very conducive to group projects and group action. Such collaborative efforts reinforce the idea that people working together can create changes. When students put their new-found awareness into constructive action, a sense of personal power and self-confidence develops. Emphasize to students that small changes *are* important, and that they can make a difference by taking action. Encourage cooperation, creativity, and perseverance when using these lessons.

The initial activities help students build the skills and confidence to foster change most effectively. In the section, "Making Changes at School," students not only create new products and experiences, but share their materials, skills, and new knowledge with other students. In the following two sections, students have a variety of opportunities to make books, packaging, and so on more fair and equal. Through skits, bulletin boards, and new materials, these improvements are shared with others. Finally, students reach out to make an impact on friends, family, and community.

Support students in finding as many ways as possible to share the results of the lessons in this chapter. Visit other classes, make displays for your school and community, and write articles for the school and local newspapers. Change is contagious!

---

> If we are honest with ourselves we will admit that our whole structure of relationships is rattling and creaking, as people of all types challenge its usefulness to humanity. The demand for a more humane structure and more humane values echoes across the land.
>
> *Human and Anti-Human Values In Children's Books, C.I.B.C., pp. 3–4.*

---

## SECTION A   GAINING CONFIDENCE AND SKILLS FOR CHANGE

### Say It So They'll Hear It _____ SS, LA, C

**OBJECTIVES**   To help students develop strategies for sharing their learning about stereotypes and the "isms" in a way that others will hear rather than reject.
To help students develop general skills for sharing opinions, convictions, and information in a positive way.

Copies of Worksheet: Strategies for Confronting Stereotypes and "Isms," p. 244; paper and pencils; video-tape equipment, if available.

Discuss with students what they have learned about stereotypes and discrimination due to sex, class, race, and age. Discuss how, when we make discoveries, we often want to share our excitement with others. Explain that one of the purposes of this unit is to encourage this, since social change is brought about when we get others thinking about promoting equality. Therefore it is important to develop positive strategies for sharing what we have learned. Emphasize that though it is not our fault that we have been taught stereotypes and the "isms," it is our responsibility to unlearn some of that—which is hard and takes practice.

Tell students that although we sometimes feel frightened about correcting stereotypes and "isms," with practice it becomes easier. The role-plays are meant to provide that practice!

STEP ONE. The class brainstorms the sorts of situations where they could confront someone who has just said or done something racist, classist, ageist, or sexist. Make a list on the board. If you need to get them going, give examples from your school or community. The class picks one example. Follow the guidelines on role-playing (p. 56) and act out the scene. Debrief carefully.

In the discussion of the situation, encourage students to discuss alternative ways of communicating. With students, make up a list of Communication Guidelines for such situations. Do and discuss several situations as a class.

## EXAMPLES OF COMMUNICATION GUIDELINES

1. Since you want people to listen to you, don't say anything in a way that attacks or puts them down.
2. Share your learning and opinions in a way that makes someone else feel glad to be learning something new.
3. Work with the other person to develop ideas of very practical ways to change.
4. Add new ideas, rather than just criticize what's there.

STEP TWO. Hand out the Worksheet. Thoroughly discuss the four types of strategies listed. Don't use the role-plays yet, but give concrete examples of each strategy, using other examples.

Divide the class into four groups, assign each group a situation from the Worksheet, and have students role-play it in front of the class. Debrief carefully. After all the situations have been tried, groups meet separately. They think of several more situations in which that particular strategy could have been followed. For each they should list what kind of reaction might have occurred.

Get together again as a class. Look at the first situation. How did students feel about the original role-play? Did the solution "work"? Was the father more open minded? Discuss more effective use of both the Communication Guidelines and the particular strategy being tried. Go on and do the same for the other situations. Remember that there is often more than one effective way to use a strategy and that a style that might work well for one student mightn't work at all for someone else.

1. Why is it hard for people to be "corrected"? Why is it hard for you to have others "correct" you?
2. What people or kinds of people do you find it easier to confront in the situations? Why? Which are harder? Why?
3. Now that you've done the role-plays, do you have some more helpful suggestions? How does role-playing help you find these? List them with our initial Guidelines.
4. In what ways is group action easier and more effective than individual?
5. In which type of situation is which strategy most effective? Why?
6. Which strategy are you most comfortable with? Why?

## From Fear to Power

**OBJECTIVES**
To have students examine internal blocks to acting for change.
To learn a strategy for feeling more confidence and power in order to stand up for one's feelings and beliefs.
To experience peer support for speaking up for equality.

**MATERIALS**
Copies of Worksheet: Recess Fantasy, p. 245; copies of Power Statement Contract, p. 246.

**IMPLEMENTATION**
Explain to students they will be practicing a way to feel confident in challenging stereotypes and "isms." It is best to do "Say It So They'll Hear It," p. 219, first.

Tell students they will be participating in a fantasy activity. Explain that you will begin a story and they should imagine it in their minds. You will stop the story and they should finish it in their own imaginations. Answer any questions about what is going to happen.

Tell students to get in a relaxed position. Some may want to lie on the floor. Tell them not to answer the questions aloud. Direct the fantasy as follows:

Close your eyes and try to relax as much as possible. [Wait ten seconds.] Get the thoughts of the day out of your mind. Concentrate on your breathing. Now I want you to imagine that you and a group of your friends are on their way out to recess. Who's with you? [Wait five seconds.] How are you feeling? Picture this in your mind. [Wait ten seconds.] Someone in the group mentions black people. Another person says, "I can't stand black people, they rot." [Substitute Puerto Ricans, kids from X neighborhood, and so forth—whatever is most relevant to your group of students.] Take as much time as you need to finish the fantasy in your mind. What happens next? [Wait one minute or more.] When you have finished your fantasy, slowly open your eyes.

Each student then fills out the Worksheet. With partners, they read or tell their fantasy and share Worksheet responses. Then come together for discussion.

**DISCUSSION**
1. First talk about each of the questions on the Worksheet.
2. Sometimes when we are trying to decide what to do there are two different voices in our heads having a conversation. This is called an "internal dialogue." For example, if you just earned a quarter, your internal dialogue might go like this:

   Voice-in-your-head #1: Oh great, I'll buy a candy bar!
   Voice-in-your-head #2: Wait, save the quarter and you can get something you really need!
   Voice #1: I'm hungry now.
   Voice #2: If I buy candy Mom will tell me I wasted my money and I'll get cavities on top of it all.

   Think back to your fantasy. What was your internal dialogue when you were trying to decide what to do in response to the remark of your friend? Who can tell us about that?
3. When we have to make a decision to stand up for our beliefs one of our voices is sometimes a scared voice that gives us "Fear Messages." Let's make a list on the board of the "Fear Messages" we sometimes give ourselves. For example: "If I say something my friends won't like me anymore." "What X said isn't right, but I'm afraid my words will get mixed up." "I should speak up, but oh well, it won't make a difference anyway."

4. Tell the students that, instead of "Fear Messages," they can give themselves "Power Statements." These are voices that give you power and remind you how important it is to stand up for what's fair. Make a list of "Power Statements" on the board. For example: "It's important to speak up for what's fair no matter what others think." "I *can* speak clearly and can get people to stop and think." "I can make a difference!"

5. What can *we* gain by speaking up for equality?

Finally, students form support pairs. They fill out a Power Statement Contract with each other and sign it. (Remind students to use the Communication Guidelines. Feeling powerful is only part of being effective.) Have a few students share their Power Statement Contracts with the class. Give them encouragement. Set a date when they'll report back to their partners and the class.

"We can *make* it fair !!!/\ "

---

In Germany they first came for the Communists and I didn't speak up because I wasn't a Communist. Then they came for the Jews and I didn't speak up because I wasn't a Jew. Then they came for the trade unionists and I didn't speak up because I wasn't a trade unionist. Then they came for the Catholics and I didn't speak up because I was a Protestant. Then they came for me and no one was left to speak up.

Martin Niemoller, "In Unity," University Fellowship of Metropolitan Community Churches, August/September 1978.

---

## You Have To Make Decisions ———————————— LA, R

**OBJECTIVES**
To help students realize that frequently they are confronted with moral dilemmas concerning issues of equality.

To encourage students to look at these dilemmas in terms of what they have learned and to make conscious decisions which promote equality.

**MATERIALS**
Copies of Worksheet: Rebekah's Journal, continued, p. 247–48; paper for additional entries; pencils.

**IMPLEMENTATION**
This follows the lesson, "A Girl on Our Team," p. 68. Do that one first. Hand out copies of the Worksheet. Students staple on additional sheets to create a notebook.

Discuss with students their sense of Rebekah from the lesson in the earlier chapter. Then have each student write journal entries as follow-ups to each of Rebekah's entries. (Tell them Rebekah has been learning about sexism, racism, class bias, and age discrimination in school. She is trying to put what she learned into practice in her life.) Next, get together in small groups. Students share what they wrote and get ideas from each other.

Re-divide into heterogenous groups of three to five students. Each group picks one original entry (be sure that each original entry is picked at least once) and thinks of alternative ways of acting in the situation described—as many ways as possible. Remind them they, like Rebekah, are trying to put what they've learned about equality into practice in their lives. They should think of the possible results of their actions and decide which of their options seems most sensible and fair. Students can either share their favorite ideas or act them out for the whole class.

**DISCUSSION**
1. When you were writing journal entries, what criteria did you use for deciding what to do or say? What values were most important to you? What worried you most?

2. Which situations were easy for you? In what ways? Which situations were harder? Why?

3. What did you think others—your friends, family, or adults—could do to help you in these situations? How could you ask for that help?
4. What could you do to help others in each situation? How could you offer that help?
5. These situations involve acting or not acting on values that support equality. Think of some similar situations you find at school, in your community, or at home. List them. What can you do in each case?
6. Tell about a time when you acted on values that supported equality? How did you feel? What did you learn?

---

I sit on a man's back, choking him and making him carry me, and yet assure myself and others that I am very sorry for him and wish to lighten his load by all possible means—except by getting off his back.

Tolstoy, *Philosophical Writings*

---

## SECTION B  MAKING CHANGES AT SCHOOL

### Calendars _____ M, SS, LA, A

**OBJECTIVES**    To encourage a multi-cultural appreciation of history and celebrations.
To have students share their learning with others.

**MATERIALS**    Large sheets of good-quality paper; rulers and yardsticks; pencils, paint or markers; calendars from a diverse group of school systems; library books with information about holidays in various cultures.

**IMPLEMENTATION**    Divide students into small groups. Each group takes one or several calendars collected from other school systems. Give each group at least one library book about holidays of other cultures. Each group lists several holidays it would like to add to the school calendar. These should acknowledge the contributions of other peoples or cultures to our history or customs. Examples are the winter solstice or International Women's Day. If students need more ideas, they can use biographies of women and people of color and pick a few people they wish to honor. For each holiday, the group writes a few clear sentences of explanation.

HERE ARE A FEW HOLIDAYS TO GET YOU GOING

Martin Luther King's birthday—January 15.
Yuan Tan, Chinese New Year—first day in the first month in the lunar calendar, between January 21 and February 19.
Maple Festival—an Iroquois celebration with songs and dances—early spring.
Lei Day—a Hawaiian holiday showing friendliness and telling old tales—May 1.
International Women's Day—commemorating women's worldwide struggle for justice—March 8.
Tet-Trung-thu—a Vietnamese holiday in honor of the moon, festivals with lanterns; fifth day of the eighth month in the lunar calendar—September or October.
Kwanza—an ancient African feast in honor of the bringing in of the first crops—begins December 26.

Then the class as a whole makes a combined calendar, using some or all of the suggested new holidays. Or, each group makes up its own calendar. Do each month neatly on large paper with the new holidays marked with pictures and names.

You might hang one large monthly calendar in a central place in the school, or make copies of the calendars and distribute to other classrooms and school systems.

**DISCUSSION**

1. How easy or hard was it to find calendars with diverse holidays? Why might this be the case?
2. How hard was it to come to a consensus on what holidays you wanted to add? Why?
3. Did you find holidays from your sources which you would consider racist, sexist, classist or ageist which you would choose not to include in your new calendar? Which ones?
4. Were there some types of holidays you think should exist, in support of a more egalitarian world, that you didn't find? What are they? Do you wish to add them to your calendar?

**GOING FURTHER**

Make enough copies of the calendar so students can take them home. Have them share them with parents and get reactions.

Celebrate at least one of these new holidays in your classroom and perhaps elsewhere in your school. Can students celebrate it at home?

Have students write up more detailed reports on some of the holidays, including suggestions for appropriate activities and reasons for celebration. Share these with others.

---

KWANZA

Kwanza is a holiday based on traditional African harvest festivals. Its American form was started in California in 1966. In Swahili, Kwanza means "first" or, in this case "first fruits." Kwanza starts on December 26, stressing its first principle of "unity." The six subsequent days emphasize the following values: "self-determination," "collective work and responsibility," "cooperative economics," "creativity," "purpose," "faith."

There are some items, preferably homemade, which are part of the Kwanza celebration. A woven straw mat represents tradition as a foundation for everything else. A seven-place candleholder, called the "kinara," represents the original stalk from which black people came. The candles stand for the seven principles of Kwanza. Corn symbolizes the children of the house. The bowl of "zawadi" or gifts symbolize the fruits of labor. These gifts stay out on the mat throughout Kwanza and are opened on the last day.

Each day the family lights a new candle and talks about the principle for the day. On the last day, there is a feast using the foods which have traditionally been part of Afro-American and southern New Year's meals.

---

YOU'RE INVITED FOR LUNCH

Here's an idea for adding a multi-cultural flavor to your school.

Your students can prepare a multi-ethnic luncheon for their parents, younger siblings, and other teachers. Look in the bibliography for multi-ethnic cookbooks. Try to get parents to help you with the cooking. Students work cooperatively in small groups to cook the foods. Use this as an opportunity to appreciate the traditions of different ethnic foods. Recipes can be put on dittoes, illustrated and collated into a class cookbook.

---

## Keep Your Rights*
SS, M, LA

**OBJECTIVES**

To give students information about the Title IX law.
To help students examine their school for compliance with Title IX.
To give students strategies to use this law to bring about a non-sexist atmosphere in their school.

**MATERIALS**

Copies of Worksheet: Title IX, p. 249; one copy of each Situation Card, p. 250; paper and pencils.

---

*Material for this lesson was adapted from *A Student Guide to Title IX*, by Myra Sadker. This is an excellent resource; we recommend that you order it.

**IMPLEMENTATION** STEP ONE:   Post a large copy of these Title IX regulations on poster board:

1. School system must have a policy saying it does not discriminate on basis of sex. This must be printed on school mailings and in the newspaper.
2. School system must have a Title IX coordinator to see that it follows the regulations.
3. School system must have a method for people to file complaints and get answers to those.
4. School system must do a self-evaluation about sex discrimination and make necessary changes.
5. If school systems ask for money from the federal government, they must fill out a form saying that they don't discriminate on basis of sex.

Discuss this with the class. Make sure they understand the vocabulary and the concepts.

Divide students into groups of three. Hand out Worksheets and go over them with the groups. Answer questions. Use examples to clarify.

Hand out one Situation Card to each group. Instruct each group to read its card and decide if any Title IX regulations have been violated. Each group prepares a short presentation for the class, explaining the situation and what regulations either have or haven't been followed. Correct answers are on p. 226.

STEP TWO:   The next day, ask each group to think of a way that your school system has been active in support of these regulations. Working in groups, write letters of praise to the people responsible. For example, if a guidance counselor is good about encouraging boys to take home economics, she gets a praise letter. Or if a physical education teacher actively supports girls' participation on the intramural basketball team, he gets a praise letter.

Then have groups think of a way that the school is not actively supporting these regulations. Have them work out a strategy for taking action. They could plan to write letters, make phone calls, make visits, enlist their parents' support, and so on. If groups have trouble, give them help or brainstorm as a class.

Make a classroom poster of guidelines to follow in making complaints. The class can generate these or you can present them with the following:

1. Remember that counselors, teachers, and administrators may be well-meaning but unaware of their responsibilities, or unaware that they are behaving in a discriminatory way.

2. Call this behavior to the adult's attention in a way that is polite and shows you are knowledgeable. Be positive and helpful.

*If that doesn't work:*

3. Go to the Title IX coordinator for the district. Share your concerns, with detailed information, and ask for changes.

*If that doesn't work:*

4. Get help from your parents and other students and other adults. File a complaint, using the correct procedure.

*If that doesn't work:*

5. File a complaint with: Director, Office for Civil Rights, Department of Health, Education, Welfare, 330 Independence Avenue, S.W., Washington, D.C. 20201. Include your name, person(s) who has been discriminated against, school district name, date, and explanation of what happened.

Finally, discuss the whole lesson with the class.

**DISCUSSION**
1. Did you know about this regulation before doing the lesson? Why or why not?
2. What did you discover about our school district?
3. Was it easier to think of positive situations or negative ones?
4. What reactions did you get to your compliment letters? to your concerns?
5. In what ways were people willing to help bring about change for sexual equality? In what ways were they not?

ANSWERS TO TITLE IX SITUATION CARDS:

1.  Maggie and Gioia—violated.
2.  Rose—not violated.
3.  Gregg—violated.
4.  Dan—violated.
5.  Ryan and Gilah—violated.
6.  Gurtney—not violated.
7.  Ming—not violated.

## Relearning About Native Americans _____ SS

**OBJECTIVES**

To give students some correct information about Native Americans.

To help students learn to look critically at what they are taught about Native Americans, encourage them to reject that which is discriminatory, and seek out correct information.

**MATERIALS**

Guidelines chart on large oaktag; books (see Bibliography).

**IMPLEMENTATION**

Some of the ideas in this activity, and the guidelines listed below come from *Unlearning "Indian" Stereotypes*, an excellent resource we highly recommend. It is advised that teachers read that booklet before teaching this lesson.

**Part One: Correcting Stereotypes**

Make an oaktag chart for "Guidelines on Native Americans" and post it.

---

GUIDELINES ON NATIVE AMERICANS

1. Don't give the idea that all Native American nations live or lived in the same manner, with the same housing, dress, customs.
2. Don't say "Mohawk Indians" which is repetitive (like "French Europeans"). Just "Mohawks" or "Navajos" is enough.
3. If talking about customs of the Cheyennes or Seneca or any specific people, say that, rather than Native Americans in general.
4. Do not use words like squaw, brave, papoose. Use woman, man, child.
5. Do not use words which describe Native Americans in ways which are frightening.
6. Do not use sentences such as "Acting like a bunch of wild Indians," "Indian giver," "Sitting Indian style," "Walking Indian file."
7. Don't use an alphabet chart with "I is for Indian," if your other letters use fruits, or objects for examples.
8. Don't talk about Native Americans only in the past—they are very much a part of today's world.
9. Don't let TV stereotypes go unchallenged.
10. Don't talk about "us" and "them."

---

Discuss this chart with the class. Look for examples in each area. Post the pictures and stories your class did for "From Feathers to Facts," p. 91. Look at these and discuss where stereotypes come from, why they're bad, and what we can do to rid ourselves of them. Ask students who have never met a Native American where they got their ideas.

Many people think of Native Americans as being of all one culture and nation. Help children to see this error by comparing to Europeans. Have them think of a characteristic of a European nation—for example, tulips in Holland. Would they think of all countries of Europe as having tulips growing all around? Now compare to Native Americans. Tipis were a form of housing on the plains but not in other areas of the country. Not all Native Americans wore feathered headdresses. Drawing a headdress on all Indians is analogous to drawing yarmulkes on all white people. Some Omahas or Winnebagos, for example, would correctly be pictured with headdresses for ceremonies, but this is not correct for all nations of Native Americans, nor for daily wear for any. Encourage students to correct friends and relatives about these stereotypes.

**Part Two:**
**Role-Plays**

Here are a few ideas for role-plays and dramatization. Develop more with your students.

ADAM NORWALL.   Adam Norwall, an Ojibway dressed in Native clothing, traveled by jet to Italy in 1973. When he got off the plane he said "In the name of the Indian people, I claim the right of discovery and take possession of this land." He said that since Columbus claimed to have discovered America when Indians were here, he could claim Italy.

Processing questions can include the following: How did you feel as Italian people? How did Adam Norwall feel? How might Native Americans have felt when Columbus "discovered" America? What new ideas do you have about Native Americans because of this role-play?

THE SETTLERS ARE LANDING.*   The Native American stands in the classroom, which represents her land. (If possible, invite a Native American to play the role.) The students play the roles of white settlers. Each time they come from the hall (ocean) into the room (land), they represent another boat of settlers. When they arrive, they ask the Native American for some land. She agrees and gives up a section of the room. They keep going out and coming in until the Native American is standing in a corner of the classroom.

Discuss with children, "Should the Native American give up her space to these new people?" Have children take roles, some as settlers and some Native Americans.

Subsequent discussion questions include the following: How fair was the taking of Native lands? What could have been done differently? Why did Native American people eventually fight the settlers? What are the current demands for Native American land rights?

---

"Indian" is so frequently found under the letter "I" that one wonders if there is a lack of other words beginning with that letter. No other group is similarly treated: the "I—Indian" is never followed by a "J—Jew" or a "P—Puerto Rican." Nor is it accompanied by an "I—Italian," even though the "I" in Indian and the "I" in Italian have the same sound. Rather, the "I—Indian" coexists with objects—Igloos, Islands, Ink, etc.

*From Unlearning "Indian" Stereotypes.*

---

**Part Three:**
**Research and Reading**

There are some good books on Native Americans for children. (See the Bibliography.) Assign students research on topics that will correct stereotypes about Native Americans, or have them read fiction that portrays Native peoples accurately and with dignity.

---

RECOMMENDED BOOKS: A BEGINNING

For students:
   *The People Shall Continue*, by Simon Ortiz
   *I Am the Fire of Time: Voices of Native American Women*, by Jane Katz
   *The Mishomis Book: Voice of the Ojibway*, by Edward Benton-Benai
   *Tonweya and the Eagles*, by Rosebud Yellow Robe

For teachers:
   *Bury My Heart at Wounded Knee*, by Dee Brown
   *The Ways of My Grandmother*, by Beverly Hungry Wolf

---

*This role-play was developed by Jane Califf and is described in depth in *Unlearning Indian Stereotypes*.

GOING FURTHER — Have students put on a role-play for another class; make a bulletin board—Correcting Stereotypes about Native Americans—for the school; or make a book display on fair and unfair portrayals of Native Americans for the PTA book fair.

## Making Learning Cooperative_____ SS, A

**OBJECTIVES**
To see how the projects given to young children affect cooperation.
To learn how cooperation among young children was encouraged in the People's Republic of China.
To have students make cooperative learning materials for younger students.

**MATERIALS**
Copies of Worksheet: To Serve the People, p. 255, one per group; materials to make cooperative items.

**IMPLEMENTATION**
Introduce the lesson by telling students that one way to encourage cooperation, instead of competition, is by providing children with materials and projects that have them work together.

Divide students into groups. Tell them they will read how such cooperation was encouraged in another country. Distribute Worksheets. After reading the Worksheet, each group answers the questions at the bottom. Join together as a class for discussion.

**DISCUSSION**
1. How do you feel about the ways the Chinese encouraged cooperation among young children?

2. How would these cooperative experiences affect children as they grow up?

3. What cooperative projects have you done? What cooperative toys have you used? How did you feel about them?

Next have groups report on their ideas for cooperative toys and materials the class could make. Discuss the practicality and creativity of the ideas. Choose one or several to make.

When the materials or toys are completed, have children bring them to a day-care center, kindergarten, or younger class. They explain them to, and use them with, young children. You can donate them to that center or class.

Discuss with students children's responses to the materials. Encourage students to write an article for the local newspaper about this cooperative project.

---

Are you interested in reading more about childcare and education in China? If so, see *Women and Childcare in China* by Ruth Sidel.

---

A society that is organized so that the individual can get ahead (accumulate wealth or power) only at the expense of the group is more likely, according to Ruth Benedict, to produce aggression. "Nonaggression occurs," she said, "not because people are unselfish and put social obligations above personal desires, but when social arrangements make the two identical." She called this quality of combining the efforts of the individual to advance the interests of the group synergy, a word which means that the combined action of a number of things produces results greater than the sum of the separate actions.

From *Developing Effective Classroom Groups*, by Gene Stanford

**OBJECTIVES** To help students see how an egalitarian vocabulary can help them think in a more open-minded way.

To help students develop vocabularies which do not have racist or sexist connotations.

To encourage students to share their learning.

**MATERIALS** Paper and pencils; dictionaries; ditto masters; student work saved from the lesson "Black Lies and White Lies," p. 163.

**IMPLEMENTATION** First, look back at the earlier lesson. Post the lists the students made for "black" and "white" phrases. Working as a whole class, brainstorm on alternative words or phrases for any of those which held positive connotations for white and negative connotations for black. For example, "white lies"—to "small or unimportant lies," "black as night"—"dark as night." If students seem to be getting the idea, have them work in small groups to continue.

In the same groups, students list words which have sexist connotations. These can be of two types—words like "mail man" or "fireman," which use sex-related words to describe all people, and words like "manmade," "manhandle." Allow about ten minutes.

Now the group thinks of one or more alternative words to the sexist one. Get together as a class and share lists. If groups came up with sexist words but not alternatives, others in the class can help them. Put all the original words and phrases and all the new alternatives on dittos.

Make a cover for your newly created class dictionary. Make a copy for each student, and others to distribute to other classes in the building. If you have a school newspaper, write a synopsis of this exercise for it. Each week your class can pick one racist or sexist word and its alternative and post both on a central bulletin board.

**DISCUSSION** 1. What harm does it cause to use words with racist or sexist connotations?

2. How does it help to change these words? How does it change our thinking?

3. For which words was it difficult to think of alternatives? Do you have any ideas why? Why were some words easier?

4. What can you do as an individual, and what can we do as a class, to encourage use of the more egalitarian words?

---

ALTERNATIVES IN LANGUAGE

| | |
|---|---|
| man | person, human being, people, women and men |
| "it's not all black and white" | "it's not one extreme or the other" |
| forefathers or fathers | precursors, ancestors, forebears |
| black deeds | evil deeds |
| brotherhood | unity, community |
| white-wash | cover-up |
| mankind | human kind |
| women's lib | women's liberation, feminist movement |

---

White is sending black men to kill yellow men to protect the land white men stole from the red man.

Preston Wilcox, *White Is*, 1970.

## SECTION C  CHANGING OUR TEXTS AND BOOKS

### Textbook Alert R, LA

**OBJECTIVE**

To give students an opportunity to carry out small action projects concerning biased textbooks.

**MATERIALS**

Paper and pencils; ditto masters; textbooks analyzed in Chapter 7.

**IMPLEMENTATION**

Remind students of their work analyzing textbooks in "Our Textbooks: Are They Fair?" p. 147. Tell students they will have a chance to take action to begin to alert people to bias in their textbooks, and to change this. There are three possible action projects. Either divide into three groups and have one group work on each, or decide on one activity for the whole class.

1. WARNING LABELS.  Just as cigarettes have a warning label, "This product is dangerous to your health," so too textbooks can have a label in the front jacket, "This book can be dangerous to equal education because . . ." Make dittos with that statement on top. For each text, students complete the label—for example, "Because women scientists are not shown," "Because Native American culture isn't represented fairly." Once students have agreed upon labels for each text, either tape them in the text or put them on a ditto for texts of multiple copies. Give labels to other classes using the same texts.

2. EQUALITY TEXTBOOK LIST.  Students go over the texts they've analyzed and make a list of those texts in each subject area that either aren't biased or are least biased. Students make an Equality Textbook List of such books and distribute to other teachers in the district.

3. LETTERS TO PUBLISHERS.  Students write to publishers of biased texts, explaining and asking for changes. Students write praise letters to publishers of textbooks that promote equality.

---

**FOURTH-GRADERS MAKE BIG CHANGES!**

Several years ago a fourth-grade class in Maryland did a project that brought changes to many other fourth-grade classes throughout their district. Here's what they did:

The class learned to analyze textbooks to discover examples of racism and sexism. Some students got so good at it that they took on a special project. They gathered all the fourth-grade textbooks used in the whole district and examined them for examples of race and sex bias. These students wrote a report about what they found and made copies of it. They distributed the report to all the other fourth-grade classes in the school district. Other teachers and students then learned to pinpoint materials that didn't portray women and minorities equally. That's a big change, and fourth-graders take the credit!

---

### Finding Better Books R, LA

**OBJECTIVE**

To give students experience and tools for choosing books which promote equality.

**MATERIALS**

Use of library; paper and pencils; copies of Worksheet: Review on Books, 1 or 2, pp. 159–60, enough for at least four per student.

**IMPLEMENTATION**  This lesson is a follow-up of "Read Me a Story" p. 156, which should be done first. Tell students that since they have learned to analyze books for equality, they now will try to find books that promote equality, and share that information with others. Hand out a Worksheet to each student, and have extras available.

If students have access to a library, they go in pairs or small groups and pick what they think might be books that promote equality to bring back to the classroom. Otherwise collect books yourself. (See Bibliography.) Still in pairs or groups, they check each book according to the criteria and fill out Worksheets. If students did "Read Me a Story" with their parents, encourage them to do this lesson with them as well.

Display the books, together with the Worksheets, around your classroom. Have students bring other books that promote equality to class to share. If you do book orders from paperback companies, ask students to review the books that are offered by these criteria.

As a class prepare a list of egalitarian books. Give copies to your school librarian, children's librarian at the public library, other teachers or parents. Involve parents actively in this lesson if they participated in "Read Me a Story."

**DISCUSSION**  1. How hard was it to find books which promote equality? Did you have to look through many to find some which meet these standards? Did you have any method for picking?
2. Did you find some books which actively fight stereotypes? Were they written by the same authors? Published by the same publishers?
3. Were certain stereotypes countered better than others? Did your books generally do better in countering sexism? racism? ageism? classism?
4. Were there any "isms" for which you couldn't find books which were fair? If so, why do you think that is?

---

Good sources of books that promote equality are the following:

Feminist Press, Box 334, Old Westbury, N.Y., 11568
New Seed Press, 1665 Euclid Avenue, Berkeley, CA, 94709
Lolipop Power, Box 1171, Chapel Hill, N.C., 27514
Asian American Bilingual Center, 1414 Walnut St., Berkeley, CA, 94709

---

## . . . And We Wrote Them Ourselves

R, LA, A

**OBJECTIVES**  To challenge students to create stories which actively promote equality.
To give students the opportunity to share their learning with others in a way that is creative, enjoyable and constructive.

**MATERIALS**  Copies of Worksheets: Book-Writing Mechanics, p. 251, and Book-Writing—Criteria for Equality, p. 252; unlined paper, pencils, pens, markers, crayons, dental floss, large needles, cardboard, fabric, wallpaper samples, glues, scissors and papercutter; books on book-binding.

**IMPLEMENTATION**  Review "Read Me a Story," p. 156. If you haven't done those activities with the children, take time to do them now.

Students can do this activity independently, in pairs, or in small groups. Allow freedom of choice. Each student or group of students writes an anti-racist, anti-sexist, anti-classist, anti-ageist, or cooperative story for younger children. Review the Worksheet: Criteria for Equality before students begin working. If starting from scratch is too difficult, the students can take a typical stereotypical fairytale, like Cinderella, and rewrite it according to the criteria. This can be fun as well as educational. Or

provide a story for them to change. For example, students could rewrite a story about a person who "works his way up on his own" so that it becomes a story in which that person works with others to change conditions that limit many people.

After students have written their rough drafts they proofread for errors in mechanics and structure. Use the Worksheet: Book-Writing—Mechanics." They then exchange stories and Worksheets and proofread each other's stories for these errors.

Students then take their own stories back and proofread them for stereotyping. Use Worksheet: Book-Writing—Criteria for Equality. Again they trade stories and Worksheets and proofread each other's. Collect drafts and check for errors and stereotyping. Then return to students, to copy over if needed.

Divide students into groups of eight to twelve. Have each group of students read the stories aloud. They listen to see if the stories will be interesting to younger children. Check for a well-developed plot and good word-choice.

Look through books on book-binding (see Bibliography). Again, students may work independently or with others. They create their books, bind them, and copy over their stories, leaving room for illustrations. Students can work in their free time to finish illustrating their books.

When the books are finished, have your class read them to younger classes, but first discuss or role-play ways of answering young children who respond to the non-stereotypical nature of the books. For example, practice answering responses like, "Women can't be doctors." This will give your students more confidence.

**DISCUSSION**

1. What were some hard parts of this project? (You may need to give examples such as "thinking of a plot," "being careful not to have any sexist words," "making it mixed culturally.")
2. What were some easy parts?
3. Did you find yourself unintentionally putting in anything that was racist, sexist, classist, ageist? How did you feel about that? What did you do about it?
4. Were you basing your stories on any real incidents in life? Why or why not? Did you base them on books you have read which you think are multi-cultural?
5. How did younger children react to your stories? Give specific examples of what they liked and didn't like.
6. How would you change your story for another time?

## Change That Class(ic) Bias  R, LA

**OBJECTIVES**

To hear and examine an example of a story that challenges class bias.
To develop a story and presentation that counters stereotypes of lower- or working-class people.

**MATERIALS**

A copy of *New Life: New Room*, by June Jordan; paper and pencils; materials for skit, story-boards, or film-strips.

**IMPLEMENTATION**

PART ONE. Ask students to review what class bias is and give some examples of ways lower-income people are sometimes portrayed or stereotyped. If you did "Find that Class(ic) Bias," p. 150, remind them of it.

Now ask students to think of a family with two parents and three or four children who live in a small two-bedroom apartment or housing project. Ask students to think of stereotypes some people might have of that situation and that family. List them on the board.

Tell students that some authors are trying to counteract negative stereotypes about low-income people by writing realistic stories about families affected by class discrimination. These stories point to the resourcefulness and creativity of people confronted with difficult living or working situations.

Over the next few days read *New Life: New Room* aloud to your class. As you go along, discuss the characters in the story and their various responses to their difficult situation. By the end of the story, be sure that you have discussed many of the questions listed below.

**DISCUSSION**

1. Describe the Robinson family. How are they like or unlike your family?
2. Choose several adjectives that you feel best describe the various members of the family.
3. The Robinsons are probably working-class people. What clues do you get in the story that might indicate this?
4. Why did the Robinsons have to stay in their small apartment, even though another child was being born?
5. What do you think should be done about the fact that there isn't enough housing for low- and middle-income people in the United States?
6. How did the Robinson family use creativity and intelligence to deal with a difficult situation?
7. How have you ever used your creativity to deal with a situation when there wasn't enough to go around?
8. How does the Robinson family compare with the stereotypes you listed at the beginning of this lesson?
9. How is the author of this story countering stereotypes through her work?

PART TWO.   Tell students that it is now their turn to develop a story that counteracts stereotypes about low-income people. Divide students into groups. First ask them to imagine a family that makes hardly enough money to live on. Then ask them to think of a problem this family might face because of unequal opportunities and resources. Finally, ask them to come up with a creative solution to this problem that is cooperative and includes people making changes in the conditions that cause their problem. Tell students they can involve more people in the solution than the original family. Remind students to check their stories to make sure that they avoid stereotypes of low-income people.

When each group has decided on the problem and on a creative, cooperative solution, have them *tell* this to other groups. Other groups should be alert for stereotypes. They listen to be sure the families are shown in a realistic, positive way. Writing groups then may make revisions in their stories, based on the feedback. Tell students that to create change it's important to share non-stereotyped stories.

PART THREE.   According to the resources you have available, ask your class to decide if they want to present their stories in the form of skits, film-strips, or story-boards.

If your class creates skits, provide practice time for a few days, then make presentations to other classes. Have one student explain the purpose of the skits to the audience, specifically as it relates to countering class bias in stories. If your class makes film-strips, these can be shown in other classes, preceded by a short rationale and followed by discussion. If your class designs story-boards, provide them large sheets of drawing paper. Story boards depict key events in a story in separate pictures, with the narrative written underneath. Post across bulletin boards in your class or in a main hall of your school a title like "Changing That Class Bias." A written description of the purpose of the project should be included in the display.

# SECTION D MAKING AN IMPACT ON THE MEDIA

## TV Turnabouts _____ LA, C

**OBJECTIVE**   To help students develop a sensitivity to what is non-stereotypic advertising and to design a project accordingly.

**MATERIALS**   Paper and pencils; possibly props and costumes.

**IMPLEMENTATION**   Divide students into groups of three to five. Each group brainstorms on a list of television advertisements which are ageist, racist, sexist, or classist—overtly or subtly.

"we've got a lot in common!!!"

FDA* ALL the WAY!!!

* Future Dishwashers of America

Each group picks one of its ideas to dramatize in a new way. (Check to see that each group has picked a different advertisement.) Ask the children to create an advertisement, using the same product, but with a script which does not put down any groups of people.

Get together as a class and review what you have learned so far about stereotypes, discrimination, and the "isms." Develop guidelines for non-stereotypical television advertisements. Small groups may then make modifications in their scripts. After rehearsal, each group performs its advertisement for the class. Then discuss it.

Another version is to have the class brainstorm on new products that people truly need, not luxury items, as there might be advertised on TV. Instead of rehearsing these, have students volunteer to act out advertisements in an impromtu manner.

**DISCUSSION**   1.   How easy or difficult was the process of thinking of stereotypical advertisements? Could you think of only a few? many? Why?
2.   What sorts of products seem to have advertisements which are most sexist? racist? ageist? classist? Were some advertisements bad in several of these ways? How?
3.   How well did your group work together? Describe the process of developing ideas and deciding on them?
4.   In what specific ways was it easy to come up with non-stereotypical advertisements? In what ways was it hard?
5.   Was it harder to re-design the advertisements for some products than others? What reasons can you give for this?
6.   How hard was it to create new products?

**GOING FURTHER**   Show your advertisements to other classes or at a school assembly.

## Let Me Tell You What I Think _____ LA, A

**OBJECTIVE**   To give students an opportunity to take action by communicating their learning and beliefs to those with decision-making power.

**MATERIALS**   Paper, pencils, envelopes, stamps, drawing paper, markers.

**IMPLEMENTATION**   Before doing this students should have done at least one of the following: "Sell, Sell, Sell, Buy, Buy, Buy," p. 166; "Please Buy Me One," p. 167; "A Firefighter, Not a Fireman," p. 168; "Stop and Look Carefully," p. 145. Ask students to think back and remember what they learned. Bring out their work as a reminder.

The class has the option of writing to advertisers, school product companies, toy manufacturers, or newspapers or magazines. Divide into pairs or trios with similar interests. Each group picks an advertisement, product, or word-use to which it objects.

Go over the discussion questions in the earlier lessons. Students need to be sure to explain in their letters 1) why they found these products, advertisements, or word-uses to be racist, classist, ageist, or sexist; and 2) why they find that offensive. They should include suggestions for improvements.

Once letters have been written in rough draft form, display them around the room along with the offending advertisements, products, bulletin board pictures, or newspaper articles. Everyone circulates around the room to read all letters and add ideas. Briefly discuss the letters and ideas for improvement. Then each pair or trio writes final copies, checking for proper mechanics. Stress that it is especially important to use correct English, spelling, and punctuation so that their letters will be taken seriously. Students may include drawings illustrating their suggestions. When writing to advertisers, students can send copies of the letters to the magazines which publish the advertisements.

**DISCUSSION**
1. How difficult was it to phrase your arguments in a convincing way?
2. How do you expect the advertisers or publishers to react? Does that tell you anything about ageism and classism in our society?
3. Do you think publishers should refuse to publish advertisements which are offensive to some people? Give your reasons.
4. What do you think might change if advertisers and publishers no longer used this kind of advertisement?

**GOING FURTHER**
Write letters to advertisers and publishers who have non-racist, non-sexist advertisements and compliment them on their good work.

## Sharing Results _____ LA, A

**OBJECTIVES**
To share with others how packaging of products perpetuates stereotypes and the "isms."
To give students an opportunity to display their learning in a way which will interest others and get students, teachers, and visitors thinking and questioning.

**MATERIALS**
Packages collected for "The Message in the Package," p. 170; file cards and/or construction paper, markers, scissors, tacks; use of a show case or, if this is not possible, a hallway bulletin board.

**IMPLEMENTATION**
This is a follow-up to "The Message in the Package" which must be done first. Students work together to sort the packages they collected either by types of products or by age, race, class, and sex displayed in the advertising on the package. Divide students into groups so that each group has a pile of packages.

Each group writes cards which either ask questions of a person viewing the package or make points to get the viewer thinking. Give a few examples: "How would you feel if you were a Native American and saw this package?" "How would you feel if you were Asian-American and saw how small a pile we have with Asian-American pictures?" "Why do you think advertisers show a woman in this pose on this package?"

After completing their cards, each group makes a mini-display of their products and cards in the front of the room. Have all the students peruse these displays. Gather as a class and discuss the cards, encouraging suggestions from everyone.

Students can now make a title banner for a display and labels for each category—either products or stereotypes. Install the display in a public place. If you use a bulletin board, open packages and flatten them.

Alternatively, students can write a script for a film-strip with comments or questions about each product. This can be read aloud or played on tape as the film is projected. Put the film in the camera and, with the cover on the lens, advance about 8 frames. This is your lead off strip to thread into a projector. Now you are ready to shoot. Two filmstrip frames fit a regular slide frame. Put down your first two frames and shoot that. Get close enough so no background interferes. Then put down the next two. Continue until you have shot your whole filmstrip, leaving leader film free at the other end. Students can make a title page and picture for the beginning and a credits page for the end. When you have the film developed tell the company *not* to cut it apart for slides. When developed, run it through a filmstrip projector. Then students either write a narrative which is read aloud, or tape a script.

**DISCUSSION**
1. What more about packaging and products did you learn while doing this? Give examples.

2. How do you expect those who look at your display or film-strip to react? Why?
3. What are some ways we can get others to look with an open, questioning mind at what we have learned? What are some pitfalls to avoid?
4. Were there conflicts your group had in designing the display or film-strip? If so what, and how did you handle them?
5. What are some other ways, besides displays, that you can share your learning with others? What are the advantages and disadvantages of these?

**GOING FURTHER**   Set up your display in other schools or community centers in town.

Call your local newspaper. Ask the reporter if she would like to do a story on your research and display or film-strip.

## We Can Design Them Ourselves _____ LA, A

**OBJECTIVES**   To help students focus on the components of egalitarian illustrations on packages, and appreciate both the difficulties in designing these and the advantages of having them.
To give students the opportunity to share the broader perspectives they have gained in a practical way.
To give students the opportunity to change competitive games to cooperative ones.

**MATERIALS**   Game boxes from home or school; paper large enough to cover the box covers; drawing materials; adhesive-backed paper or laminating film.

**IMPLEMENTATION**   Ask students to bring in games from home. These can be complete or have missing pieces. Collect some classroom games. If you need more, used games can be bought at yard sales. Use games with content that is not discriminatory.

STEP ONE.   Students divide into groups of three or four. Each group picks one or several games. First, using scrap paper, they sketch ideas for new game box covers that aren't either racist, sexist, classist or ageist. They m    need to try out many scrap paper ideas before finding one which is actively egalitarian and artistically appealing, and which would sell. They then sketch out their idea on a piece of paper which would cover the box. Remind students that they also need a design along the sides of the box, a catchy slogan somewhere on the box, a title, and the name of the manufacturer. After designs are drawn and colored in, preserve them. If laminating, do so before sticking them to the boxes. If using clear contact paper, put the new covers on the boxes first, then cover them.

This chapter encourages sharing. Therefore, display the new game covers in the library, in a showcase, or at a school or library fair. Set up the display in the community at the public library, banks, community center and so on.

Another action option is to enclose color photographs of the covers in letters to the game manufacturers. In these, students explain why they didn't like the old covers and why they feel theirs are fairer. See "Let Me Tell You What I Think," p. 234, for further guidelines for such letters.

STEP TWO.    Most games foster competition rather than cooperation. Choose games that still have all their parts. Divide students into groups of three or four and give each group a game. Students revise the rules to make it a cooperative game—a game where people win as a group by working together. Each group plays their own game. Have all the games available for rainy-day recesses or activity periods.

If this activity is too difficult for your students, redesign some games yourself, and have students play. In either case, discuss their reactions.

**DISCUSSION**
1. What criteria did you use for an egalitarian design? Did you have some disagreements in your group over what was acceptable? Give examples. How did you resolve those?
2. What are some of the hard points about this kind of design? How did you overcome those?
3. In what ways would these designs sell the product better? In what ways would they hinder its sale?
4. If there are some ways they would possibly hurt sales, what arguments could you give manufacturers that these are still good changes to make?
5. If you are part of the group normally portrayed on the box cover of a particular game, how do you feel about the changes? How about if you are a part of a group normally neglected?
6. How would changes like this help to change the way children and adults choose games and play with them? How could those changes affect ways children see themselves and others?
7. Describe the process of making competitive games cooperative. How did you overcome any problems?
8. How did you like playing your cooperative game? How were your feelings the same or different from those during a competitive game?

---

**SPREAD THE WORD**

Have you tried getting articles about your students' efforts to provide equality into the local newspapers? If you live in a city, perhaps there is a neighborhood newspaper. Often a reporter assigned to schools will be willing to come to your classroom on request, take photographs, and write up captions. Start by inviting a reporter when you are doing activities such as "The Equal School," p. 29; "Seeing Eye Glasses," p. 72; "Assignment: Research Papers," p. 132; "Sharing Results," p. 235, since those are particularly noticeable in the newspapers.

---

# SECTION E   REACHING OUT: FRIENDS, FAMILY, AND THE COMMUNITY

## Won or Fun? _____ PE

**OBJECTIVES**   To have students learn about ways people are revising sports and games to make them cooperative.
To have students experience, and then develop, cooperative sports.

**MATERIALS**  Red rubber ball and a net or rope, or regular volleyball equipment; equipment for the games students develop.

**IMPLEMENTATION**  If possible get a copy of *The Cooperative Sports and Games Book* (see Bibliography). The many fine ideas provide good background for this lesson.

Tell students that across the country many people are revising traditional sports and games to make them more cooperative. Describe the following example:

> The American Youth Soccer Organization (AYSO) is dedicated to the motto "Everyone Plays." AYSO is young boys and girls, from five to eighteen years old, playing soccer, not because they're good or bad athletes, but because they want to play. AYSO is a non-profit organization dedicated to the philosophy that everyone plays at least one half of every game on balanced teams. Some people have suggested that this philosophy promotes "mediocrity" in the level of youth soccer. Statistically this has not proven to be true. There is an almost equal percentage of highly skilled soccer players coming from competitive and cooperative-based organizations.

STEP ONE.  Students think of ways to make a game of soccer more cooperative. Here are some examples: give a point to a team that passes the ball to all the players in the course of getting the ball down the field; rotate players between teams every time out; keep team rather than individual scores (for example number of shots on goal by all forwards, number of assists); make a rule that four different players must make a goal before the team can win.

Then go to the playground or gym and play the new variation. Discuss. Play another new variation the next day. Discuss again. Continue until all alternatives have been tried.

**DISCUSSION**  Be sure to encourage equal discussion from those who usually do well in sports and those who don't.

1. How did you like these versions of cooperative soccer? What did you like about them? What didn't you like about them?
2. What were some feelings you had while you were playing? How are these feelings different than those you experience when you play more competitively?
3. What is the difference, if any, in your feelings about cooperative and competitive sports, if you're a skilled player, or a less skilled player?
4. In what ways is including everyone and having fun important to you? Why? In what ways is winning important to you? Why?
5. How do you think our society as a whole would be different if people grew up playing more cooperative sports?

STEP TWO.  Divide students into heterogenous groups (be sure to mix males and females) and have each pick another sport or game and redesign it to make it cooperative. Groups share their new rules with each other and choose a few to try out at recess. After, discuss their assessment of the new sports and their feelings while playing.

Students teach these cooperative sports or games to their families and neighborhood friends.

*And now more follow-up ideas for action with friends and family...!*

## Using Privilege for Change _____ LA, SS

**OBJECTIVES**  To have students learn about people who have used their privilege to create changes. To have students think of ways they can use the privilege they have to create changes.

**MATERIALS**  Copies of Worksheet: Using Privilege for Change, pp. 253–54, one per group.

**IMPLEMENTATION**  Introduce the lesson by reminding children of the definition of the word "privilege." Explain that a privilege is a special advantage, benefit, or bonus that some people or groups of people have. People don't always earn privileges; often they are born with them.

   Have children think of some privileges they have in school, their family, or community. For example, because they are older they may have certain playground privileges that others don't. Explain that some groups of people often have more privileges because society gives that group more chances and opportunities than others. For example, white people's skin-color is a privilege because it keeps them from facing the racism black people do.

   Divide students into groups of four and give each student one section of the Worksheet. Each person first reads her account to herself and then to her group. Each is an example of a person who had a privilege and used it to help create change. Some readings are harder than others, so distribute sections accordingly. Encourage students to ask each other the definition of words they don't know.

   After children have read the accounts aloud, have them brainstorm on ways they could use the privileges they have to act for change. Even if your students come from the least privileged groups in society, remind them that they have some privileges based on age, sex, or lack of handicaps. Come together as a class to discuss the accounts and share ideas.

**DISCUSSION**  1.  What did the people in the stories gain from using their privilege for change? (Discuss each separately.)
   2.  What did other people gain by their actions?

3. What are some ideas you came up with to use your privileges for change?
4. How can you help each other put some of those ideas into practice?
5. When will people report back to the class and tell us what happens?

---

STUDENTS USING PRIVILEGE FOR CHANGE

1. Students who can walk have the privilege of mobility. Some decided to change the rules of their recess games so that a wheel-chair-bound student could join them in play.
2. In a certain class, skin-color privilege kept white students out of trouble. When there was a conversation going on when there shouldn't have been, the teacher tended to blame the Puerto Rican students rather than the white students. To change that, some white students spoke up and were honest when they were the ones talking.
3. In some families, male privilege allows boys to avoid cooking, doing dishes, and helping with the younger children. Some boys decided to split those responsibilities so everyone would be doing their fair share of housework.
4. Young people whose parents could afford to pay to join the summer pool had class privilege. Some kids got their friends, parents and teachers to organize a petition for the town to run the pool with tax money, so that everybody could keep cool in the summer!

---

## Removing Those Hurdles _____ C, SS

**OBJECTIVES**
To give students an opportunity to investigate barriers to equality in their community.
To learn a process for cooperatively confronting a barrier to equality.
To develop a collective action project to deal with one of those hurdles.

**MATERIALS**
Copies of Worksheet: Community Problem-Solving, p. 256.

**IMPLEMENTATION**
Review with students case histories, "The Hurdles of Life" p. 132. Remind students that institutional discrimination sets up barriers or hurdles for people that makes it hard for them to achieve their goals. Review some of those hurdles. Tell students they will be using a cooperative process to pinpoint and attempt to solve a community problem. Go over the Worksheet together.

Divide students into groups of about five. Have each group pick a group of people in society that often faces special hurdles—women, minorities, older people, low-income people and so on. Assign one such group to each student group.

STEP ONE. For the next few days, students will conduct interviews with members of the population their group is focusing on. (Review the lessons on interviewing, pp. 50, 62. They will ask members of that group, "What hurdles and barriers do you and members of your group face that hinder you from gaining equality in your community?" Each student interviews at least two persons and brings a written summary to class.

Alternatively (or additionally), invite a member of each population group to class where students can interview that person together. For example, a member of a welfare rights group might represent low-income persons, or a member of a Latino civic association represent that minority group.

After interviews are completed, students work together in their group to identify the hurdles mentioned most often. As a class, list the hurdles, by population group, on the board. The class picks one problem area that they want to work on further.

STEP TWO. As a class, brainstorm about what to do to help get rid of this hurdle. Next, students try to reach an agreement on a practicable project that they could organize or take part in, toward that end. For example, one hurdle for women, especially low-income and minority women, to gaining equality in the workplace is lack of after-school child-care. Many women, therefore, can take only part-time jobs. The class might choose one of a number of alternative solutions to this problem. They might document the need, write articles and try to encourage the school system and community groups to start an after-school program. They might research all the available after-school opportunities and make a booklet "After-school Programs for Children in Our Community," to be distributed.

STEPS THREE THROUGH FIVE. Now students make contact with a wide variety of groups and individuals with whom to work. Guide students as they plan their steps to implement the project. Help them organize themselves so everyone has a role and is working together toward a common goal. Have them evaluate each step as they go along. Most importantly, help students see that they can work together toward removing hurdles to equality, no matter how small the project may be.

---

Think about the kind of world we want to work and live in. What do we need to know to build that world? Let's teach each other.

Adapted from Peter Kropotkin,
Peace Calendar, War Resistors League, 1977

---

---

COOPERATIVE VENTURES AT WORK IN YOUR COMMUNITY

It is important that students learn that cooperative endeavors can work in daily living. If there is a food cooperative, recycling cooperative, or any other type of cooperative project operating successfully in your community, invite members from that group to visit your class to describe their aims and processes. There may be a way that students can take part in the ongoing work of that cooperative.

---

## New Village                                                                           A, LA

**OBJECTIVES**  To imagine and design social institutions in a community that would provide equality for all.
To depict these institutions in stories and art work.
To share this envisioned community with friends, family, and community members.

**MATERIALS**  Art supplies for a large mural: mural paper, paint, markers, scissors, and so on.

**IMPLEMENTATION**  PART ONE. REVIEWING AND ENVISIONING. Tell students that they will review what they've learned about racism, sexism, class bias, ageism and competitive individualism in order to create a fair and just community—one that gives everybody an equal chance.

The class decides on a name for its community. Here it is named New Village. Divide students into small groups of four or five. Have each group choose one institution to work on—family, school, media, business, or community groups. Make sure that each institution is being covered by at least one group. (Notice that these are the same areas covered in Chapters 7 and 8.)

Groups make a list of the specific ways they've learned that institutions can discriminate on the bases of race, sex, class, age, or competition. For example if the area is the media, the group can write, "Very few positive pictures of older people on TV." If students have reports or projects from previous lessons, they should review those for information as well.

Then students make a list of how those examples of inequality would be changed in a just society. Encourage them to be specific. For example, "Older adults will be shown in the media in non-stereotyped ways." Circulate from group to group helping students as needed. Students read the lists to the whole class. Group members ask others for additional suggestions.

**DISCUSSION**

1. In what specific ways was it hard or easy to think of ways to change things that supported inequality? Why?
2. How do you think you would feel living in New Village? Why?

PART TWO. WRITING.   Students now write about their view of a just society, focusing on the institution they have chosen to work on. Students choose one or two of their group members to write a paper describing the institution—for example, "Schools in New Village." The remaining students choose to be a person of a race, sex, or age different from their own. Then write about a day in their lives in that institution—for example, "My Day in School in New Village."

Students within groups read their papers to each other to make sure that all papers fit together to present a consistent picture. They check each others' papers for grammar and punctuation. These papers will be posted on the bulletin board with an accompanying mural.

**DISCUSSION**

1. In what ways was it hard or easy to write a clear picture of your institution in New Village? Give reasons and examples.
2. How hard or easy was it to write from the point of view of a person of a different race, sex, or age? Why? What did you learn?

PART THREE. CLASS MURAL.   The third step of the project is to make a class mural depicting New Village. Each group plans, designs, and draws a section showing the institution they've focused on. Each group completes its section and then puts it together with others' sections. Students place their stories beneath or around the mural.

**DISCUSSION**

1. What were some of the decisions groups had to make in planning the mural?
2. How did you show that all people had equal opportunities in your institution?
3. Let's look at the sections of the mural. Where do we see people of different races, sexes, ages, and class backgrounds? Are people who should be there missing?
4. What can we do to make our families, schools, the media, and total more like New Village?

PART FOUR. SHARING.   Invite other classes to your room to see the mural. Class members describe how New Village depicts a just community. Answer questions other students raise.

Move the mural to a bulletin board in the hall or at the entrance to the school. Students explain the mural to visitors, at a PTA meeting or at parents' nights.

Display the mural in your community. The library, community center, post office, or a bank are possible locations. Write an article about the mural for your local newspaper. Invite a photographer from the paper to take a picture.

Convince your friends, family, and community members that equality is possible and together *we can make changes!*

Worksheet: STRATEGIES FOR CONFRONTING STEREOTYPES AND "ISMS"

1. Provide Correct Information

Situation: Your father is watching a TV movie in which the army is gunning down Native Americans. He is rooting for the military and calling the Native Americans barbarians.

You say and/or do                              He reacts


2. State How You Feel  (Use feeling messages)

Situation: Your friend Robert calls Rodney a sissy because he won't play a rough game with you.

You say and/or do                              He reacts


3. Encourage a group of people to speak up together

Situation: You notice that the crossing guard outside your school is nasty to black children. You're scared to say something to her yourself.

You, with others, say and/or do        She reacts


4. Take creative, cooperative action

Situation: Your school's PTA is having a book fair. You know many of the books being sold include stereotypes and "isms."

You, with others, say and/or do        People at the fair react

Worksheet:  RECESS FANTASY

1.  What feelings did you have at the very beginning of the
    story?

2.  What feelings did you have when your friend made the
    negative comment?

3.  What different ideas went through your mind when your
    friend made that comment?

4.  In your fantasy, what did you say or do, if anything, after
    your friend made that comment?

Worksheet:  POWER STATEMENT CONTRACT

1.  Here's a situation where I might have to stand up for what
    I believe and challenge a stereotype or "ism":

2.  The Fear Statements I could tell myself are:

3.  The Power Statements I could tell myself, instead, are:

4.  The Guidelines for Communication I'll remember when I
    state my feelings are:

5.  I contract that I will tell myself a Power Statement next
    time I hear a stereotype or "ism."  I'll report back to
    you, my partner, what I do and what happens.

                              Signed_____


Partner's Statement

    I'll encourage you to think of your Power Statements and
give you support.  If you hear your Fear Statements, let me
know and I'll remind you of your Power Statements.  We'll talk
about how things are going soon.

                              Signed_____

October 27

Dear Diary,

Halloween this year sure is giving me lots of problems. A bunch of us decided to go trick or treating together. Serena and Sherisse are coming over to meet Tammy and me and then we're going to Angela's house. We were trying to decide the best places to go then. I especially wanted to go to Mrs. Rivera's house up on Union St. When we were little kids we were always scared of her. She's old and walks with two canes and her legs look all knotted up. To make it even worse, she lives in an old house with a porch that's falling in.

One day, years ago, Scott let go of our dog, Muffin, and Muffin ran up on to Mrs. Rivera's house. Scott wouldn't go get her and I was afraid Dad would be furious if he had to do that for us, so I went. Mrs. Rivera's hard to understand, I think most of her teeth are gone, but she was really glad to see me and really friendly.

I keep wanting to go there but I don't want to make a big deal with the other kids. They're always saying I'm such a "goody-goody." They'll make fun of me for wanting to do something kind on Hallowe'en when it's supposed to be a holiday just for fun for kids.

Well, I guess I'll have to decide soon.

Love,
Rebekah

---

October 18

Dear Diary,

We were discussing Hallowe'en in school today. Some of the kids think they are too old to get in costumes but I think that, secretly at least, most of us still like to do that and especially like to go trick or treating. Tammy and I were having lunch with a bunch of kids including Lester and Derek. They said they were going to dress up like "wild Indians." We didn't say much. I wondered why they hadn't outgrown that, it sounded more like the two little boys I babysit for.

Later when we were at Tammy's house working on our costumes--she's going to be a computer and I'm a ditto machine (have you ever tried to make a ditto machine costume?)--we were talking about how those two still think of Indians in such an unfair way. Last year in school we studied a lot about all the things the white settlers learned from the Native Americans and about how the Native Americans only fought them because the settlers were taking their land.

Should we say anything to them? What should we do?

Love,
Rebekah

November 8

Dear Diary,

Dumb, dumb, dumb! Sometimes people are so dumb. Scott came home from school today all upset about something. Now that he's thirteen, he won't talk to me about stuff very much. That's dumb too, he thinks that teenage boys aren't supposed to talk about stuff when they're upset. But that wasn't what I was going to write about.

He did say a little--I guess he was too upset to hide it all. I think I'm glad he told me what was wrong, but now he won't discuss it. Some of the boys in his class have been making comments about Dad. It's not his fault that he is bringing us up alone. And he's doing a good job of it. But they were saying all these stupid things about Dad's cooking and cleaning, and going places with us when all the other grown-ups are mothers. I think they were calling him names.

Scott's just sitting in his room sulking and says I should leave him alone. I don't know what to do, but I don't want to just do nothing.

We're supposed to be getting tulip bulbs in the ground today. Maybe he'll get more talkative while we're digging into the almost frozen ground. I guess I'll stop writing and go get him.

Love and confusion,
Rebekah

---

November 19

Dear Diary,

Guess what, Norbert's coming to visit us over Thanksgiving. I can't wait. And Tammy's cousins who live in Alaska are coming to her house! And it looks like it might snow! And we're having tacos for dinner!

Last night while we were eating, a man came to the door with a petition for Dad to sign. They are planning to build a low-income housing project in this neighborhood and the man who came around was against that. He kept saying how property values would go down. He said it wouldn't be safe to play around the streets anymore. He said the neighborhood would get messy and dirty and noisy. He wanted Dad to sign.

After he left we talked about it. We all think that it would be good for them to build the project here. I know from stuff we've done in school that this town needs much more low-income housing. There would be families with kids there and I'd love to have more kids around. I don't think it's fair that people have all these ideas in their minds about low-income people and won't give them a chance.

I'd like to get together with some kids from school and see if we can do anything to help the project get built. I wonder if I dare do it. Some kids won't like the idea.

You should see the great pumpkins we grew for Hallowe'en. We're going to all help make pies out of them.

Love,
Rebekah

Worksheet:   TITLE IX


Physical Education

1.   Equal requirements.

2.   Classes open to girls and boys.

3.   Classes co-ed except for ability groups or contact sports.

4.   Standards for sucess clearly stated and fair.

5.   Wide range of activities.


Guidance and Counseling

1.   Graduation requirements the same for both sexes in all
     courses.

2.   Vocational courses all co-educational.

3.   Descriptions and pictures include males and females in
     all courses.

4.   Counselors avoid sex-role stereotyping.

5.   Counseling provides wide range of courses and ideas for
     males and females.


Treatment of Students

1.   Prizes and honors open to both sexes.

2.   No segregated activities except Scouts and Ys.

3.   Equal use of all school equipment.

4.   Equal punishments for school rule violations.

Situation Cards:  TITLE IX - to be placed on separate file cards

Maggie and Gioia wanted to take wood shop.  They both helped their parents cook at home and felt that they wouldn't learn much that was new in home economics.  Neither one had parents who were good at fixing things so they thought woodworking would be a good skill to learn in school.  The guidance counselor said they could take it if they wanted to but that he wouldn't recommend it and that he was sure the shop teacher would not be happy to have them in the class.

---

Rose wanted to play tennis, which she'd never played before. When she got into her beginners' tennis class, she found that all the other students were also girls.  After class, she was walking by the courts looking at the intermediate and advanced classes and found that the advanced class was all male.  She complained that that was segregating by sex and wasn't fair.

---

Gregg was looking through booklets about jobs in his school's guidance office.  He'd been planning to do the mini-course on nursing so that he could work as a volunteer nurse's aide at the local hospital.  When he looked at the pictures, he realized that all the nurse's aides were female.  He felt silly taking a course where he expected only girls.  So he decided to take an auto mechanics workshop which didn't interest him, but where at least there'd be lots of other guys.

---

The principal told Dan he would be suspended from school until he cut his hair.  The principal said that he could tolerate shoulder length hair in a boy, although he wasn't happy about it, but he certainly couldn't allow him into school with hair longer than that.  Dan's sister Tara went to the same school and had hair down to her waist.  Dan insisted that wasn't fair and that he should get to wear his hair however he wanted.

---

Gilah got pregnant while she was in high school.  The assistant principal said that as soon as it became obvious that she was pregnant she couldn't come to regular classes.  Gilah's parents complained saying that as long as she had a doctor's note saying she was healthy, she should get to come to school.

---

Gurtney wanted to join Boy Scouts, which met at her school, since she didn't like the kind of activities they did in Girl Scouts.  The scout leaders and the administrators of her school both said that it was legal to separate scout troops by sex and that she couldn't join Boy Scouts.

---

Your school has had eleven teams for boys and only four for girls.  One of the girls' teams is archery.  Ming wants to be on what has been the girls' archery team since there aren't enough boys who are interested to start a boys' team.  The coach says no, that there are plenty of sports for boys and she wants to keep this for girls only.

---

Worksheet:  BOOK WRITING MECHANICS CHECKLIST


Title_____


Author (s)_____


                                         Author   Proofreader


1.  Go through the story looking for
spelling errors.  Mark not only the
words you are sure are wrong but those
that might be.  Then either use a dictionary or ask someone how to spell
these.


2.  Start again at the beginning and
read the story quietly to yourself.
Look for run-on sentences.  Put in
periods and capitals where needed.
Look for sentence fragments and
sentences beginning with "And" or
"Then", and change them.


3.  Check for capital letters for names
of people and places.  Put in ones that
are needed.  Take out capitals where
they are incorrect.


4.  Check the verbs in the story.
Were you careful about keeping in the
present, past, or future?  Change these
so that they make sense.


5.  Does the story have an exciting
first sentence?


6.  Do the characters in the story
seem real?  Are they described enough so
that they are interesting?  Do they seem
real?

Worksheet:  BOOK WRITING--CRITERIA FOR EQUALITY CHECKLIST

Title_____

Author (s)_____

|                                                                                                                    | Author | Proofreader |
|--------------------------------------------------------------------------------------------------------------------|--------|-------------|
| 1.  Look at the female and male characters.  What kinds of personalities do they have?  What kinds of tasks are they doing?  Are the tasks anti-sexist? | ____ | ____ |
| 2.  Look at the ages of the people.  Are there elderly people and young people? Are they doing different interesting things?  Do they have the freedom to be different sorts of people? | ____ | ____ |
| 3.  Does the book show people of different incomes?  Do people of different classes take leadership and make decisions? | ____ | ____ |
| 4.  Does the book include people of different races?  Have stereotypes been avoided? | ____ | ____ |
| 5.  Do people work cooperatively together? Do they make changes to promote equality? | ____ | ____ |

Worksheet: USING PRIVILEGE FOR CHANGE

1. Ann is a teacher who lives in New York. In 1964 she knew
that, in the South, black people weren't allowed to ride in the
same buses as whites, to use the same bathrooms, or drink from
the same water-fountains.

Ann said to herself, "Because I'm white I can ride on any
bus I want. It's not fair that black people can't. I have a
privilege black people don't have. I want to do something
about this."

Ann decided to become a Freedom Rider. Freedom Riders were
black and white people who went on buses from the North into
the South. They went into segregated bus stations and used any
water-fountain and toilet they wanted. They were sometimes
beaten by people who wanted segregation. A few Freedom Riders
were beaten so badly they were crippled for life.

The Freedom Riders made people more aware of segregation,
and many other Americans became angry. Their courage was an
important cause of the ending of segregation.

---

2. Roderick is a social worker. He is very proud of his two-
year-old daughter, Latisha. He spends many hours in the evening feeding her, bathing her, and playing with her. The only
problem is when Latisha gets sick, Vivian takes time off from
work. Then Roderick got to thinking. "Why should Vivian be
the one who always loses a day at work when Latisha is sick?
Some people think that the woman should always be the person to
stay home with a sick child. That's not fair! I have a
privilege that women don't have. I want to do something about
this."

The next time Latisha was sick Roderick said, "Vivian,
let's take turns staying home with Latisha when she's sick.
I'll do it today and you can do it the next time. I know my
boss won't like it, but I'll have to teach him. It can't be a
man's world forever!"

3.  Theresa is thirty-five and the mother of a young daughter.
She had a happy childhood.  Her family could pay for music
lessons, camp, vacations, and college.

For many years, Theresa worked for a large company and
earned a good salary.  But Theresa saw how unfair the company
was.  People with important jobs made a lot of money.  The
other workers, who worked just as hard, were paid very little.
The company spent lots of money trying to keep a union out.  A
union fights for more pay and better conditions for the low-
paid workers.  Theresa decided she didn't like what the company
was doing.

Theresa said to herself, "Because I'm middle-class and have
an education, I can earn a good salary.  It's not fair that
other people can't.  I have a privilege poor people don't have.
I want to do something about this."

Theresa decided to change jobs.  She took a job working for
a union that was organizing workers.  She earned less money,
but she felt better.  "I have many skills I gained because of
my middle-class background.  I want to put them to use to make
changes so everybody can have a good life."

---

4.  Ed works in a hospital.  He loves his work because he's
helping people.  He works with many older people, and he has
learned about many of the problems older people face.

Many older people can't find housing because they live on
a "fixed income."  Workers like Ed get raises at their jobs as
prices get higher.  Older people get Social Security or a pension.  This amount of money stays nearly the same.  Many older
people can't keep up with prices that keep getting higher.

Ed said to himself,"Because I'm working age and have a job,
I can pay to live in a nice house.  It's not fair that many
older people can't.  I have a privilege older people don't
have.  I'm going to do something about this."

Ed decided to rent the extra bedroom in his house to an
older person at a price that person could pay.  "I wasn't using
that room.  Now I'm making good use of it, and at least one
older person can have a better life."

Worksheet:  TO SERVE THE PEOPLE

In the People's Republic of China during the late 1960s and early 1970s, schools helped children learn to cooperate. Chinese teachers taught young children to care for, to love, and to teach each other.  They taught the children to "serve the people" - to think of other people before themselves.

The Chinese had very creative ways for young children to learn to cooperate.  Here are some examples:

1.  Buttons on children's coats were put in the back.  Students had to help each other button up before going outside.

2.  Blocks in the nursery school were made too heavy for one child to carry.  Children would have to work together and help each other in order to build a block project.

3.  Children were taught to respect all kinds of work--especially work with their hands.  Children in kindergartens spent a few hours a day working to make things that would be used by other Chinese people.  For example, one kindergarten made a game set (like checkers) that was sold.  The money was used to buy things the class needed.


1.  How do you feel about these ways to build cooperation among young children?  Write down those feelings.




2.  Brainstorm ideas for cooperative toys or materials that your class could make for a day-care center or kindergarten in your community.  List the ideas here.

Worksheet:    COMMUNITY PROBLEM SOLVING

Step 1.    Problem

What is the problem we're concerned
about?_____

How is it defined by members of the
group affected?_____


Step 2.    Proposed Change

What can we do about it?_____

Is our plan possible?  Why?_____

Are we committed to following through?_____

How do we know?_____


Step 3.    Allies

Who can work with us?_____

What members of the
group affected by the problem
are we cooperating with?_____


Step 4.    Activities

What are all the activities we need to
do to accomplish our plan?_____

Who will take responsibility for
each activity?_____


Step 5.    Evaluations  (Questions to ask after every few steps)

How effective is our problem solving?_____

What do we need to change before
moving on?_____

# ANNOTATED BIBLIOGRAPHY

## SOURCES OF MATERIALS

Sources of materials and ideas that will help you promote equity in your teaching and living.

Akwesasne Notes, Mohawk Nation, Rooseveltown, NY. Information, books, art work of Native American peoples.

Arachne Publishing, P.O. Box 4100 Mountain View, CA 94040. Cartoons on sexism and other forms of inequality by Bülbül.

Asian American Bilingual Center, Berkeley Unified School District, 1414 Walnut St., Berkeley, CA 94709. Curriculum materials and books (some bilingual) about Asian-Americans. Newsletter.

Bilingual Publications Company, 1966 Broadway, New York 10023. Books in Spanish—many about Puerto Rican and Chicano people and culture—for all grade levels.

Children's Book Press, 1461 Ninth Ave, San Francisco, CA 94122. Source of stories and folklore of many peoples of color now living in North America.

Community Change Inc., 14 Beacon St. Rm 709, Boston, MA 02108. Short articles, simulations and other resources regarding racism. Newsletter.

Continental Press, Elizabethtown, PA 17022. Booklets, exercises, and study posters on Native Americans, Hispanics and African leaders.

Council on Interracial Books for Children and the Racism and Sexism Resource Center, 1841 Broadway, NY 10023. Excellent books, pamphlets, filmstrips, and in-service materials on racism, sexism, and other forms of inequality in education.

El Camino Real, P.O. Box 25426-C Denver Federal Center, Denver, CO 80225. Materials on minorities, particularly Chicanos; books, posters, literature, bilingual education.

Education Exploration Center, 3104 16th Avenue, Minneapolis, MN 55407. Resources, information, curriculum on social change; particular focus on racism and sexism.

Feminist Press, Box 334, Old Westbury, NY 11568. Non-sexist children's books, feminist books, materials for in-service training and curricula. Catalogue.

Feminists Northwest, 5038 Nicklas Pl. NE, Seattle, WA 98105. Non-sexist materials for various grade levels.

Gray Panthers, 3700 Chestnut St., Philadelphia, PA 19104. Information and materials on older Americans and advocacy.

Institute for Peace and Justice, 2747 Rutger, St. Louis, MO 63104. Curriculum and media dealing with racism, sexism, and peace education.

Indian House, Box 472, Taos, NM 87571. Records, cassettes and tapes of Native American music from many nations.

Japanese American Curriculum Project, P.O. Box 367, 414 E. Third Avenue, San Mateo, CA, 94401. Non profit educational organization that develops and distributes Japanese-American and Asian-American curriculum materials.

Lollipop Power, Box 1171, Chapel Hill, NC 27514. Non-sexist children's books.

Mid-Atlantic Center for Sex Equity, American University, Washington, DC 20016. Source of resources and support for promoting sex equity in schools.

National Association for Asian and Pacific American Education, 1414 Walnut St., Berkeley, CA 94709. Monographs and articles for educators. Catalogue.

National Women's Studies Association, University of Maryland, College Park, MD. Source of materials on feminist education of all levels K–higher education.

Navajo Curriculum Center Press, Rough Rock Demonstration School, Star Route One, Rough Rock, AZ 86503. Source of fine materials on Navajo culture.

New Seed Press, 1665 Euclid Ave., Berkeley, CA 94709. Non-sexist children's books.

Racism, Sexism Resource Center for Educators, 1841 Broadway, NY 10023. Excellent resources, curricula, materials. Catalogue (project within Council on Interracial Books for Children).

Resource Center on Sex Roles in Education, Council of Chief State School Officers, 400 N. Capital St., N.W., Washington, DC 20001. Non-sexist curriculum materials, in-service training, and technical assistance.

Women's Action Alliance, 370 Lexington Ave., R. 601, NY 10017. Toys and manipulative materials that are non-sexist, multi-racial.

Women on Words and Images, P.O. Box 2163, Princeton, NJ 08540. Pamphlets and slide shows on sexism in children's readers, career education materials.

Women's Educational Equity Act Publishing Center. Educational Development Center, 55 Chapel St., Newton, MA 02160. Curriculum and in-service materials for addressing sex inequities in education. Catalogue.

## RESOURCES FOR TEACHERS

*Ageism: Special Issue of Bulletin of CIBC*, Vol. 7, # 6, 1976. Council on Interracial Books for Children, 1841 Broadway, New York, 10023. Informative material about ageism in books and curriculum materials.

*Becoming Sex Fair: The Tredyffin/Easttown Program*, by Marilyn Calabrese, Women's Educational Equity Act Program, 55 Chapel St., Newton, MA 02160. Program offering procedures for selecting, developing, applying, and evaluating techniques for improving sex-fairness in all areas of school life.

*The Bookfinder: A Guide to Children's Literature*, by Sharon Spredemann Dreyer. American Guidance-Service, Publishers Building, Circle Pines, MN 55014. Resource book of children's literature, listing many topics relevant to equality, such as aging, working mothers.

*Books for Today's Young Readers*, by Jeanne Bracken and Sharon Wigutoff. Old Westbury, NY. Feminist Press, 1981. An annotated bibliography of recommended fiction for ages 10–14.

*Channeling Children: Sex Stereotyping in Prime Time TV*. Women on Words and Images, Princeton, New Jersey. Study of sex-role stereotyping in programming during family viewing. Twenty shows and commercials are analyzed.

*The Chicanos*. North American Congress on Latin America, 151 W. 19th St., 9th floor, New York 10011. Account in comic book form of current struggles of the Chicanos.

*The Cooperative Sports and Games Book*, by Terry Orlick. New York, Pantheon, 1978. An excellent book full of cooperative physical activities and ways to make traditional sports more cooperative.

*Cracking the Glass Slipper: PEER's Guide to Ending Sex Bias in Your School*. N.O.W. Legal and Defense Fund, 1029 Vermont Avenue, NW Suite 800, Washington, DC 20005. Packet of materials to use to deal with sexism in schools.

*Developing Effective Classroom Groups: A Practical Guide for Teachers*, by Gene Stanford. New York, Hart Publishers, 1977. A down-to-earth book of ideas and strategies to make your classroom function as an effective group.

*Dick and Jane as Victims: Sex Stereotyping in Children's Readers*. Women on Words and Images, Box 2163, Princeton, NJ 08540. A survey of children's books documents sex-role stereotyping.

*A Different Look at Word Problems*, by Margaret Rogers. *Mathematics Teacher* 68 (4), 285–288 1975. An analysis of math books for sexism.

*Eliminating Ethnic Bias in Instructional Materials*, by Maxine Dunfee. Association for Supervision and Curriculum Development, 225 N. Washington St., Alexandria, VA 22314. A booklet containing commentary, evidence of bias, efforts of change, resources for educators.

*Equal Their Chances* by June Shapiro, Sylvia Kramer, Catherine Hunerberg. Englewood Cliffs, NJ, Prentice-Hall, 1981. Children's activities for non-sexist learning.

*Equity in Physical Education* by Annie Clement and Betty Hartman. From Women's Educational Equity Act Program, Newton, MA 02160. Booklet to aid teachers in planning an equitable co-educational program.

*Fact Sheet on Institutional Racism*. Council on Interracial Books for Children, 1841 Broadway, New York 10023. Detailed booklet of facts documenting institutional racism.

*Feminist Resources for Schools and College*, by Carol Ahlum and Jackie Frolley. Old Westbury, NY, Feminist Press, 1973. A bibliography for teachers of feminist materials.

*The Girl Sleuth: A Feminist Guide*, by Bobbie Ann Mason. Old Westbury, NY, Feminist Press, 1975. A book that analyzes the general mystery series with women heroines for sexism.

*Guidelines for Selecting Bias Free Textbooks and Storybooks*. Racism and Sexism Resource Center, 1841 Broadway, New York 10023. A complete and useful manual containing a variety of forms and criteria with which to examine books.

*Human and Anti-Human Values in Children's Books*. Council on Interracial Books for Children, 1841 Broadway, 10023. Analysis for sexism, racism, elitism, individualism, materialism, and ageism of 238 children's books published in 1975. Valuable statement of criteria.

*Human Teaching for Human Learning*, by George Brown. New York, Viking, 1971. Theory and practice of confluent education—combining cognitive and affective learning.

*Institutional Racism in American Society: A Primer*. Mid-Peninsula Community House, East Palo Alto, CA. A concise, direct explanation of institutional racism in pamphlet form.

*Joining Together: Group Theory and Group Skills*, by David and Frank Johnson. Englewood Cliffs, NJ. Prentice-Hall, 1975. Theory and practice of group dynamics—a comprehensive volume.

*Learning Together and Alone: Cooperation, Competition, and Individualization*, by David W. Johnson and Roger T. Johnson. Englewood Cliffs, NJ, Prentice-Hall, 1975. An extremely valuable guide to providing rationale and practical strategies for structuring learning cooperatively.

*Little Black Sambo: A Closer Look*, by Phyllis Yuill. Racism, Sexism Resource Center, 1841 Broadway, New York 10023. A thoughtful study of Helen Bennermen's well-known, controversial children's book.

*Minority Women: An Annotated Bibliography*, by Gloria Kumagai. Women's Educational Equity Act Publishing Center, Education Development Center, 55 Chapel St., Newton, MA 02160. Very practical resource to locate "hard-to-come-by" materials about minority women.

*Multicultural Education: Theory and Practice*, James Banks. Boston: Allyn and Bacon, 1981. Theoretical basis for developing multicultural education programs.

*Multi-Ethnic Education: Theory & Practise*, by James Banks. Rockleigh, NJ, Allyn & Bacon, 1981. Theoretical statement concerning the field with practical examples and full bibliography.

*The New Games Book*, by Andrew Fluegelman. Garden City, NY, Doubleday, 1976. A rich resource of both cooperative and competitive games, for all numbers and all ages.

*Playfair: Everybody's Guide to Non-Competitive Play*, by Matt Weinstein and Joel Goodman. San Luis Obispo, CA, Impact Publishers. Resourcebook of cooperative games.

*Project on Sex Stereotyping in Education*, by Patricia Campbell. Women's Educational Equity Act Publishing Center, 55 Chapel St., Newton, MA 02160. Self-contained in-service program of 13 modules to develop increased awareness of sex-role stereotyping in many subject areas such as science, American history, math.

*Puerto Rican Resource Units*. State Education Department, Bureau of Bilingual Education, Albany, NY 12234. A guide for elementary and secondary school teachers of Puerto Rican studies. Contains very comprehensive bibliography.

*Racism in Career Education Materials*, by Racism and Sexism Resource Center, 1841 Broadway, New York 10023. A thorough analysis of 100 institutional materials presently used in career education. Effecitve practical change strategies included.

*Racism in the English Language*, by Robert Moore. Racism and Sexism Resource Center, 1841 Broadway, New York 10023. Informative essay on ways our language perpetuates racism and lesson plan to use with students.

*Reaching Out: Interpersonal Effectiveness and Self-Actualization*, by David Johnson. Englewood Cliffs, NJ, Prentice-Hall, 1972. A basic source book of communication skills.

*A Self-Study Guide to Sexism in Schools*. Pennsylvania State Department of Education, Harrisburg, PA. Comprehensive guide for examining one's school for sexism.

*Sex Equity Handbook for Schools*, Myra and David Sadker, New York: Longmann, 1982. A comprehensive resourcebook for recognizing and dealing with sex bias in classrooms and schools, including a curriculum unit on the effects of sexism on men.

*Sex Fairness in Career Guidance*, by Linda Stebbins, Nancy Ames, Ilana Rhodes. Abt Associates, 55 Wheeler St.,

Cambridge Mass., 02138. Packet of materials for guidance counselors and teachers on family and occupational roles.

*Sexism and Racism in Popular Basal Readers*, by Baltimore Feminist Project Racism and Sexism Resource Center, 1841 Broadway, New York 10023. A thorough study that looks at both racism and sexism.

*Sexism in Career Education Materials*, by Women and Words and Images. Racism and Sexism Resource Center, 1841 Broadway, New York, 10023. Documents sexism in career education. Also available on slide-tape.

*Stereotypes, Distortions and Omissions in U.S. History Textbooks*. Racism and Sexism Resource Center for Educators, 1841 Broadway, New York 10023. Volume providing analysis of racism and sexism in recent history books with helpful criteria for educators ongoing use.

*Student-Team Learning Curriculum Materials*, by Robert Slavin. Center for Social Organization of Schools, Johns Hopkins University, Baltimore, Md. 21218. Ready-made materials in various subject areas to be used in structured small group, teaching and learning situations.

*Teacher Training Manual for Integrating Cultural Diversity into Non-Sex-Biased Curriculum*, Gloria Kumagai Women's Educational Equity Act Publishing Center. 55 Chapel St., Newton, MA 02160. Plans and strategies for teachers for dealing with racism and sexism.

*Teaching the Black Experience: Methods & Materials*, by James Banks. Belmont, CA. Fearon Publications, 1970. Written from a historical perspective, this book provides suggestions on curriculum organization, implementation, and materials.

*Teaching Ethnic Studies: Concepts and Strategies*, edited by James Banks. National Council for The Social Studies, Washington, DC, 1973. An anthology focussing on racism, cultural pluralism, social justice and teaching about ethnic minority culture.

*Teaching Human Dignity: Social Change Lessons for Every Teacher*, by Miriam Wolf-Wasserman and Linda Hutchinson. Education Exploration Center, P.O. Box 7339, Minneapolis, MN. 55407 1979. Sourcebook for teachers about various forms of inequality and educational strategies for change. A useful bibliography.

*Teaching Strategies for Ethnic Studies*, by James Banks, Rockleigh, NJ, Allyn and Bacon, 1975. A comprehensive volume providing helpful resources and curriculum for teaching ethnic studies, k-12.

*Ten Quick Ways to Analyze Children's Books for Racism and Sexism*. Council on Interracial Books for Children, New York, N.Y. Short flyer with clear criteria concerning racism and sexism. Useful for parents.

*Toward a Humanistic Education*, by Mario Fantini and Gerald Weinstein. New York, Praeger Publishers, 1970. Combines theory and practical strategies for dealing with students' feelings and needs in teaching.

*Unlearning "Indian" Stereotypes*. Council on Interracial Books for Children, 1841 Broadway, New York 10023. Booklet and 15 min. film-strip. Valuable resource for teaching accurate information about Native Americans to elementary students. (Booklet can be ordered separately.)

*Values and Teaching*, by Louis Raths, Merrill Harmin, Sidney Simon. Columbus, OH, Charles Merrill, 1966. Philosophical rationale and practical exercises for the values clarification approach.

*Values Clarification: A Handbook of Practical Strategies*, by Sidney Simon, Leland Howe, Howard Kirschenbaum. New York, Hart Publishers, 1972. Numerous values clarification activities to use with both students and adults.

*Violence, the Ku Klux Klan and the Struggle for Equality*. Council on Interracial Books for Children, 1841 Broadway, New York 10023. A very valuable resource for teaching about the history and activities of this white supremacist organization.

## CURRICULUM MATERIALS

*Again at the Looking Glass*. Feminists Northwest, 5038 Nickels Pl. NE, Seattle, WA 98105. Language Arts suggestions for combating sexism.

*American Indian Study Prints*. Instructor Publications, Danville, NY 14437. Contemporary American Indian Study Prints with teacher guides.

*Asian American Women* by Yolanda Yokota and Linda Wing. Berkeley Unified School District, Berkeley, CA. A teaching unit on the history and experience of Asian women in this country, grades 5-8.

*Being A Man: A Unit of Instructional Activities on Male Role Stereotyping* by David Sadker. U.S. Government Printing Office, Washington, DC, middle school.

*Black is Beautiful*, by Ann McGovern. Scholastic Books. A short, creative picture book exemplifying the beauty of blackness.

*Changing Learning–Changing Lives: A High School Women's Studies Curriculum from the Group School* by Barbara Gates, Susan Klaw, and Adria Steinberg, Old Westbury, N.Y.: Feminist Press, 1978. Fine background information and ideas; geared for working-class female students; adaptable to lower grades.

*Chinese Americans Past and Present*, Japanese American Curriculum Project, San Mateo, CA. A book of 20 stories for students 9-12 with activity sheets, book, teacher guide, and activity sheets.

*Crowell Biography Series*, New York, Thomas Y. Crowell Co. Many books in this biography series focus on blacks, minorities, and women—e.g. Malcolm X, Mother Jones, Emma Goldman, Wilt Chamberlain—all levels.

*Elementary Curriculum Guide for Integrating Cultural Diversity into Non-Sex-Biased Curriculum* by Gloria Kumagai. Education Development Center, 55 Chapel St., Newton, Mass., 02106. Very useful curriculum dealing with both racism and sexism.

*Famous Black Americans* by Morrie and Letha Turner. Judson Press, Valley Forge, Pa. 19481. Accounts of the lives of black Americans told by WEE PALS, stars of the cartoon series. Informative and fun.

*The First Americans*, by Virgil Vogel. Continental Press, Elizabethtown, Pa. 17022. Short essays on a cross section of American Indian peoples with comprehension questions.

*Free to Be You and Me*, by Marlo Thomas et al., New York, McGraw Hill, 1974. Book of nonsexist songs and stories—elem.

*The Friendly Classroom for a Small Planet: Handbook for the Children's Creative Response to Conflict Program*, by Priscilla Prutzman et al. Children's Creative Response to Conflict, Nyack, N.Y., 10960. Activities for working with children to resolve conflict non-violently.

*Growing Up Female in America: Ten Lives*, by Eve Meriam, New York, Dell, 1971. An anthology of 10 lives of American women of various backgrounds as recorded in their personal writings.

*A Handbook of Personal Growth Activities for Classroom Use* by Robert and Isabel Hawley. Educational Research Associates, Box 767, Amherst, MA 01002. Activities and lessons to enhance self concept, decision making, and values clarification for older students.

*Hypatics Sisters: Biographies of Women Scientists—Past and Present*. Feminists Northwest, Seattle Washington. Illustrated biographies.

*"I Am Loveable and Capable"* by Sidney Simon. Argus Press, 7440 Natchez Ave., Niles, IL 60648, 1973. Short pamphlet with the complete text of the original "I Am Loveable and Capable" story.

*An Illustrated History of the Chinese in America* by Ruthanne Lum McCunn. San Francisco, CA, Design Enterprises, 1979. Available from J.A.C.P. Well-illustrated account includes history, community, role models—for young readers.

*In Search of Our Past,* by Susan Groves. Women's Educational Equity Act Publishing Center, 55 Chapel St., Newton, MA 02160. Multi-ethnic materials for junior high students present women involved in three periods of American history and three eras in world history.

*The Interdependence Journal*. Philadelphia Affective Education Project, Philadelphia Public Schools, 21st and Parkway, Philadelphia, PA, 19104. A handbook of ideas for teachers to enable them to work together more cooperatively.

*The Japanese Americans: An Inside Look*. Japanese American Curriculum Project, 414 E 3rd Ave., San Mateo, CA 94401. Program covers experience of Japanese Americans, issues of citizenship, racism, etc. Two film strips, casette/record available also in Japanese.

*Labor Heroines: Ten Women Who Led The Struggle* by Joyce Maupin. Union Wage P.O. Box 40904, San Francisco, CA 94140. Information on a variety of labor leaders. Jr. High.

*La Chicana Curriculum* by Susan Groves and Clementine Duron. Berkeley Unified School District, Berkeley, CA. Lessons and activities about Mexican-American women.

*A Manual on Nonviolence and Children* by Stephanie Judson. Friends Peace Committee, 1515 Cherry Street, Philadelphia, PA 19102. Describes program and activities that help children resolve conflicts nonviolently.

*Matsuri Festival: Japanese-American Celebrations and Activities* by Nancy Arcki and Jane Horii. Heian International, San Francisco, CA, 1978. Available from JACP. 150 pages of "how to" activities for classroom.

*NonSexist Curricular Materials for Elementary Schools* by Laurie Olsen. Feminist Press, Old Westbury, NY. Packet of nonsexist teaching materials for the elementary school class including student workbook and curriculum units.

*North American Indian Personalities*. Instructor Publications, Danville, NY. 20 full color posters featuring 10 historic and contemporary Indian personalities. Brief biography on each poster.

*Reading Exercises and Study Posters*—"History and Culture of Puerto Rico," "African Leaders," "Spanish Americans," "Mexican Americans." Continental Press, Elizabethtown, PA. 30 short accounts of biographical sketches of 4th grade reading level with follow-up exercises. Booklet and study posters.

*A Student Guide to Title IX* by Myra Sadker. Resource Center on Sex Roles in Education, 400 N. Captial St. N.W., Washington, DC, 20001. A 45 pg. booklet written for students to monitor Title IX.

*Tales of the Iroquois*, Tehanetorens, Akwasasne Notes, Mohawk Nation, Rooseveltown, NY 13683. Teaching legends that depict values of the natural world and human life and that negate standard stereotypical images.

*The Together Book*. Philadelphia Affective Education Program, Philadelphia Public Schools, 21st and Parkway, Philadelphia, PA 19104. An excellent resource book of activities to help students improve group skills—grades 5-8.

*Winning Justice For All: A Supplementary Curriculum Unit on Sexism and Racism: Stereotyping and Discrimination*. Racism and Sexism Resource Center, 1841 Broadway, New York, N.Y. Excellent curriculum focussing on stereotypes and race and sex discrimination in history, books, and work. Curriculum unit, 3 filmstrips (including student workbook & teacher guide). Curriculum booklet can be ordered separately.

*Women in America Series*. New York, Thomas Crowell. Biographies of Women—Margaret Sanger, Fanny Kemble, Bessie Smith, Lydia Maria Child, Emma Goldman, Mary Cassatt, Pearl Buck, Rachael Carson, Mother Jones, Gertrude Stein. Upper elem. and ms.

*Women Who Shaped History* by Henrietta Buckmaster. New York, Collier Books, 1976. Describes lives of six women in 19th Century—Blackwell, Crandel, Dix, Eddy, Stanton, Tubman.

*Won For All: A Cooperative Board Game About Women and Minorities in American History* by Nancy Schniedewind and Ellen Davidson. Women's Educational Equity Act Publishing Center, Educational Development Corporation, 55 Chapel St., Newton, MA. An educational and fun game for students or home that teaches about persons typically left out of history books. Jr. H. and older.

## MEDIA

*America's Women of Color Filmstrips*. 1. "America's Women of Color: Past, Present, and Future." 2. "American Indian Women." 3. "La Mujer Hispana: Mito Y Realidad/The Hispanic Woman: Myth and Reality." 4. "Asian American Women." 5. "Not About to Be Ignored." Women's Educational Equity Act Publishing Center, Education Development Corporation, 55 Chapel St., Newton, MA 02160. Excellent filmstrips on minority women.

*And Ain't I A Woman: 200 Years of Feminist Literature*. Warren Schloat Productions, 150 White Plains Rd., Tarrytown, NY 10591. Through writing and speeches of 30 women from colonial times to present, feelings, views and visions of women are depicted. Six-part filmstrip and cassette, 13 min. each.

*Anything You Want to Be*. New Day Films, Box 315, Franklin Lakes, NJ 22147. A short creative film challenging the myth that a girl can become 'anything she wants to be', 15 min.

*Asian American Study Prints*. Asian American Bilingual Center, Los Angeles, CA 1979. Ten photo essays on life and work of different Asian American men and women.

*Bill Cosby on Prejudice*. Budget Films, 4590 Santa Monica Blvd., Los Angeles, CA 90029. A biting monologue by Cosby that hits home regarding prejudice, 25 min.

*Black and White Rabbits*. Warren Schloat Productions, 150 White Plains Rd., Tarrytown, NY 10591. Short cartoon allegory re: black/white relations in our society.

*Black History, Lost Stolen or Strayed*. Kit Parker Films, P.O. Box 227, Carmel Valley, CA, 93924. Powerful account of how the black race has been dehumanized through media and history. 60 min.

*Black Thumb*. University Michigan AV Center, 416 Fourth St., Ann Arbor, MI 48103. A short film that enables the viewer to confront her tendency to stereotype.

*Chinese Americans: Realities and Myths*. Institute for Peace and Justice, 2747 Rutger, St. Louis, MO 63104. Set of 4 filmstrips and cassettes dealing with historic and present day realities of life for Chinese Americans.

*Contributions of Native People*. Awkwasane Notes, Mohawk Nation, Roosevelt Town, NY 13683. On this cassette Tehanetorens describes the many contributions of Native people. Fine for young people unlearning Indian stereotypes.

*Crystal Lee Jordan*. Indiana University AV Center, Bloomington, IN. From the perspective of a strong woman union leader, a view of the organizing struggle of blacks and whites at the J.P. Stevens Mills in the South.

*Eye of the Storm*. Xerox, 245 Long Hill Rd., Middletown, CT 06457. An in-the-classroom view of a 4th grade public school teacher using the blue-eye/brown-eye experience to effectively teach discrimination, 30 min.

*The Fable of He and She*. Learning Corp. of America, 1350

Avenue of Americas, New York, 10019. A short animated story of men and women freeing themselves from their sex role definitions—elem-m.s.

*Fannie Lou Hamer*. Rediscovery Productions, 2 Halfmile Common, Westport CT 06880. A short film about this Civil Rights Activist, 10 min.

*Free to Be You and Me*. McGraw-Hill Films, Film of stories, songs, dances, emphasizing human potentialities for boys and girls and women and men, 42 min. K-12.

*Free to Be You and Me*. Bell Records, New York. Record of non-sexist songs and stories, elem.

*Help Wanted*. Women on Words and Images, Box 2163, Princeton, NJ 08640. Slideshow containing content analysis for sexism of 100 sets of career education materials, 30 min.

*Hey Cab*. BFA Educational Media, 2211 Michigan Avenue, P.O. Box 1795, Santa Monica, CA 90406. A short, poignant vignette describing a black man's attempt to get a cab and the driver's subsequent rationalizations for his discrimination, 10 min.

*I Am Somebody*. Contemporary Films, McGraw-Hill. A documentary film of the 1969 Charlestown hospital workers strike. Strikers are mainly black women fighting for civil rights and union representation.

*Identifying Sexism and Racism in Children's Books*. Racism and Sexism Resource Center, 1841 Broadway, NY 10023. Two filmstrips demonstrate both blatant and subtle ways racist and sexist messages are transmitted to children in the books they read.

*Images of Males and Females in Elementary Tests* by Diane Rizzo and Lenore Weitzman. Feminist Press, Box 334, Old Westbury, NY. An excellent slide tape documenting the portrayal of men and women in elementary texts.

*Indians of North America*. Society for Visual Education, 1345 Diversey Parkway, Chicago, Ill 60614. Filmstrips that explore the culture of Native Americans in various regions; the Northeast, Southeast, Plains, Northwest Coast, Southwest, and Far North.

*In the Best Interests of the Children*. Iris Films, Box 5353, Berkeley, CA 94705. Describes life experiences of lesbian mothers and their children.

*Jobs and Gender*. Guidance Associates, Pleasantville, NY 10570. Two filmstrips with tapes focussing on opportunities for, and barriers to, work for men and women.

*Masculinity*. Warren Schloat Productions, 150 White Plains Rd., Tarrytown, NY 10551. Focus on the roles, stereotypes and new directions for men today, 4 filmstrips about 12 min.

*Masculinity-Femininity*. Guidance Associates, Pleasantville, NY 10570. Two filmstrips and tapes describing the myth and reality of the differences between females and males.

*Men's Lives*. New Day Films, P.O. Box 315, Franklin Lakes, NJ 07417. Introductory film depicting the socialization of men in our society.

*Miguel: Up From Puerto Rico*. Learning Corporation of America, 1350 Avenue of the Americas, New York 10010. Story of young Puerto Rican boy living in New York City who uses his knowledge of Spanish to earn money to get his father a special birthday treat, 15 min.

*Oh Freedom*. Rediscovery Productions, 2 Halfmile Common, Westport, CT 06880. A comprehensive documentary of the Civil Rights movement, 28 min.

*Other Women: Other Work*. Churchill Films, 662 N. Robertson Blvd., Los Angeles, CA 90069. Women working in traditionally male fields are interviewed and shown in their work—e.g., roofer, pilot, marine, biologist, veterinarian, reporter, carpenter, 20 min.

*People on the Job*. Mind Openers, Box 2948 Rockridge Station, Oakland, CA 94618. A set of pictures showing men and women, white and minority doing a wide variety of jobs.

*The Point*. McGraw-Hill Films, 110 15th St., Del Mar, CA 92014. Film about a child who is different in his community, 75min.

*The Punishment Fits the Crime*. Warren Schloat Productions, 150 White Plains Rd., Tarrytown, NY 10591. Short cartoon allegory regarding justice and injustice in society.

*Rosa Parks*. Institute for Peace and Justice, 2747 Rutger, St. Louis, MO. 63104. A 15 min. filmstrip/cassette on the story of Rosa Parks.

*Six Native American Families*. Society for Visual Education, 1345 Diversey Parkway, Chicago, Ill. 60614. Separate filmstrips narrated by family members of Native Americans of 6 nations—Mohawk, Sioux, Seminole, Navajo, Pueblo, Kwakiutl. Six filmstrips.

*Sometimes We Feel*. Barr Film, Post Office Box 7-C, Pasadena, CA 91104. A young Indian tells of the proud history of his people and how they are reduced to a life of sorrow, poverty and neglect on their desert reservation. 10 min.

*Songs of the Suffragists*, Folkway and Scholastic Records, 906 Sylvan Ave., Englewood Cliffs, NJ, 07632. Ballad documentary history of women's suffrage movement.

*The Sooner The Better*. Third Eye Films, 12 Arrow St., Cambridge, MA. Film on non-sexist preschool education—also can be used with students, 20 min.

*The Trial of Susan B. Anthony*. BFA. Educational Media. A dramatic rendering of the trail of Anthony for her crime of voting—a "You Are There" special, 22 min.

*Understanding Institutional Racism*. Racism and Sexism Resource Center, 1841 Broadway, New York 10023. Clear, descriptive filmstrip on institutional racism.

*Unlearning "Indian" Stereotypes*. Council on Interracial Books for Children 1841 Broadway, New York 10023. Valuable resource for teaching accurate information about Native Americans to elementary students. Filmstrip and booklet, grades 3–6.

*Union Maids*. New Day Films, P.O. Box 315, Franklin Lakes, NJ 07417. Account of 3 women workers in Chicago and their histories as union members—vibrant music backs up a moving film. 45 min. Jr. Hi. and above.

*When Women Get to Hurting*. WNET/13 Media Services, 356 W. 58th Street, New York 10019. Moving account of women who created their own alternatively-structured factory with the needs of the workers as primary, 3/4" video. m.s. and up.

*Women on the March*. National Film Board of Canada, 16th floor 1251 Avenue of the Americas, New York 10020. A documentary of the women's rights movement in Britain and the U.S. An energizing film. 30 min.

*Women In American History*. Encyclopedia Britanica, 425 North Michigan Avenue, Chicago, Ill. 60611. Series of 6 filmstrips and tapes tracing the history of women in America concluding with the current women's movement.

*Women in American History*, Educational Activities, Inc., Freeport, NY 11520. Women's struggle for justice and equality, 6 filmstrips, 3 cassettes, activity sheets, guides.

*Women's Work America: 1620–1920*. Warren Schloat Productions, 150 White Plains Rd., Tarrytown, NY 10551. Historical survey of some of diverse roles occupied by women and document of women's fight for equality with men. Four film strips about 15 min.

*Wrinkled Radical*. Indiana University Film Center. A documentary film about Maggie Kuhn, the spirited leader of the Gray Panthers.

## PERIODICALS FOR TEACHERS

*Akwesasne Notes*. Mohawk Nation, Rooseveltown, NY 13683. Comprehensive news journal written from an Native American perspective, information on new resources, good coverage of struggles of native peoples.

*Asian American Bilingual Center Newsletter*. 1414 Walnut St., Berkeley, CA 94709. Newsletter with information from Asian American perspective—geared toward educators.

*The Black Scholar*. Box 908, Sausalito, CA 94965. Scholarly journal focussing on black studies, the black experience.

*Bulletin: Council on Interracial Books for Children*. 1841 Broadway, New York 10023. High quality publication concerned with fostering equality in education. Particularly useful book reviews and practical ideas for teachers.

*Civil Rights Digest*. U.S. Commission on Civil Rights, Washington, DC 20425. A quarterly focussing on current issues in civil rights.

*Ebony*. Johnson Publishing Company, 820 S. Michigan Avenue, Chicago, IL. Popular magazine about black Americans.

*Ebony Jr*. Johnson Publishing Company, 820 S. Michigan Avenue, Chicago, IL. "Ebony" for children.

*Freedomways*. 799 Broadway, New York 10003, A quarterly journal of the civil rights movement in South and North. Reflects Pan-African consciousness as well.

*Gray Panther Network*, 3635 Chestnut St., Philadelphia, PA 19104. Newsletter of the Gray Panthers.

*Journal of Non-White Concerns in Personnel and Guidance*. American Personnel and Guidance Association, 1609 New Hampshire Ave. NW, Washington, DC 20009. A journal describing issues in counselling of particular concern to minority group members.

*M. Gentle Men for Gender Justice*, 306 N. Brooks, Madison, WI 53715. A journal dealing with men and sexism.

*Ms*. 370 Lexington Avenue, New York, 10017. Popular monthly magazine aimed at a broad audience reflecting a variety of perspectives on women. Includes "Stories for Free Children."

*Off Our Backs*. 1724 20th St. N.W., Washington, DC 20009. A monthly newsjournal of the feminist community, coverage of national and international events.

*Quest: A Feminist Quarterly*. 1909 Que St. NW, Washington, DC 20009. Quarterly feminist journal focussing on feminist theory and politics.

*Southern Exposure*. P.O. Box 531, Durham, NC 27702. Periodical with special attention to Southern struggles.

*TABS: Aids For Ending Sexism in School: A Quarterly Journal*. 744 Carrol St., Brooklyn, NY 11215. Practical journal with useful ideas, resource, and strategies for readers.

*Women: A Journal of Liberation*. 3028 Greenmount Avenue, Baltimore, MD 21218. Quarterly feminist journal often with special topic focus.

*Women's Studies Quarterly*. Feminist Press, Box 334, Old Westbury, NY 11568. Articles and information on women's studies and feminist curriculum for both the college level and k-12 teachers.

*WIN Magazine*. 326 Livingston St., Brooklyn, NY 11217. A biweekly journal documenting current activities to foster social change in many areas.

## BACKGROUND READING FOR TEACHERS

Akwesasne Notes, *Voices from Wounded Knee* Rooseveltown, NY, Mohawk Nation, 1974. Account of the history and background of Native Americans at Pine Ridge with a focus on the Wounded Knee struggle.

Anyon, Jean, "Ideology in U.S. History Textbooks", *Harvard Educational Review*, 49 (3), 361–386, 1979. A study of history texts revealing an ideology that supports those in power and discourages working class consciousness.

Apple, Michael, *Ideology and Curriculum*. New York, Routledge, Kegan, Paul, 1979. A radical theoretical analysis of ideological basis of curriculum, providing a framework for evaluating curriculum from the point of view of whose societal interests it serves.

Arnow, Harriette, *The Dollmaker*. New York, Avon, 1954. One of the best characterizations of a working class woman and her family.

Aronson, Elliot, "Bussing and Radical Tension: The Jigsaw Route to Learning and Liking". *Psychology Today*, Feb., 1975. An excellent case study of the use of cooperative grouping of students to encourage racial understanding.

Asian American Studies Center, *Asian American Women*, Los Angeles, CA, U.C.L.A. A resource book by and about Asian American women.

Asian American Studies Center, *Counter Point: Perspectives on Asian Americans*. Los Angeles, CA, U.C.L.A., 1976. Articles, poems, illustrations, photos showing Asian American and Pacific peoples as active participants in making history.

Babcox, Deborah, Madeline Belkin, *Liberation Now*. New York, Dell, 1971. Excellent anthology of early writings from the women's liberation movement.

Babson, Steve and Nancy Brigham, *What's Happening To Our Jobs*. Somerville, MA. Popular Economics Press (Box 221), 1976. A concise and easy-to-understand account of the reason people are losing jobs—good treatment of racism and sexism.

Babson, Steve and Nancy Brigham, *Why Do We Spend So Much Money?* Somerville, MA. Popular Economics Press (Box 221), 1972. Books for adults and older students providing clear critique of normative economic policy. Good material for math problems for upper grade levels.

Baxandall, Rosalyn, Linda Gordon and Susan Reverby, *America's Working Women: A Documentary History—1600 to the Present*. New York, Vintage, 1976. Primary source materials about working women through U.S. history with very useful commentary.

Beauvoir de, Simone, *The Second Sex*. New York, Bantam, 1961. A classic, comprehensive account of the history and socialization of women.

Blocki, Benjamin, *The Joyful Community*. Baltimore, Penguin Books, 1971. A detailed account of a Christian pacifist community, the Bruderhof Community.

Bloom, Benjamin, *Human Characteristics and School Learning*. New York, McGraw-Hill, 1976. Provocative book detailing the potential capacity of almost all students for equal learning, advocates mastery learning.

Brown, Dee, *Bury My Heart at Wounded Knee*. New York, Bantam, 1975. The very comprehensive story of the Native American side of the ledger of American history.

Boston Women's Health Collective, *Our Bodies Our Selves*. New York, Simon and Schuster, 1976. A thorough, practical handbook for women providing factual information about their bodies and discussion of women's health issues.

Bowles, Samuel and Gintis, Herbert, *Schooling in Capitalist America*. New York, Basic Books, 1976. Comprehensive argument that the function of schooling is to preserve the economic and political status quo.

Bülbül, *I'm Not For Women's Lib, but*. Mountain View, CA, Arachne Publishing Com., 1976. Booklet of poignant cartoons depicting ways men "keep women in their place."

Bülbül, *Sugar Daddy's a Sticky Myth*. Mountain View, CA, Arachne Publishing Com., 1976. A fine booklet of cartoons about men and power.

Bunch, Charlotte, Nancy Myron, *Class and Feminism*. Oakland, CA, Diana Press, 1974. A series of clear, personal articles relating women's experiences of class to feminism.

Burton, Cynthia, et al, *Women Taking Change: New Ways to Economic Power*. Washington, D.C., Strongforce Inc. (2121 Decator Pl. NW) 1978. Accounts of alternatively-structured cooperatives and businesses run by women.

Butler, Robert, *Why Survive? Being Old in America*. New York, Harper and Row, 1975. Good overall account of effects of ageism on lives of older Americans.

Chin, Frank et al, *Aiieeee!: An Anthology of Asian-American Workers*. Washington, D.C. Howard University Press, 1974. Literary works of 14 Americans of Japanese, Chinese and Filipino descent.

Council on Interracial Books for Children, *Chronicles of American-Indian Protest*. New York, C.I.B.C., 1980. Comprehensive collection of documents that recounts American Indians struggle for survival.

David, Deborah, Robert Brannon, *The Forty-Nine Percent Majority: The Male Sex Role*. Reading, MA, Addison Wesley, 1976. Analysis of the effects of sexism on men.

Deloria, Vine, *Custer Died For Your Sins: An Indian Manifesto*. New York, Avon, 1970. Prominent American Indian's description of the Native Americans' situation in the U.S., past and present.

deLone, Richard and The Carneige Council on Children, *Small Futures: Children, Inequality and The Limits of Liberal Reform*. New York, Harcourt, Brace, Jovanovich, 1979. Powerful documentation of the effect of economic inequality on children's development.

Dorris, Michael, *Native Americans: 500 Years Later*, New York, Thomas Crowell, 1975. Valuable for hundreds of photos of Native American life around the country today.

Dowd, Douglass, *The Twisted Dream: Capitalist Development in the United States Since 1776*. Second edition. Cambridge, Mass., Winthrop Press, 1977. A study of the nature and evolution of the U.S. capitalist political economy over the last 200 years.

Dreeben, Phillip, *On What is Learned in School*. Reading, MA, Addison Wesley, 1968. An analysis of the hidden curriculum of our nation's public schools.

Frazier, Nancy and Myra Sadker, *Sexism in School and Society*, New York, Harper and Row, 1973. An analysis of both sexism in our society and ways in which sexism is concurrently manifested in schools.

Frazier, Thomas, *The Underside of American History*. New York, Harcourt, Brace, Jovanovich, 1974. Readings in American history focussing on blacks, women, Indians, the poor, and radical whites.

Franklin, John Hope, *From Slavery to Freedom*. New York, Alfred Knopf, 1967. A standard history of blacks in America.

Freire, Paulo, *Education for Critical Consciousness*. New York, Seabury Press, 1973. An account of the integration of theory and practice in education for literacy and political empowerment.

Freire, Paulo, *Pedagogy of The Oppressed*. New York, Herder and Herder, 1968. A provcative book about the relationship between education and social change—the theoretical basis of Freire's work.

Gonzales, Rodolfo, *I Am Joaquin*. New York, Bantam, 1972. An epic poem of the Chicano people.

Gordon, Thomas, *Parent Effectiveness Training*. New York, Peter Wyden Publishers, 1970. Strategies for productive communication between people, particularly parents and children.

Haley, Alex, *The Autobiography of Malcolm X*. New York, Grove Press, 1964. Powerful, comprehensive account of the life of Malcolm X.

Hamilton, Charles, Carmichael, Stokeley. *Black Power: The Politics of Liberation in America*. New York, Vintage, 1967. A political framework and ideology for black liberation.

Harth, Dorothy, Baldwin, Lewis, *Voices of Aztlan, Chicano Literature of Today*. New York, New American Library, 1974. An anthology of contemporary Chicano literature.

Hooks, Bell, *Ain't I A Woman: Black Women and Feminism*. Boston, MA, South End Press, 1981. An examination of the impact of sexism on black women both historically and currently with a focus on black women's involvement with feminism.

Hungry Wolf, Beverly, *The Ways of My Grandmothers*. New York, Morrow, 1980. Experiences of the lives of women of the Blackfoot Nation during the recent past.

Jacobs, Paul, Landau, Saul, Pell, Eve, *To Serve The Devil*. New York, Vintage, 1971. Two volumes of historical analysis documenting American's racial history—includes blacks, Native Americans, Chicanos.

Joseph, Gloria, Lewis, Jill, *Common Differences: Conflicts in Black and White Feminist Perspectives*. New York, Doubleday, 1981. Exploration of the similarities and differences in experiences and perspectives of black and white women.

Jones, Ron, *Finding Community: A Guide to Community Research and Action*. Cupertino, CA, James Freel and Associates (10370 Saratoga-Sunnyvale Rd.), 1975. Well-developed guide for researching the community—can be easily applied to issues of race and sex.

Kahn, Si, *How People Get Power*. New York, McGraw-Hill, 1970. Short paperback describing strategies for social change.

Kanter, Rosabeth Moss, *Men and Women of The Corporation*. New York, Basic Books, 1977. An analysis of the dynamics of a typical corporation, with particular focus on the effects of instituional sexism.

Kerner Commission, *Report of National Advisory Commission on Civil Disorders*. New York, Bantam, 1968. A well-documented analysis of the mid 60's racial crisis—well developed account of conditions of the "two Americas."

Knowles, Louis, Kenneth Prewitt, *Institutional Racism in America*. Englewood Cliffs, N.J., Prentice-Hall, 1969. A comprehensive account of the way racism pervades various institutions of our society—a basic book.

Kovel, Joel, *White Racism, A Psychohistory*. New York, Vintage, 1970. A complex, scholarly, and ultimately pessimistic study focussing on the psychological roots of racism in America.

Kozol, Jonathan, "Great Men and Women—Tailored For School Use". *Learning Magazine*, Dec., 1975. A provocative article manifesting how Americans working for fundamental social change have been watered down in school texts.

Kozol, Jonathan, *The Night is Dark and I'm Far From Home*. Boston, Houghton Mifflin, 1975. Kozol exposes the political implications of policies and principles common to American education and asks hard questions of teachers.

Ladner, Joyce, *Tommorow's Tomorrow: The Black Woman*. New York, Doubleday, 1972. A thorough study of black womanhood that challenges many established theories about the black family and women.

Lerner, Gerder, *The Black Woman in White America: A Documentary History*. New York, Vintage, 1973. Anthology of the life experiences of black women, as recorded in primary sources throughout American history.

Lerner, Gerda, *The Women in American History*. Menlo Park, CA, Addison Wesley, 1971. Short, comprehensive survey of the role of women in American history.

Levine, Alan with Eve Carey and Diane Divoky, *The Rights of Students: An ACLU Handbook*. New York, Avon, 1973. Basic guide to public school student's rights.

Lignori, James, "*The Role of Women's Soccer in Humanizing Athletic Competition*." Unpublished paper, SUNY New Paltz, 1980. The philosophy and rationale of a cooperative, humane athletic program is put forth.

Magdelina, Mora, Adelaida Del Castillo. *Mexican Women in U.S. Struggles: Past and Present*. Los Angeles, CA, 1980. Chicano Studies Research Center, UCLA, A fine overview of the history and current struggles of Chicanas.

Manuel Madonado-Denis, *Puerto Rico: A Socio-Historic Interpretation*. New York, Vintage, 1972. Account of historical and current social, economic and cultural conditions affecting Puerto Ricans.

Martin, Del and Phylis Lyon, *Lesbian Women*. New York, Bantam, 1972. Two lesbians write about their lives and the lives of other lesbians.

Meier, Matt and Feliciano Rivera, *The Chicanos: A History of Mexican Americans*. New York, Hill and Wang, 1972. A comprehensive historical account of The Chicano experience in America.

Moody, Ann, *Coming of Age in Mississippi*. New York, Dell, 1970. Account of this black woman's experience growing up in the deep South.

Moraga, Cherrie and Gloria Anzaldua, *This Bridge Called My Back: Writings by Radical Women of Color*. Watertown, MA, Persephone Press, 1981. A powerful anthology of writings of women of color, with particular emphasis on interplay of racism, sexism, and homophobia.

Morgan, Robin, *Sisterhood is Powerful*. New York, Vintage, 1970. An excellent anthology of early writings from the women's liberation movement.

Morrison, Toni, *The Bluest Eye*. New York, Simon and Schuster, 1970. A very powerful novel describing the effects of racism and sexism on a black family.

O. M. Collective, *The Organizers Manual*. New York, Bantam Books. Filled with sources of information, resources, to deal with community problems.

Ortiz, Roxann Dunbar, *Great Sioux Nation*. Berkeley, CA, Moon Books, 1977. Historical and contemporary account of Lakota (Sioux) people with many primary sources and photos.

Pogrebin, Lettie Cottin, *Growing Up Free: Raising Your Kids in the 80's*. New York, McGraw-Hill, 1980. A useful guide to help create sex-fair living and learning situations.

Pohl, Constance, "Rocking The Dock: Women on the Waterfront." *Heresies* 1979. #7, Vol 2 #3 p. 73. A description of the struggle to get women into cargoworker jobs on the New York City waterfront.

Raths, Louis, Merrill Harmin, Sidney Simon, *Values and Teaching*. Columbus, Ohio, Charles Merrill, 1966. Philosophical rationale and practical exercises for the values clarification approach.

Rist, Ray, "Student Social Class and Teacher Expectations: The Self-Fulfilling Prophecy in Ghetto Education". *Harvard Education Review*, 1970. 40,3, pp. 411–450. A powerful study on the effects of teachers' attitudes about class on student achievement.

Rosenthal, Robert, Lenore Jacobson, *Pygmalion in The Classroom*. New York, Holt, Reinhardt and Winston, 1968. Analysis of the effect of teacher expectations and the self fulfilling prophecy effect on student learning.

Rubin, Lillian Breslow, *Worlds of Pain: Life in the Working-Class Family*. New York, Basic Books, 1976. Interviews with working class women and men with clear, provocative analysis.

Ryan, William, *Blaming The Victim*, New York: Vintage, 1976. Analysis of how white society blames the victims of racism and poverty for "their problems" rather than change its own policies.

Sadker, Myra and Sadker, David, *Beyond Pictures and Pronouns: Sexism in Teacher Education Textbooks*. Women's Educational Equity Act Publishing Center, 1980. Newton, Mass. Analysis of ways teacher education texts reinforce sexism.

Sadker, Myra and David Sadker, *Now Upon a Time: A Contemporary View of Children's Literature*. New York, Harper and Row, 1977. Children's literature text that focuses on books for and about blacks, Native Americans, other minorities and women.

Sadker, Myra and David Sadker, *Sex Equity Handbook for Schools*. New York, Longman, 1981. Methods for detecting and combatting sex bias in schools.

Schwartz, Barry and Robert Disch, *White Racism*. New York, Dell, 1970. An excellent anthology of readings forcefully documenting the practice of white racism in America.

Seifer, Nancy, *Nobody Speaks for Me! Self Portraits of Working Class Women*. New York, Simon and Schuster, 1976. Interviews with working class women who describe their life experiences.

Sennett, Richard, Jonathan, Cobb, *The Hidden Injuries of Class*, New York, Vintage, 1972. Through a series of conversations and generalization the authors define a new form of class conflict in America—The conflict within blue-collar workers who compare their lives to those society values.

Selye, Hans, *Stress Without Distress*. Philadelphia, PA, Lippincott, 1974. Explanation of the physiological mehanisms of stress and advice for avoiding stress that is harmful.

Sidel, Ruth, *Women and Childcare in China*. Baltimore, MD, Penguin Books, 1973. Account of women's changing roles and cooperative educational programs during the Cultural Revolution.

Silan, Juan Angel, *We The Puerto Rican People: A Story of Oppression and Resistance*. New York, Monthly Review Press, 1971. Comprehensive account of colonization and struggle for liberation of Puerto Rican people.

Simon, Sidney, Leland, Howe, Howard Kirschenbaum, *Values Clarification: A Handbook of Practical Strategies*. New York, Hart Publishers, 1972. Numerous values clarification activities to use with both students and adults.

Slavin, Robert, Nancy Madden, "School Practices That Improve Race Relations." *American Educational Research Journal*, Vol 16 #2 pp. 169–80, 1979. A review of the literature that points to cooperative interaction as the strategy most likely to improve race relations.

Smedley, Agnes, *Daughter of the Earth*. Old Westbury, NY, Feminist Press, 1973. A very powerful account of a working class woman's life from childhood to womanhood. Excellent combining of personal and political perspectives.

Stacey, Judith, Susan Bereaud, Joan Daniels, *And Jill Came Tumbling After: Sexism in American Education*. New York, Dell, 1974. A complete anthology of readings documenting the existence of sexism of all levels of education.

Stalvey, Lois, *The Education of a WASP*. New York, Morrow, 1970. A compelling and honest account of one women's discovery of her racism and subsequent struggle to act upon these new learnings.

Stalvey, Lois, *Getting Ready*. New York, Bantam, 1975. Provocative account of a parent's growing awareness of white racism in education through the experiences of her family in inner city schools.

Terry, Robert, *For Whites Only*. Detroit, MI, William. B. Eardmans Publishing Co., 1970. A book that enables white people to examine their own racism and define alternatives to it.

Tutko, T., *Sports Psyching: Playing Your Best Game All of the Time*. Los Angeles, CA, J. P. Tarcher, 1976. Study of attitudes, values, and motivation on effectiveness in sports, with an emphasis on cooperative approaches.

Vida, Gina, *National Gay Task Force, Our Right to Love: A Lesbian Resource Book*. Englewood Cliffs, NJ, Prentice-Hall, 1978. A comprehensive resourcebook about lesbians—an excellent educational tool.

Vocations for Social Change, *Work Liberation*. Cambridge, MA, Vocations for Social Change. A provocative pamphlet that encourages the reader to redefine the meaning and goals of work and examine the implications for self and society.

Wagenheim, Kal, *Puerto Rico: A Profile*. New York, Praeger, 1970. A good book for basic information about Puerto Rico.

Walker, Alice, *In Love and Trouble: Stories of Black Women*. New York, Harcourt Brace, 1967. An anthology of powerful short stories about black women.

Wilcox, Preston, *White Is*. New York, Grove Press, 1970. A short, poignant book satirically pointing to examples of white racism.

Wright, Richard, *Native Son*. New York, Harper and Row, 1940.

Wright's very compelling novel capturing the anguished emotions and sufferings of black Americans.

Wright, Richard, *Uncle Tom's Children*. New York, Harper and Row, 1936. A superbly written short novel graphically depicting the struggle in the lives of black people.

Yette, Samuel, *The Choice*. New York, Berkeley Books, 1971. A provocative analysis of racism as institutional genocide in America.

**FICTION FOR CHILDREN**

Many of the titles listed below have been reviewed in depth in the *Bulletin* of the Council on Interracial Books for Children. The authors urge teachers to use that valuable resource and we thank the Council writers for their efforts that are reflected in this Bibliography. Key: Y-Younger, M-Middle, U-Upper.

Adoff, Arnold, *Black is Brown is Tan*. New York, Harper and Row, 1973. Warm picture book about an interracial family (Y).

Anker, Charlotte, *Last Night I Saw Andromeda*. New York, Henry Z. Walck, Inc., 1975. Strong anti-sexist and anti-racist, middle class families, high adventure. (M,U.)

Atkinson, Mary, *Maria Teresa*. P.O. Box 1171, Chapel Hill, NC 27514: Lollipop, 1979. A sensitive book about a Chicana girl moving to Midwest and coping with discrimination for the first time. (Y)

Baylor, Byrd, *Hawk, I'm Your Brother*. New York, Charles Scribner and Sons, 1976. Shows the oneness between human beings and nature in exploring the relationship between a Chicano or Native American boy and a hawk. (Y,M)

Bosse, Malcolm, *The 79 Squares*. New York, Crowell, 1979. Shows the friendship between a 14 year old boy and an 82 year old man, anti-ageist and anti-materialistic, compelling. (U)

Brenner, Barbara, *A Year in the Life of Rosie Bernard*. New York, Harper and Row, Inc., 1971. An historical novel with a feminist "survivor" for a focal character. (M)

Charlip, Remy and Burton Supress, *Harlequin and the Gift of Many Colors*. New York, NY: Parents Magazine Press, 1973. A beautifully told and illustrated story on the value of love and cooperation. (Y)

Cleaver, Vera and Bill, *Where the Lillies Bloom*, 1969. *Ellen Grae*, 1967. *Grover*, 1970. All New York, New American Library. *Queen of Hearts*, New York, Bantam, 1978. The Cleavers write about children growing up in low income rural homes and how they cope with their lives, divergent family situations. (M)

Clifton, Lucille, *My Friend Jacob*. New York, Harper and Row, Inc., 1980. Friendship between an 8 year old boy who is black and his friend a retarded white teenager, strong, not sentimental. (Y)

Coutant, Helen, *First Snow*. New York, Knopf, 1974. Very sensitive portrayal of a Vietnam American family dealing with grandmother's death, beautiful. (Y)

Delton, Judy, *My Mother Lost Her Job Today*. Chicago, Whitman, 1980. Child's perspective of a mother, in a single-parent home, losing her job, deals with children's fears. (Y)

Dunahoo, Terry, *Who Needs Espie Sanchez?*. New York, Dutton, 1977. Working class Chicana teenager who is strong and realistic, but some problems in cultural authenticity. One of the best available about Chicanos, sequel to this is not as good. (U)

Evans, Mari, *JD*, Garden City, NY, Doubleday, 1973. A set of stories about a 12 year old growing up in poor family, good outlook and survival skills, good family love, excellent discussion stimulator. (M)

Fogel, Julianna, *Wesley Paul, Marathon Runner*. New York, Lippincott, 1979. Story of an Asian-American boy who is a long-distance runner. (Y)

Forman, James, *Freedom Road*. New York, Franklin Watts, 1979. Fictionalized version of first week in Freedom Summer in 1974 when three civil rights workers were killed. (U)

French, Michael, *The Throwing Season*. New York, Delacorte, 1980. Good characterization on a Cherokee boy high school athlete, value of working for what is right. (U)

Getz, Arthur, *Tar Beach*. New York, Dial, 1979. Depiction of one hot Saturday in a low income Latino and black urban neighborhood, good interconnectedness of people. (Y)

Goffstein, Marilyn, *Two Piano Tuners*. New York, Farrar, Straus and Giroux, 1970. Story of an 8 year old girl, living with her grandfather, she begins to learn to be a piano tuner, anti-sexist, anti-ageist. (Y)

Gonzalez, Gloria, *The Glad Man*. New York, Knopf, 1975. Respect for being different, and independent; feminist, anti-ageist, sense that you can fight city hall. (M,U)

Gould, Lois, *X: A Fabulous Child's Story*. New York, Grosset and Dunlap, 1980. Story of a child whose parents tell no one if the child is male or female—shows how different and more open life can be. (Y)

Graham, Lorenz, *Return to South Town*. New York, Crowell, 1976, The struggle of a black doctor who returns to work with the poor in his home town, people meeting one another on human ground. (U)

Greenfield, Eloise, *Talk About a Family*. New York, Scholastic, 1980. A look at a child's coping with her parents' divorce, beautiful. (M)

Hall, Carol, *Super-Vroomer!*. Garden City, NY, Doubleday, 1978. Cooperative, creative story about three black children, realistic on race and class, slight problem with stereotyping of black females. (Y)

Hall, Lynn, *Sticks and Stones*. New York, Dell, 1972. Powerful description of what name calling and stereotyping can do to individuals and to friendships. (U)

Hamilton, Virginia, *The Long Ago Tales of Jahdu*. New York, Macmillan, 1969. A magical folk hero tale told by an elderly neighbor, anti-racist, anti-ageist. (M)

Hamilton, Virginia, *Zeely*. New York, Macmillan, 1967. Set in current, rural South, this is the story of black children and their admiration for a regal looking black woman neighbor, good self-acceptance. (M)

Holland, Isabelle, *The Man Without a Face*. New York, Bantam Books, 1972. Sensitive story about a teen age boy's friendship with a gay man.

Hopkins, Lee Bennett, *Mama*. New York, Knopf, 1977. Main character is a woman who steals to support herself and two sons, good for discussion. (M)

Hunter, Kristin, *Soul Brothers and Sister Lou*. New York,

Scribner, 1968. A courageous black girl growing up in poor urban setting, action filled. (U)

Hurwitz, Johanna, *Once I Was a Plum Tree*. New York, Morrow, 1970. Set in 1947 this shows a Jewish girl searching for her roots, strongly feminist, shows dilemmas a child faces. (M,U)

Irwin, Hadley, *The Lilith Summer*. SUNY/College at Old Westbury, Box 334, Old Westbury, NY 11568: Feminist Press; 1978. A 12 year old girl spends the summer with a 77 year old woman, good understanding of aging, loneliness and insecurity. (M,U)

Irwin, Hadley, *We are Mesquakie: We Are One*. SUNY/College at Old Westbury, Box 334, Old Westbury, NY 11568: Feminist Press, 1980. Based on historical fact, story of girl in early 19th century and her people's ways, coupled with the new problems they were facing. (M,U)

Jordan, June, *His Own Where*. New York, Crowell, 1971. A boy whose single parent father is very sick meets a girl who is being placed in a shelter, written in Black English. (U)

Jordan, June, *New Life: New Room*. New York, Crowell, 1975. A family must make arrangements for a new sibling, good strong problem solving in a low income city family. (Y)

Juster, Norton, *The Phantom Tollbooth*. New York, Random House, 1961. A superb story giving the reader a whole new look at reality, choices, values. (M,U)

Kent, Deborah, *Belonging*. New York, Dial, 1978. Realistic, unsentimental book about the adjustment of a girl who is blind to public high school, appropriate for disabled and non-disabled students. (U)

Kerr, M. E. *I'll Love You When You're More Like Me*. New York, Dell, 1977. The protagonist's friend is gay and has come out; not the focus of the story but presents this as acceptable and part of life. (U)

Klein, Norma, *Breaking Up*. New York, Pantheon, 1980. A teenage girl chooses to live with her lesbian mother in spite of father's serious attempts to prevent that; mother's relationships is not presented in depth, but is positive and very much part of her life. (U)

Lester, Julius, *Long Journey Home*. New York, Dell, 1975. Six stories told through eyes of mother and grandmother on blacks during slavery and emancipation, struggles and sacrifice, courage, humor and sadness. (M)

Levy, Elizabeth, *Something Queer at the Ball Park: A Mystery*. New York, Delacorte, 1975. A non-sexist, racially mixed mystery, fast moving, appealing, amusing. (Y)

Litchfield, Ada, *A Button in Her Ear*. Chicago, Albert Whitman, 1976. Well handled, upbeat anti-racist, anti-sexist book on hearing loss. (Y)

Little, Lessie Jones and Greenfield, Eloise, *I Can Do It By Myself*. New York, Crowell, 1978. City black family, good family relations. (M)

McCannon, Dindga, *Wilhelmina Jones, Future Star*. New York, Delacorte, 1980. The growing up of a black artist in the 1960's, hopeful but still realistic. (U)

McLeniglon, Valjean, *I Know You Cheated*. Chicago, Children's Press, 1977. Third world boys and third world teacher, realistic, good for discussion on cooperation and competition. (Y)

Mann, Peggy, *The Street of the Flower Boxes*. New York, Coward, McCann, and Geoghegan, 1966. A nine year old boy leads a neighborhood in working cooperatively to improve quality of life there. (Y,M)

Martel, Cruz, *Yagua Days*. New York, Dial, 1976. Culturally authentic, Puerto Rican family in New York City and on visit to Puerto Rico. (Y)

Mathis, Sharon Bell, *Listen for the Fig Tree*. New York, Viking, 1974. A 16 year old black girl copes with her father's death, mother's depression and her own blindness; a strong, fighting focal character. (U)

Mathis, Sharon Bell, *Sidewalk Story*. New York, Viking, 1971.

Strong friendship between two black girls and assertive action helps a family being evicted. (Y)

Maury, Inez, *My Mother and I Are Growing Strong*. P.O. Box 3016, Stanford, CA 94305: New Seed Press, 1978. The way a Latino family handles a father's being sent to prison for his response to a racist insult, and a mother and daughter's growth. (Y,M)

Miles, Betty, *All It Takes Is Practice*. New York, Knopf, 1976. The story of the friendship of two boys, one white, one biracial and their coping with racism in their town in Kansas. (M)

Miles, Betty, *Maudie and Me and the Dirty Book*. New York, Knopf, 1980. Deals realistically with prejudice and censorship and how two sixth grade girls are able to stand up for their choices. (M)

Monjo, Ferdinand, *The Drinking Gourd*. New York, Harper and Row, Inc., 1970. A simple story about one stop on the Underground Railroad. (Y)

Myers, Walter Dean, *Fast Sam, Cool Clyde, and Stuff*. New York, Viking Press, 1975. Black and Hispanic, working class, city, slight problems with sexism. (U)

Myers, Walter Dean, *The Young Landlords*. New York, Viking, 1979. Teenagers unwillingly become the landlords of a Harlem tenement, high adventure, good characterization, good for discussion. (U)

Nolan, Madeena Spray. *My Daddy Don't Go To Work*. Carol Rhoda Books, 241 First Ave. N., Minneapolis, MN 55401, 1978. An urban black family deals with a father's unemployment, strength, sensitivity, and a direct dealing with emotions. (Y)

O'Dell, Scott, *Island of the Blue Dolphins*. Boston, MA, Houghton Mifflin, 1960. 19th Century Indian girl grows up alone for 20 years on an island off the California coast, excellent as anti-sexist; high adventure story.

Paek, Min, *Aekyung's Dream*. Chicago, Children's Press, 1978. A Korean-American girl develops a stronger self-image and pride as she identifies herself as Korean and as she learns English. (Y)

Patterson, Katherine, *The Great Gilly Hopkins*. New York, Crowell, 1978. Funny, very well written, strong female roles, excellent on class, race, education being nonstereotypical. (M,U)

Pinkwater, Manus, *Wingman*. New York, Dodd, Mead & Co., 1975. A Chinese American boy copes with his white neighborhood, good father-son relationship. (M)

Robinson, Tim, *An Eskimo Birthday*. New York, Dodd, Mead & Co., 1975. The story of a close-knit Eskimo family during a winter storm, good on both the commonalities we have with Eskimo life style and the differences. (Y)

Rockwood, Joyce, *Long Man's Son*. New York, Holt, Rinehart, Winston, Inc., 1972. Authentic novel about Cherokee life and culture. (U)

Stern, Patti, *There's a Rainbow in My Closet*. New York, Harper and Row, Inc., 1979. Good combatting of ageism and conformity, some problems in portrayal of mother. (M)

Taylor, Mildred, *Roll of Thunder, Hear My Cry*. New York, Dial, 1976. Southern black 9 year old girl hero, very strong book. (M,U)

Taylor, Mildred, *Song of The Trees*. New York, Dial, 1973. Set in the depression, this story shows an intact black family actively defending itself and caring for each other. (U)

Thomas, Ianthe, *Hi Mrs. Mallory!* New York, Harper and Row, Inc., 1979. Story of love and caring between black girl and elderly white woman shows age, race and economics not necessarily preventing people's relating to each other. (Y)

White, Edgar, *Children of the Night*. New York, Lothrop, Lee and Shepard Books, 1974. Black boy living in poverty in NYC, dreams of freedom and faces the dilemmas brought about by urban riots.

Wilkinson, Brenda, *Ludell*, (1975) *Ludell's New York Time*. New York, Harper and Row, Inc., (1980). What it was like to grow up black in the South in the 1950's, good general issues of maturing, poverty, racism, 2nd book shows her in NYC. (U)

Uchiola, Joshiko, *Journey Home*. New York, Atheneum, 1978. Excellent look at concentration camps where Japanese Americans were put during World War II, strong female characters, very informative culturally. (M,U)

Yep, Lawrence, *Child of the Owl*. New York, Harper and Row, Inc., 1977. A very strong moving book about a 12 year old Chinese American girl's growing up, counters race, sex, and age stereotypes effectively. (M,U)

Yep, Lawrence: *Dragonwings*. New York, Harper and Row, Inc., 1975. Set in San Francisco's Chinatown in early 1900's, a man and his son build a flying machine, consciously counters stereotypes. (U)

Yep, Lawrence, *Sea Glass*. New York, Harper and Row, Inc., 1979. Chinese-American "average" boy, good on self acceptance and non-competitiveness, counters race, sex, and age biases. (M,U)

## NON-FICTION FOR CHILDREN

Adams, Barbara, *Like It Is: Facts and Feelings About Handicaps From Kids Who Know*. New York, Walker, and Co., 1979. Sensitive and understanding information about disabled children, mostly narrated by the children, photos and text capture the children, not just the disabilities. (M,U)

Aliki, *Corn is Maize*. New York, Crowell, 1976. Science information book on maize, excellent for showing strength of Native American culture. (Y)

Ayson, Sasha, *Young, Gay and Proud*. Order from Carrier Pigeon, 75 Kneeland St., Room 309, Boston Mass., 02111, 1980. Primarily for gay and lesbian teens but worthwhile for all—positive, supportive, informative. Illustrations however, are all white and text does not consider problems of third world gays. (U)

Ancona, George, *Growing Older*. New York, Dutton, 1978. Biographies of older Americans from tremendously varied walks of life and living very different lives now, counters stereotypes. (M)

Benton-Banai, Edward, *The Mishomi's Book: The Voice of the Ojibway*. Indian Country Press and Publications Inc., 560 Van Buren St., St. Paul, MN, 1979. A rediscovery of the Ojibway way of life, centered on respect for all living things, spiritual and historic. (U)

Blood, Charles and Martin Link, *The Goat in the Rug*. New York, Parents' Magazine Press, 1976. Told through the eyes of a Navajo goat this book tells the story of Navajo rug weaving, charming, good appreciation of Navajo culture. (Y)

Clymer, Theodore, *Four Corners of the Sky*. Boston, Little, Brown and Co., 1975. Anthology of Native American oral expression, the sky, earth, religion, and daily lives of many different nations. (Y)

Coy, Harold, *Chicano Roots Go Deep*. New York, Dodd, Mead and Co., 1975. Useful introduction to past and present Chicano history, slight problems with stereotyping.

Falcon, Luis Nieves, *Yucayeque*. Bilingual Publications Co., 1966 Broadway, New York, NY 10023, 1980. Daily lives of Taino Indians—food, clothing, ceremonies, politics. (U)

Fish, Byron, *Eskimo Boy Today*. Alaska Northwest Publishing Company, Box 4 EEE, Anchorage, Alaska, 99509, 1971. Excellent photography and interesting text about changing life of Alaskan Eskimos. (M)

Green, Paul; *I AM Eskimo *Aknik My Name*. Alaska Northwest Publishing Company, Box 4 EEE, Anchorage, Alaska, 99509, 1973. A collection of traditional stories told by an Inuit living in a northern Alaskan village (M,U)

Greenfield, Eloise, Lessie Jones Littles, Pattie Ridley, *Childtimes: A Three Generation Memoir*. New York, Crowell, 1979. A beautiful book of shared memories of three generations of black women, strongly feminist and with strong family ties. (M,U)

Grimes, Nikki, *Growin'*. New York, Dial, 1978. City black families, good on race and sex roles and on acceptance of nonconformity. (M)

Hanckel, Frances and John Cunningham; *A Way of Love, A Way of Life*. New York, Lothrop, Lee and Shepard Books, 1979. Informs teenagers about being gay as a way of living—especially useful for those who think they may be gay, but informative for everyone. The section which interviews 12 gay men and lesbian women shows a good cross section economically and racailly. (U)

Katz, Jane, ed., *Let Me Be a Free Man. A Documentary of Indian Resistance*. Minneapolis, MN, Lerner Publication, Inc., Anthology of orations by Indian patriots, also good background information. (U)

Katz, Jane, *I Am The Fire of Time: The Voices of Native American Women*. New York, Dutton, 1977. An anthology of personal accounts and poetry from Native American women today. (U)

Leiner, Katherine, *Ask Me What My Mother Does*. New York, Franklin Watts, 1978. Information about types of work, tools, interactions with children, reader projects included. (Y)

Meltzer, Milton, *The Chinese Americans*. New York, Crowell Junior Books, 1980. Well researched, comprehensive study of Chinese in America, good for breaking down stereotypes and for increased awareness. (M,U)

Minfong, Ho, *Sing to the Dawn*. New York, Lothrop, Lee and Shepard, 1975. Set in a rural Thai village, this is a moving account of a young girl's struggle to continue her education in the face of traditional views of women's role.

Ortiz, Simon. *The People Shall Continue*. San Francisco, CA., Children's Book Press, 1977. Simple and powerful account of the history of Native people to the present—well illustrated and presented as an epoch.

Pugh, Ellen Tiffany, *The Adventures of Yoo-Lah Teen*. New York, Dial, 1975. Growing up of Salish Indian boy, strong and accurate historically. (M,U)

Rosenberg, Janet, *Being Poor*. Carolrhoda Books, 241 First Ave. N., Minneapolis, MN 55401: 1973. A short, poignant series of responses to the open-ended statement, "Being poor is ........" Fine multi-racial illustrations. (Y,M,U)

Shanks, Ann Zane, *Old is What You Get: Dialogues on Aging by the Old and the Young*. New York, Viking, 1976. Interviews with old and young people of many socio-economic and racial backgrounds, dispels ageist myths. (U)

Simon, Norma, *Why Am I Different?* Chicago, IL, Albert Whitman, 1976. Explores many types of diversity in people's lives, shows appreciation of differences. (Y)

Sobol, Harriet Langsam, *Grandpa—A Young Man Grown Old*. New York, Coward, McCann, and Geoghegan, 1980. Parallel soliloquies by a 17 year old girl viewing her grandfather and the grandfather viewing his life. (M,U)

Sterling, Dorothy ed., *The Trouble They Seen*. Garden City, NY, Doubleday, 1976. Counters lies and stereotypes about the South during Reconstruction. (M,U)

Yee, Sylvia and Lisa Kokin, *Got Me a Story to Tell*. St. John's Educational Threshold Center, San Francisco, CA, 1977. Five stories told by children who are black, Latino, Chinese, Hindustani and Filipino. (M)

## POETRY AND LEGENDS FOR CHILDREN

Baylor, Byrd, ed. *And It Is Still That Way: Legends Told by Arizona Indian Children*. New York, Scribner's, 1976. Some of oldest and best known Indian legends, good respect for environment. (Y)

Greenfield, Eloise, *Honey, I Love and Other Poems*. New York, Crowell, 1978. Poems exploring loving relationships with family and friends as experienced by a young black girl. (Y)

Grimes, Nikki, *Something on My Mind*. New York, Dial, 1978. Poetry about problems and joys of growing up. (Y,M,U)

Hausman, Gerald, *Sitting on the Blue-Eyed Bear: Navajo Myths and Legends*. 520 Riverside Ave., Westport, CT 06880: Lawrence Hill & Co., 1976. Navajo world view, history, art, enviromental issues, well told and well illustrated. (U)

Jones, Hettie, ed., *The Trees Stand Shining*. New York, Dial, 1971. Songs, printed as poems, from many generations of Native Americans.

Tehanetorens, *Tales of the Iroquois*, Akwesasne Notes, Rooseveltown, N.Y.. Legends that teach the value of the natural world and the proper way for human beings to live together.

Thomas, Marlo, *Free to Be You and Me*. New York, McGraw-Hill, 1974. Poems, songs, stories and pictures about growing up with non-stereotypic sex roles.

Widerberg, Siv, *I'm Like Me: Poems for People Who Want to Grow Up Equal*. Old Westbury, NY 11568: Feminist Press; 1973. Candid poems on subjects that concern children everywhere. (M,U)

Yarbrough, Camille, *Cornrows*. New York, Coward, McCann and Geoghegan, 1979. A poem-story in African Praise Tradition about legends relating to cornrows, beautiful illustrations. (Y,M)

Yellow Rose, Rosebud. *Tonweya and the Eagles*. New York, Dial, 1979. A collection of Lakota legends as gathered and told by the author.

## STUDENT RESOURCE BOOKS

Alkema, Chester Jay, *Puppet-Making*. New York, Sterling Publications Co., Inc., 1971. Basic book with good variety of puppets (Y,M)

Ault, Roz and Parents Nursery School, *Kids are Natural Cooks*. Boston, MA, Houghton Mifflin, 1972. Healthy recipes in a well organized, fairly easy to read format. (Y,M)

Cooper, Jane, *Love at First Bite*. New York, Knopf, 1977. A very easy to read, creative cookbook not necessitating use of an oven. (Y)

Cooper, Terry Touff and Marilyn Ratner, *Many Hands Cooking*. New York, Crowell, 1974. A UNICEF cookbook featuring single recipes from many different nations, attractive design and good cultural information. (Y,M)

Hooper, Grizella, *Puppet Making Through the Grades*. New York, Davis Publications, 1966. Clear directions for a wide variety of types of puppets (Y,M,U)

People's Fund, *The People's Philadelphia Cookbook*. 1427 Walnut St., Philadelphia, PA 19102, 1976. Ethnic foods from the Philadelphia community. (Y,M,U)

Purdy, Susan, *Books for You to Make*. New York, Lippincott, 1973. Excellent book with book binding from very simple to very complex and professional looking, good directions with details, good list of materials. (M,U)

## BIOGRAPHIES FOR CHILDREN

*Jane Addams*. Keller, Gail. New York, Crowell, 1971.
*Jane Addams*. Peterson, Helen Stone. Westport, CT, Garrard, 1965.
*Benjamin Bannekar: Genius of Early America*. Paterson, Lillie. Nashville, TN, Abingdon, 1978.

*Mary McLeod Bethune*. Greenfield, Eloise. New York, Crowell, 1977.
*Mary McLeod Bethune*. Anderson, LaVere. Westport, CT, Garrard, 1976.
*Louis Braille*. Davidson, Margaret. New York, Hastings House, 1971.
*Cesar Chavez*. Franchere, Ruth. New York, Crowell, 1970.
*Roberto Clemente*. Rudeen, Kenneth. New York, Crowell, 1974.
*Escape to Freedom: A Play About Young Frederick Douglass*. Davis, Ossie. New York, Viking, 1978.
*Charles Drew*. Bertol, Roland. New York, Crowell, 1970.
*Ray Charles*. Bell, Sharon Mathis. New York, Crowell, 1973.
*Jane Fonda*. Fox, Mary Virginia. Minneapolis, MN, Dillon, 1981.
*Charlotte Forten*. Douty, Esther. Westport, CT, Garrard, 1971.
*I Always Wanted to be Somebody*. Gibson, Althea. New York, Noble and Noble, 1967.
*Horace Greeley: The People's Editor*. Faber, Doris. Englewood Cliffs, NJ, Prentice-Hall, 1964.
*Fannie Lou Hamer*. Jordan, June. New York, Crowell, 1972.
*Lorraine Hansberry*. Scheader, Catherine. Chicago, IL, Children's Press, 1978.
*Langston, Hughes*. Walker, Alice. New York, Crowell, 1974.
*Anne Hutchinson*. Faber, Doris. Westport, CT, Garrard, 1970.
*Chief Joseph*. Johnson, R. P. Minneapolis, MN, Dillon Press, 1975.
*Coretta Scott King*. Taylor, Paula. Minneapolis, MN, Creative Education, 1975.
*Martin Luther King*. Paterson, Lillie. Westport, CT, Garrard, 1967.
*The Education of Little Tree*. Carter, Forest. New York, Dell, 1967.
*Maria Martinez*. Nelson, Mary Carroll. Minneapolis, MN, Dillon Press, 1975.
*Maria Mitchell*. Wilkie, Katherine. Westport, CT, Garrard, 1966.
*Morrison, George*. Kostich, Dragos D. Minneapolis, MN, Dillon Press, 1975.
*Mott, Lucretia*. Faber, Doris. Westport, CT, Garrard, 1971.
*Nampeyo, Daisy*. Fowler, Carol. Minneapolis, MN, Dillon Press, 1977.
*Noguchi, Isamu*. Tobias, Tobi. New York, Crowell, 1974.
*Osceola, Blassigamo*. Wyatt. Westport, CT, Garrard, 1967.
*Owens, Jesse*. Kaufman, Mervyn. New York, Crowell, 1973.
*Parks, Gordon*. Harnan, Terry. Westport, CT, Garrard, 1977.
*Parks, Rosa*. Greenfield, Eloise. New York, Crowell, 1973.
*Red Cloud*. McGaa, Ed. Minneapolis, MN, Dillon Press, 1977.
*Robeson, Paul*. Greenfield, Eloise. New York, Crowell, 1975.
*Robinson, Jackie*. Rudeen, Kenneth. New York, Crowell, 1970.
*Ross, John*. Harrell, Sara Gordon. Minneapolis, MN, Dillon Press, 1979.
*Seattle, Chief*. Montgomery, Elizabeth Rider. Westport, CT, Garrard, 1966.
*Sequoyah*. Campbell, C. W. Minneapolis, MN, Dillon Press, 1973.
*Sitting Bull*. Knoop, Faith. Minneapolis, MN, Dillon Press, 1975.
*Oh Lizzie*. Faber, Doris. New York, Lothrop, Lee, and Shepard, 1972 (Elizabeth Cady Stanton).
*Tecumseh*. Schraff, Anne. Minneapolis, MN, Dillon Press, 1979.
*Tecumseh*. McCague. Westport, CT., Garrard, 1970.
*Sojourner Truth*. Paterson, Helen Stone. Westport, CT, Garrard, 1972.
*Sojourner Truth*. Ortiz, Victoria. New York, Lippincott, 1974.
*Harriet Tubman*. Epstein, Sam and Beryl. Westport, CT, Garrard, 1968.

*Harriet Tubman*. Grant, Matthew. Minneapolis, MN, Creative Education, 1974.

*Nat Turner*. Griffin, Judith Berry. New York, Coward-McCann, 1970.

*Annie Wauneka*. Nelson, Mary Carroll. Minneapolis, MN, Dillon Press, 1973.

*Sarah Winnemucca*. Kloss, Doris. Minneapolis, MN, Dillon Press, 1981.

*Phillis Wheatley*. Fuller, Miriam Morris. Westport, CT. Garrard, 1971.

*Malcolm X*. Adoff, Arnold. New York, Crowell, 1970.

*Whitney Young*. Mann, Peggy. Westport, CT, Garrard, 1972.

## BIOGRAPHY COLLECTIONS FOR CHILDREN (ALL UPPER GRADES)

Bowman, Kathleen, *New Women in Media*. Mankato, MN, Creative Education, 1976. Short biographies of Barbara Walters, Katherine Graham, Judith Viorst, Annie Lebervitz, Connie Goldman, Anne Chevelier, Loretta Long.

Bowman, Kathleen, *New Women in Medicine*. Mankato, MN, Creative Education, 1976. Short biographies of Mary Calderone, Katherine Nichol, Anna Ellington, Mary Louise Robbins, Estelle Ramey, Margaret Hewitt, Elizabeth Kubler-Ross.

Bowman, Kathleen, *New Women in Politics*. Mankato, MN, Creative Education, 1976. Short biographies of Bess Myerson, Elizabeth Holtzman, Dolores Huerta, Patsy Mink, Barbara Jordan, Yvonne Burke, Ella Grasso.

Biddle, Marcia, *Labor*. Minneapolis, MN, Dillon Press, 1980. Biographies of Mother Jones, Mary Heaton Vorse, Francis Perkins, Addie Wyatt, and Dolores Huerta.

Brin, Ruth, *Social Reform*. Minneapolis, MN, Dillon Press, 1980. Biographies of Harriet Tubman, Frances E. Willard, Jane Addams, Florence Kelley, Margaret Sanger, and Eleanor Roosevelt.

Emberlin, Diane, *Science*. Minneapolis, MN, Dillon Press, 1980. Biographies of Annie Cannon, Lillian Moller Gilbreth, Margaret Mead, Rachel Carson, Ruth Patrick, Eugenie Clark.

Gleasner, Diana. *Women in Sports: Track and Field*. New York, Harvey House, 1977. Essence of what sports can mean to all people, good biographies and photographs, vivid. Except for *Swimming*, other books in this series are not strong.

Greenbaum, Louise, *Politics and Government*. Minneapolis, MN, Dillon Press, 1980. Biographies of Jeanette Rankin, Margaret Chase Smith, Clare Booth Luce, Martha Griffiths, Ella Grasso, Barbara Jordan.

Haber, Louis, *Black Pioneers of Science and Invention*. New York, Harcourt, Brace, Jovanovich, 1977.

Haber, Louis, *Women Pioneers of Science*. New York, Harcourt, Brace, Jovanovich, 1979.

Jacobs, William Jay, *Mother, Aunt Susan, and Me*. New York, Coward, McCann, and Geoghegan, 1979. Biography of Elizabeth Cady Stanton, Susan B. Anthony, and Sojourner Truth.

Lee, Essie, *Women in Congress*. New York, Julian Messner, A Simon and Schuster Division of Gulf and Western, Corporation, 1971. Biographies of Shirley Chisholm, Linda Hale Boggs, Bella Abzug, Barbara Jordan, Elizabeth Holtzman and 15 others.

Savitz, Harriet May, *Wheelchair Champions*. New York, Crowell, 1978. Stories of wheelchair sports show disabled people as athletes in control of their own lives, photos are sex and race equitable.

# ACTIVITY CHART

| | LESSON | GRADE LEVEL | SKILL | PAGE |
|---|---|---|---|---|
| **2** | Name Game | 3rd–8th | C | 23 |
| | Concentric Circles | 3rd–8th | C | 23 |
| | People Scavenger Hunt | 3rd–8th | C, M, A | 25, 35 |
| | I Feel Good About Myself | 4th–8th | C | 26 |
| | Listening–Checking | 4th–8th | C | 27 |
| | Adjective Attributes | 4th–8th | C, LA | 28, 36 |
| | The Equal School | 4th–8th | C, A | 29, 37, 38 |
| | Gum Drop Inventions | 3rd–8th | C | 30, 41 |
| | Who's Doing the Talking? | 3rd–8th | C | 31 |
| | Color Me Lovable and Capable | 3rd–6th | C | 32, 39–40 |
| | Feeling Messages | 3rd–8th | C | 33, 42 |
| **3** | Brainstorming | 3rd–8th | LA, C | 44 |
| | The Bean Jar | 3rd–8th | C, M | 45 |
| | No Interrupting | 3rd–8th | C | 45 |
| | Helpful Hints for Helping | 4th–8th | C | 46, 60 |
| | Zebulon's Fall | 5th–8th | S, R | 49, 61 |
| | Intriguing Interviews | 3rd–8th | C, LA | 50 |
| | Hello, I'd Like to Know | 4th–8th | C, LA | 51, 62 |
| | Fantasy Problem Solving | 3rd–8th | C, LA, S | 54 |
| | We All Own the Problem | 4th–8th | C | 55 |
| | Role-Play Guidelines and Techniques | 3rd–8th | C, LA | 56 |
| **4** | It's All in How You Look at Things | 4th–7th | R, LA, A | 64, 75 |
| | What's in the Picture | 4th–8th | C, LA | 65, 77, 78 |
| | The Nine Dot Problem | 4th–8th | LA, M | 66 |
| | If I Were . . . | 4th–8th | R, LA, C | 67, 76 |
| | A Girl on Our Team! | 3rd–7th | LA, R | 68, 81–82 |
| | That's What You Brought for Lunch? | 4th–7th | LA, A, SS | 68, 79, 80 |
| | Falling Behind | 4th–8th | LA | 70, 83 |
| | If Only We Had More Money | 3rd–8th | C, SS | 70 |
| | Seeing-Eye Glasses | 4th–8th | R, C | 72, 84 |

*(continued)*

*(continued)*